THE
BEAUTIFUL
MACHINE

A Life in Cycling, from
Tour de France to Cinder Hill

GRAEME FIFE

MAINSTREAM
PUBLISHING

EDINBURGH AND LONDON

First published in Great Britain in 2007 by
MAINSTREAM PUBLISHING COMPANY (EDINBURGH) LTD
7 Albany Street
Edinburgh EH1 3UG

ISBN 9781845963149

A catalogue record for this book is
available from the British Library

Typeset in Frutiger and Garamond

Printed in the UK by CPI William Clowes Ltd,
Beccles, NR34 7TL

THE BEAUTIFUL MACHINE

This book is dedicated to:

Bosia, Jo, Katy and Roger, for heart-cockle-warming affection
Richard and Carol, dear friends of long date and lasting care
Geoff and Gill, who blessedly came out of the blue and stayed on
Simon and Silvana, for Accrington, Timbuktu, Mongolia and open doors
Luke and June, for unfailing good humour and dependable sanity
Dave and Carol, for the incalculable gift of being there
Bob and Linda, who happily announced themselves one day
To you all I say: Hurray

Graeme Fife is a full-time writer who has worked much in radio and written a number of books on a variety of subjects, published in the UK, the USA and Holland, including the bestselling *Tour de France: The History, the Legend, the Riders* and *Inside the Peloton: Riding, Winning and Losing the Tour de France*. A keen cyclist, he has ridden most of the celebrated cols of Tour legend.

Contents

Introduction

Cycling along a lane towards Kemsing on a bright crisp morning in early December, needing to cleanse my system and clear my head as delivery time for this book approached – like the *peloton* hunting down a break in the closing kilometres of a Tour stage – I was overtaken by another cyclist, who said good morning and streaked on. I assessed his speed: not that quick but certainly a lot quicker than I was going this dozy interim. I pondered chase, no more than reminding myself that I can respond, at least, to challenge. The will is not always there, nor the energy either, but something pricked my spirit. I gave chase, caught him some distance along and, as he turned left (thank goodness) up towards Kingsdown Hill, I wished him a pleasant ride and continued, at brisker pace now, towards the slighter cusp of my own loop via Watery Lane, Oak Bank, Bitchet Green, Fawke Common and the southern perimeter of Knole Park to Sevenoaks. And I reflected: 'When your concentration starts to flag, what do you do? You pick a fight . . . with yourself.'

I live in Bat and Ball, which is a sort of wart on the chin of Sevenoaks, but I wish to scotch the ugly rumour that Bat and Ball is twinned with l'Alpe d'Huez . . . as being another dead end.

I was in the Pyrenees not long ago. I spend a lot of time out in the mountains on a bike, cycling around, avoiding the sort of people who creep round with pamphlets of dubious intent to knock on my front door and ask: 'Have you found God?' to which the only sensible answer is: 'No, have you lost him?' In early December 2006, I went out to France to reconnoitre a climb to be included in the Tour de France route for the first time ever in 2007: the Port de Balès. Since I was, at the time, also finishing a big book about the great cols of the Pyrenees and hadn't mentioned the Port de Balès, its sudden appearance among the climbs of legend was a bit of a bugger, to be frank. I thought that must be my fault – not that the Tour had found it but that I had missed it. So I did the needful and went down to scout it.

Since I was also working on this book to a tight deadline – which is worse than a tight waistline because you rarely do anything pleasurable to deserve a tight deadline – I was very short of leisure for gallivanting. However, I flew to Pau and on the way surveyed this rogue climb on the map . . . it didn't exist, which is why I had excluded it. The eastern approach petered out on the pass into a squiggly thin black line as if the Michelin cartographer had dozed off after a good lunch and let the pen run on down the paper. No metalled way, just a forest track. Well, I went up the road that was there from the east and, lo, at the summit, another road joined it, up from the other side. 'What do I do now?' I thought. 'Sue Michelin? Sue the Tour de France? Burst into tears?' No, I braced up and continued on down the 5.88km of new tarmac, all shiny black and no graffiti, though I don't rule out the local foresters coming out with their pails of white paint and brushes and daubing 'Make tracks not Tour' instead of the more usual 'The bears are back, get your rifles out' to the hunting brothers.

I stayed overnight in Bagnères-de-Luchon. The baths were shut and so was most of the rest of the place, but I found a hotel and then asked at the tourist office what was this about the Port de Balès, which seems to have been welcomed back like a prodigal. Turns out the Tour de France has had its eye on the crossing for a year or two, and, by the usual methods – money – it finally coerced the local asphalters – you know, the blokes who pitch up to suburban houses at eight o'clock at night with an offer of a new drive or else a hole suitable for a swimming pool on the front lawn – to lay a new road. That's what happened. One day, no road and the village at the head of the valley is all full of itself for being a sort of El Dorado destination up an inaccessible mountainside. Next morning, they wake up and there's a rush hour flying past down the new throughway where there used to be a donkey ride.

At first light the next day, I drove back over the Port de Balès and stopped in a village on the other side that had probably resented not being a cul-de-sac for years but could now gloat because the smug bastards on the other side had lost their exclusivity at last. I talked to a couple of locals about this and that and bike races and cross-country skiing and what they call 'cuckoo-time snow' and other things, and the man said: 'We don't get many cuckoos down here now, it's all helicopters and not much skiing, and you ask a lot of questions.' To which I replied that I was the foreigner and isn't that what foreigners do, ask questions – which was a bit Jewish, really, now that I think about it, because they are famous for answering questions with another question.

At that, the woman said: 'You look as if you've just come back from Pontoise,' which is French for 'You're a bit out of touch, aren't you?' She said it quite nicely, and it may, of course, be true . . . perhaps it's not for me to say whether it is or not. But the weird thing, the really odd thing, is that Sevenoaks is *twinned with Pontoise*, though in my view it might be better off having a sale or return agreement with Bagnères-de-Luchon. Well, all that aside, as to being out of touch, here in this book is the most recent evidence whether I am or not.

All I can say for sure is that from the time when I first rode a bicycle, I was in touch with something with which I have stayed in touch ever since, a something which has enriched my life to an immeasurable degree. It has imbued me with a pleasure that was, is and, I trust, ever will be, as firm as the treads of that first very far from beautiful machine – nevertheless a bike – upon which I sat and pedalled and moved. It had solid galvanised-rubber tyres fastened round wheels tensioned with spokes the size of knitting needles, set in a frame made from what looked like dismantled railings painted the seaside-villa blue of an old tart's eyeshadow.

All I knew about bikes to that point was that if you didn't hold onto them, they fell over. Being only six years old, I was not yet acquainted with what Albert Einstein had said about life resembling a bicycle in that you have to keep moving to stay upright. However, neither had I plumbed the basic mystery as to how staying upright happened. Until the chance to try the two-wheeler arrived, I rode a kid's tricycle, and on that I was adept, fearless and speedy, and I could handle it flat out round right-angle bends. It had no brakes, so I learnt not to need them. But here on the quiet byway in Finchley outside the house where I lived was my pal Christopher Thompson's two-wheeled machine – no great aesthetic appeal, for sure, but I knew it held something that I wanted: the key to the road.

One

The Long Lone Break

I knew what that bike promised: it promised freedom.

In all the years of my childhood and youth, I can't remember a time when I didn't want to escape from what I was obliged to call home. It was more like *a* home, for the maladjusted. The atmosphere was almost unrelievedly tense, oppressive and bristling with anger. I was born in August 1946 – a long hot summer, apparently, followed by a long cold winter. The drop in temperature persisted at 5 Dudley Road, Finchley. My father, not many months demobbed after war service as an army sergeant, was used to ordering lower ranks around. Not that he was a leader. He was more of a scoutmaster. My feeling is that he had been promoted above his sense of humour. The only way to learn to command is to learn to obey. It is a matter of respect and understanding personal worth – your own as well as the other person's.

I didn't get spanked for being naughty, I got beaten about the head and face for being there at all – backhand, forehand, without a hint of finesse. I think he couldn't cope with my childhood and then the angularities of my youth because he hadn't been able to cope with his own. His elder brother saw through him. 'One day,' he warned him, 'that boy is going to leap out on you and stab you in the back.' My sunny disposition and wilful spirit got up his nose – it was an extremely large nose – and my mother's devotion to me made him bilious with envy and jealousy. There was no excuse, apart from his own mother, and she wasn't so much an excuse, more a *casus belli*. We all have a duty to get over our parents, but he never succeeded. The sergeant's stripes got in the way.

My mother's favourite joke was the line from Mrs Henry Wood's *East Lynne*, declaimed with histrionic mock despair: 'Dead, and never called me Mother', at which she'd grin but with the manic rictus of fear. Her pliant nature grew stubborn, worn ragged by my father's erratic mood swings and sulphuric temper, and she was deeply unhappy. It wasn't really in her spirit to be harsh, but she became so by contagion. The unguarded flame of her gentler heart did not stand up well in the chill wind that prevailed. There was, in that poky, ill-lit house of stiff locks, very little kindness. Even the ceiling at the top of the stairs fell down one morning in protest, and when the bottles of home-made ginger beer exploded overnight in the sitting room, the liquid sugar, if not the writing, was on the wall.

As if being cooped up with two pathologically irritable and choleric parents were not enough, there was the lodger, the Gothic extra. For some time after we moved in, an old lady occupied the back bedroom overlooking the garden where the crimson peony grew. An unsavoury miasma of senility seeped out onto the landing from under the door: a frowsty blend of old onions, cheap talcum powder and a pungent stale lacing of BO and drying urine. I recognised that last odour from my own chronic bed-wettings.

I never saw our resident Miss Havisham, but just knowing she was in there, the sinister muffled noise of her moving about, cooking and doing whatever unspeakable things she was doing, spooked me. Since her door lay in ambush on the direct passage between me, the bathroom and escape down the stairwell, I dreaded its opening and a fire-eyed hag in black bombazine and a fright hairnet with horny nails and nicotine-yellow teeth darting out to grab me and stuff me up the chimney.

After they were married, my father took my mother north to meet his parents in Tyneside for the first time. His mother, who was to composure what a lighted match is to a naked gas jet, opened the front door, took one look at my mother and burst into tears. Since Nan Fife was alone onstage under the proscenium arch of the doorway, such histrionic attention-seeking was hardly necessary. My mother's instant thought (in her words) was: 'My God, I've made the most terrible mistake.' It was a conclusion she later revised but never wholly spurned. I can't complain, being the direct result of that mistake, if not quite a little bastard.

They stayed married for 56 years, but serial abuse doesn't get less obnoxious the longer it goes on. They were, it seems, all along, stuck, like a seat pillar fused into a frame.

Apparently, some time around my third birthday, we were in a crowded railway compartment heading for a seaside holiday when I announced to the other passengers: 'We're going on a honeymoon.' If only. Not for the last time, naive optimism got the better of me. Guileless romanticism obscured the bleaker facts staring me in the face.

Mother's maiden name was Muriel Hilda Lickorish. This, by playground spoonerism, turned into Luriel Mickorish and she became, thenceforward and forever, Mick or Micky. She never much believed in herself, I think, but whatever lame opinion she had of herself, she didn't deserve it. She had a remarkable gift for friendship. Her headmistress summoned her, aged 12, to assign her the duty of looking after a new girl, 'because I think you are a responsible girl'. Mother said she didn't feel at all *responsible*, but her friendship with the new bug, Joan

Smith, ended only at her death, 64 years later. The autumn before she died, she was cycling home through Leiston in Suffolk, saw an old lady of her acquaintance and stopped for a chat. The woman said how bounteous the apple crop was and how sad she was not to have a tree in her garden. Next morning, she found a basket of apples from one of Mother's trees on her doorstep.

Joan said that the front door of the Lickorish house, 145 Long Lane, Finchley, was always open, expectant and welcoming of visitors. It's the same in this house. The front door has a handle and no Yale lock, not something I took note of when I arrived here but a throwback, for sure, to the Lickorish tradition of good cheer and a buoyant take on most things.

My father's parents were not so blessed.

Aside from the inadvertent joke in saddling their diminutive second child with the forenames John Thomas, former slang for a flunkey or a penis, I recall nothing in the way of levity in them, nor of humour, apart from the ill variety. They were the sort of people who see witticisms by appointment only. They may have laughed but never at themselves. Scorn was more their line, and my father inherited it.

He sometimes used a bike, he never enjoyed one. Considering himself upwardly mobile, he bought a succession of cars that were only ever intermittently forwardly mobile. Unheated, unreliable and sulkier than Mary Jane, the black Ford, Austin, Morris and Hillman planted in me a deep wariness of automobiles early on. I helped push every one of them for accumulated miles around the streets near home on cold damp mornings, afternoons and smoggy evenings in a vain effort to coax some spark out of their sluggish plugs, some carbonic wheeze out of their asphyxiated carburettors. My father, increasingly hysterical, would put his shoulder to the door posts, then, as forward momentum gathered, scramble into the front seat yelling 'faster, faster' at me, head down over the rear bumper, and slip the clutch. A bark and hiccup would follow, as internal combustion flashed briefly along the cam and then dissolved in a belch of petrol fumes up the front of my shorts.

So indelibly etched across my psyche are those appalling jalopies that I remember their number plates to this day. I won't repeat them, for fear of triggering some extremely foul atavistic karma.

Mother never learnt to drive. Just as well: she'd have been a menace. She rode a bike, reliving, perhaps, the gaiety, pranks and liberty of her days in the Women's Land Army.

Five Dudley Road wasn't quite Dotheboys Hall, but life in that house was clammed with restrictions, actual and virtual. Children generally accept their circumstances – domestic chaos, the poisonous hatred or indifference of parents, the ugly pustulence of wanton beatings – as normal. I didn't. I knew there was something very wrong, very sickly about it, and I knew I had to get out.

One Sunday afternoon in summer – sorry, *Sabbath*, *pace* my father (no games, no playing, no fun on the Sabbath) – when I was not much more than two, I made my first lone break. I know I was two because those who kept the records, taking it for a joke, told me so. Except that it was no joke. As for the escapade itself, I remember it vividly.

On Sundays after lunch, I was invariably sent to bed to sleep for an hour. I know now, of course, that this was to allow my parents the chance to go to bed for some sex. A very working-class thing, that: the afternoon nap on the only non-working day in the week.

Both my mother and my father came from what could marginally be called working-class backgrounds, with decidedly middle-class leanings: Mother's father was a milkman, her mother a wages clerk. My paternal grandfather, a browbeaten recluse, worked in a Tyneside shipyard, Nan, vain, not very bright, served in a shop and was a part-time mannequin.

My mother passed matriculation and could, therefore, have gone to university but was shamefully denied. Her parents could not afford to send both her and her younger sister, albeit she was no bluestocking, so they sent neither. My father, an unreconstructed Presbyterian, was far less well educated, duller in intellect. He also exhibited some ugly ingrained working-class traits typical of the Geordie patriarchy in which he grew up: plateful of tea hurled at the wall if it didn't appear as soon as he sat at the table . . . scrogulating his bitch of a wife for not kowtowing . . . tyrannising the kids as if their very existence questioned his authority. 'Do what you're told or, so help me, I'll knock your block off', in other words. Typical exchange:

HE: Eat your bread.

ME: I can't. It makes me retch. (The sliced bread in the pantry always went stale, mouldy, crumbly and indigestible, but not one slice could be thrown out till the loaf was finished.)

HE: Eat your bread or go hungry.

ME: I'll go hungry.

HE: [screaming and raising the back of his hand across my face] Eat. Your. Bread.

Since I was born into the infamous 'post-war austerity', I think of early life as insipid, grey as a cheap box-camera monochrome photograph, grey as the shrivelled, desiccated, stringy, overcooked joints of roast beef my mother heaved out of the oven, grey as the coarse woollen socks I was compelled to wear pulled up to my knees, itchy as measles. Colour came in jars of loose boiled sweets, or bakers' sprinkle toppings called hundreds and thousands, or the red-, white- and blackcurrant bushes in Grandma and Grandad's allotment.

Both my father and my mother always worked – I was packed off to a nursery school from the age of three, blessed spells of release and of independence – but although there was more spending power to their hand than most, not much spending went on. They did a lot of jumble sales. Hand-me-downs from alien households. Cut your jacket to suit your cloth. Joyless scrimping. Thrift . . . how I hate that word, that pinched and petty hungry self-denial. True, my father remembered kids walking around with newspapers tied round their feet because they had no shoes. If it had been a trauma, he used it, rather, as a reminder that I was wrapped in cotton wool, feather-bedded, didn't know I was born. '*Difficilis, querulus, laudator temporis acti/ se puero,*' as Horace puts it: 'Testy, querulous, always banging on about how great things were when he was a kid.'

That Sunday afternoon, I let myself out of the house and set off purposefully for Grandma and Grandad's house about a mile away. Their door knocker was surely out of my immediate reach, but I managed either to jump up and flip it with my outstretched fingers or perhaps I simply hammered on the door. Shades of the famous painting of the terrified fugitive grasping the Sanctuary Knocker on the great north portal of Durham Cathedral.

Grandma came to the door, gazed down at me in surprise and said: 'What are you doing here?'

'Daddy and Mother want you to come to tea,' I said, looking her straight in the eye. Do I need to gloss the subtext of that?

Grandma squinted at me quizzically and ushered me inside the house where I always felt safe, where, for the first year of my life, I had lived with my parents. They used to bathe me in the kitchen sink – with or without the washing-up, I don't remember, though the fact that my father's economising insisted that for shampoo we had to use diluted washing-up liquid suggests the former.

Grandad rang home to ask what was going on, and I could hear the muffled cold steel rasp of my father at the other end of the line: 'Send him back.'

It seems incomprehensible now that my grandparents, the most dependable people in my world at the time, should have sent me back unaccompanied – didn't they *know*, didn't anyone *know* what was going on? I set off back alone, my knees wobbling as my own beloved Lucy's knees wobbled when she walked away from me alone into the primary school on her first day, some 30-odd years later. Along Squires Lane, past the indoor swimming pool, towards the humpback bridge over the Northern line and there, cresting its brow, in silhouette against the sun, like one of the Horsemen of the Apocalypse, except on a bicycle, tall and threatening, I saw my father coming for me.

It was the bicycle that made his 5ft 3in. look unnaturally tall. And why would he so mistreat a bicycle as an instrument of terror? It had never done anything to him. I kept walking. As he drew alongside, he leant down, scooped me up and plonked me rudely on the crossbar, spat some grisly 'you wait till I get you home' bollocks at me, then wheeled round and rode back.

Another time, we were visiting my father's mother and her second husband in North Shields. The former husband, his father, seems to have died of incessant badgering. He used to lock himself in the kitchen and fry onions. Perhaps peeling them gave him a legitimate excuse to shed the tears he did not dare release in public, for shame. They all sat down to lunch and then someone noticed that I was missing. They caught me at the wheel of my step-grandfather's car, handbrake released, rumbling down the slope of Tudor Avenue. I was also once dragged out of a sweet shop trying to buy toffees for two girls I had met in the park, without a penny in my pocket. What killjoy bastard welshed on me?

***

So, squaring up to the first bicycle I had ever mounted, Chris holding it by the saddle, I knew exactly what was on offer: it would get me out of prison further and faster.

In the early days of the velocipede craze, enthusiasts attended bicycle classes. One of the catchphrases lauding the pleasure of the freedom to be enjoyed with the amazing new machine was 'Straddle a saddle then paddle and skedaddle'. This was it, then. I straddled the saddle, planted my feet on the pedals, Chris steadying me, then a forward thrust and the bike started rolling down the slight incline of Dudley Road on the hump of the camber, gathering speed, Chris running along behind. I knew the set of the hill from the manic descents on the trike, and the feel of the pedals under my toes was familiar, too, but suddenly I realised that an entirely new sensation was coursing through me. I was riding free. Balancing unaided. Chris had let go of the saddle and left me to natural instinct and providence. Brakes? Fat chance, but stopping didn't signify, motion did. My trike-handling saw me through a neat left-hand sweep at the bottom onto the flat of Rosemary Avenue, where the bicycle slowly rolled to a halt and I plonked my feet down on the tarmac. The thrill, the exhilaration was unimaginable then, but it has stayed with me ever since. The liberty of the bike.

I turned back radiant with glee and rode up to where Chris stood with a big grin on his face, sharing in my triumph. I was a cyclist, a skedaddler. Now, there's a good word. It dates from the American Civil War, first use recorded in 1861, describing soldiers fleeing the battlefield. A nineteenth-century slang dictionary says that the root is classical Greek *skedannumi* (to scarper, run like hell) and the neologism was probably 'set afloat by some professor at Harvard'.

The first bike I ever owned was a step up from the solid-tyred item: pneumatics, square-bracket handlebars with pomegranate pink foam sponge grips, sprung saddle, black frame, calliper brakes. It even had a front-mounted shopping basket. We carried no locks in those days. I guess bikes got stolen, but they were still the commonest mode of transport. This meant that virtually no one driving a car did not also know what it was to ride a bike. That didn't stop one imbecile opening his car door in my face as I rode past and knocking me to the deck, but the closest I have come since to the feeling of safety on a bike on a town road was years later in Holland.

The bike underpinned an essential contradiction between my solitary nature and gregarious propensity. I still enjoy riding both alone and in company. My first girlfriend was Diana Muncaster, who lived next door. She sometimes shared the madcap trike rides, standing on the crossbar at the rear of the frame into which fitted the wheel axles, crouched over me, her hands on the bars. We hurtled down the road to Breakneck Corner whooping like marauding Picts. And one day, as we lay side by side on my bed, she also introduced me to the pleasure located between my legs by telling me about the pleasure that lurked between hers. It was an entirely theoretical lesson leading to solo experiment. But she moved away and, around the time I first rode the bike, Susan Jackson came into my life:

> When I was five, at primary school
> I fell in love. I hadn't far to fall, being small.
> At the time I shared a desk with a boy
> Who took a whole line to write 'Nebuchadnezzar'.
> I tell you that to show you the kind of thing
> That impressed me then. So, anyway,
> I fell in love, with Susan Jackson and she with me.
> A love that was destined to carry us both
> Through all the times tables, sticklebacks,
> 'Olly olly in' and games of jacks,
> Christmas pageants, IQ tests,
> Games of rounders in Aertex vests,

The 11-plus into grammar school
Where our paths divided: single sex.
But it was all a wondrous delirium till then.
She'd steal my cap. I'd have to kiss her
To get it back. Snatching for it was out of the
question.
I had to kiss her, which was a nice thing to do,
In the cloakroom, nobody looking,
Which is where I learnt about the lovers' secret
world,
Although at the time it was also a matter
Of retrieving a uniform hat that didn't fit.
And in class I would write her notes and
'Please pass to Susan Jackson'.
Which is where I learnt about love letters,
Although at the time it was also a case
Of boyish bravado. Isn't it always?
And the notes read (invariably read):
'I love you'. They were short notes.
Perhaps they'd also say: 'Dear Susan'.
I can't remember. Did we promise 'forever'?
One day I can recall for sure
She sent me a reply to my latest note.
A reply. Imagine.
I was already learning about one-way mail,
Although, at the time, it was also a matter
Of seizing on trifles. Isn't it always?
And her reply said: 'Can't you think
Of anything else to say?' I couldn't.
At the time, I couldn't.
Since then, of course, the bottles of ink
Run into thousands, the paper would cover
Most of England . . . words, words, words
In search of anything else to say.

Some things you never learn at school,
Even when you had the luck, the timeless,
The outlandish, astonishing, difficult luck
To fall in love. Even if it wasn't far to fall.
So long as you fell right in, all the way.
PS Surviving which
Can be a bitch.

I spent April 1956 with my uncle and aunt in Bûr Taufiq, the Port of Suez. George was an engineer in the merchant navy. His eldest son was at boarding school in England and lodged with us most holidays. I went in exchange. Their cook, Ahmed, about 18 years old, was like the protective older brother I never had, part of his remit, undoubtedly, to look after the master's family. When he cooked eggs, Ahmed just reached for them in the boiling water. He was a font of warmth, and I felt the full blast of his devotion one day. As I cycled past a gang of Syrian boys on the bike my aunt hired for me, one of them turned, his face taut with hostility, and flung a stick through my front spokes. My blond hair and pink face marked me out as English? French? At any rate, an intruder. I crashed to the tarmac. The bike damaged but rideable, I raced back to find Ahmed. The rage surged in him like shook champagne. He grabbed another bike, flew off at furious speed, knees wide, me cycling behind, and came off. I collided with him and went down again. He remounted, I remounted, and off we rattled once more to the scene of the assault. I pointed to my tormentor. Ahmed ran across, djellabah flapping, grabbed the boy by the scruff of his neck and dragged him into the hire shop to exact reparation. In the crisis of action, I had kept my sangfroid. Ahmed's burly defence and rescue suddenly overwhelmed me and I burst into tears. I learnt something that day about the unthinking nature of kindness, even friendship, and later, more complicatedly, how bitter to compromise both by sectarian, national, religious, political divide. Yes, we fucked up badly in Suez and we're still doing it.

The first 11-plus exam: English. I bent over to scan the question paper and one of my spectacle lenses plopped out onto the desk. The distraction of refitting the loose lens in the frame probably helped calm any nerves picking at me. I passed, anyway – one of only seven from a class of forty-two. The headmistress came into the class to announce the results and spin the fatuous line that not passing didn't mean failing. We all knew what not passing meant: instead of the grammar school and a rosy future, it was the rubbish basket of the secondary modern, the despised technical drawing, infant-level maths, starting life as a second-rater. The rank snobbery which promoted academic subjects above non-academic was a disgrace. A penchant for book learning is not innately superior to manual skill. Educationalists preached doctrines of excellence but neither promoted nor instilled them in the vast number of children who didn't match up to the elitist criterion of bookish scholarship.

My father asked me what I would like as a prize for getting into Christ's College, Finchley. (Motto: *Usque proficiens*, which may be translated as 'never give up'. I go along with that.) This generosity was unexpected. I was discombobulated. 'How about a bicycle?' he said.

'I already have a bicycle,' I replied.

'How about a new one?' he urged.

We went to the bike shop, chose a red and silver, chrome and steel sit-up-and-beg Humber (I think), with Sturmey Archer triple gears and a front-wheel hub dynamo. White wall tyres. Cable brakes. Sensible. Sleek for its kind.

Actually it was the third bike I owned. A few years before, a cousin of my father's, back from Australia, probably on parole, had bequeathed me a mulberry-red Coventry Eagle racing bike with drop handlebars. It was far too big for me, so it went into storage. Patting the saddle in farewell, my relative assured me: 'Lightest bike on the road,' which it had never been. However, pushing its antique weight delivered pretty good conditioning. I never used it for the daily journeys to school, but it took me, aged 14, on a school trip to Belgium, Germany and Luxembourg. (Stricken with an attack of appendicitis, I had to stay behind in the German youth hostel and missed out on the day excursion into the Duchy. The appendicitis proved useful later. Having had the inflamed bit of me surgically removed, I eked out the post-operation convalescence for two weeks' truancy in the house on my own so as to miss the annual school exams, about which I kept quiet. My father went berserk.)

Heading for our first stop from the ferry in Ostend to Bruges, along a canalside cycle path, we had a pile-up. Stuart Dobson, our self-appointed mechanic, went down. He was carrying a pair of spare wheels attached to a hub-mounted bracket and secured at his bar ends with straps. That first evening, most of us strolled out into the Bruges night, practising our chat-up line (never voiced) for the local girls (there were none) – '*Voulez-vous promener avec moi ce soir?*' – and left Dobson in the foyer of the hostel patiently truing the accumulation of buckled wheels. He worked for Claud Butler in Hendon on Saturdays and already had that unfussed way with machines and components that I have always envied. My own efforts at repair usually led to extreme frustration and puerile tantrums: hurling stuff about, cursing fugitive ball bearings, knocking out spokes that wouldn't straighten under the key, trying to force bits into other bits that wouldn't take them.

Two masters were in charge, both called John (history and maths). Since we were all riding bicycles and I had the idea that we were therefore equal, age and status immaterial, I asked them if they wouldn't mind being called by their first name for the duration of the holiday. They agreed. I've never much liked being called mister, or, when I was a schoolmaster, sir. It was a convenience, no more. When I made friends with particular boys who comfortably called me by my first name *outside* school, their reverting to 'sir' when we were *in* school was a useful way of establishing the different context. As for mister, the origins of my objection are easily traced: it's how my father addressed me when he was angry. He'd spent time with the US Army during the war and got the practice from them. Senior officer to offending junior: 'You're dismissed, mister.'

Marshalled by the two Johns, we cycled through Belgium into Flanders, over the Ardennes, down into the Rhine valley, past the steep Lorelei rock near St Goar, south of Koblenz. About 140m high, famous for its remarkable echo, it's the traditional haunt of a siren who lures boatmen to their death. We stayed in youth hostels, got barked at by the gauleiter of one *Jugendherberge* for not putting our blankets round the right way on the bunks: '*Gott in Himmel*. You the *Fussende* to the *Kopfende* have put. Ziss against the rules is.' And again for not doing the washing-up in accepted fashion: by numbers, forks before knives and after plates.

It was on that trip that I realised I had a talent. We crossed what the two Johns told us was the highest peak in the Belgian Ardennes, the Baraque de Fraiture, or Plateau des Tailles, 652m, site of a crucial engagement on 23 December 1944 between the Americans and Germans during the Battle of the Bulge. The climb sits on the road between Liège and Bastogne and sometimes features in the famous there-and-back classic one-day race linking the two towns. The Ardennes hills aren't high – mountains start at 1,000m – but they are steep enough, and the Baraque de Fraiture was certainly the steepest and longest hill I'd ever encountered – some 50km of climbing in all from the northern approach, the final ascent around 15km.

The Coventry Eagle and I didn't fly up it, but we soon

went ahead of the rest in warm spring sunshine. It was my first long lone break on the bike. At the top, I dismounted and sat under a tree to wait. Had there been an ice-cream kiosk, I would have done a Bahamontes and bought a cone. Finally they appeared, the shattered bunch, all on foot. They flung their bikes to the grass and flopped down to recover. Someone asked me if I'd ridden all the way. Of course, I said, and Perkins, a 17-year-old club cyclist – smart machine, all the latest componentry – unfastened his saddlebag in an access of fury, cycled halfway down the hill then rode back up, just to prove that he had done it too. Except that he hadn't.

I never pursued the talent. I didn't have any friends in clubs and the idea of joining one never occurred to me. I doubt if I would have been allowed to. Financial as well as social constraints applied. My Saturdays were taken up with spare-time jobs, such as delivering meat for a butcher's in Finchley. The shop had an old bike – made of discarded domestic plumbing by the look of it – with a massive wicker basket in a cage on the front which, because it masked the undersized front wheel, made steering a puzzler at first. Turn the handlebars and the basket stayed pointing resolutely ahead while the bike veered sideways. Moving fast in rain down a wet road, I pedalled hard backwards to engage the rear brake, only for the wheel to lock, leaving me to slide helplessly straight for a junction with a busy main road, the bike out of control, the basket heavily laden with Sunday roasts, liver, bacon and sausages, but I contrived to stop, somehow.

Two

Taking to the Water

By now, the hormones were erupting, testosterone of the
endogenous variety kicking in, and though I never did go
in for time-trialling, I did a sort of against-the-clock most
weekends on the way home from my girlfriend's house. The
curfew was strict and policed by the in-house jailer with a sort
of itchy-finger, watchtower-guard fanaticism. Alleyne lived in
Belmont, about ten miles away with a cruel hill, Bittacy, en
route. Saying goodnight to her was like a slow and inexorable
countdown on the start line and the rides it launched were
always frenetic. The second hand of the clock moved in the
same slow-motion arc as my father's hand clubbing me about
the head. Get in past the deadline and the click of the front-
door latch would signal his hurtling down the stairs to give me
a frenzied belting. But, those merciless home runs taught me
how to ride out of my skin, acquainted me closely with that
suppression of physical stress in the mental focus on speed.

I learnt more about that peculiar phenomenon in a racing
shell on the River Wear in Durham, and it was taking to
the water which led me to forsake the bike for a while. The
president of the University Boat Club was a second-year
undergraduate in my college, and our instant friendship
inspired me to become an oarsman. As to going to Durham

University, I had all along intended to go to Sandhurst. My school cadet corps was highly militaristic, run by ex-regulars and TA, and sent a stream of boys to the Royal Military Academy. I was good at this amateur soldiering, passed an Officer Selection Board (pass rate less than 20%) at the age of sixteen, two years ahead of time, and enjoyed the *esprit de corps*. The word 'infantry' comes from a Scottish general who referred to his men affectionately as his children (*mes enfants*) and I found considerable comfort in the military family as opposed to the civvy version. I was almost certainly too bolshie in temperament to have been a good career officer. I once got a severe dressing-down from the regimental sergeant major (a friend of mine, it happened) when I told a young cadet he most certainly did *not* have to carry a weighty kitbag nearly as big as him to the three-ton lorry as ordered by a loutish warrant officer. That the WO was an up-his-own-arse jerk and I couldn't stand him probably showed, and the egalitarian spirit did not chime with regulations.

It was Alleyne who saved me from a life of regimental orders, mess-room hierarchies and parade-square uniformity. I walked her to the bus late one Saturday night, and, apropos of nothing, she suddenly said: 'You'd do well at university,' and that was that. *University*. Open sesame. A miraculous sudden widening of my mind to a possibility which I had never even contemplated but instantly recognised as being right. It was a massive relief. That Monday, I resigned from the corps without explanation and diverted all the energy I had hitherto expended on the military to academia. The stakes went up immediately. To get into Sandhurst, I needed no more than two A level passes. Now I not only needed good grades, I also signed up for S level English, the original state scholarship, with another boy. My results got me into Durham University's Bede College.

At Durham, I discovered a sport I adored and excelled in. The cross-country running at school suited me well, but it was on the water that I felt most at one with myself and in the gym that I gauged the full depths of my physical and mental tolerance. Unleashing my competitive aggression in the gruelling torture of circuit training lacked subtlety and science, of course. After the first session of weights, I was so stiff that I couldn't stand up straight for a fortnight. Told that one particular exercise with the barbell was good for the slabs of shoulder muscle, I felt above my collarbone: I didn't have any slabs of shoulder muscle. They came, eventually, as did the neatness of my bladework and, at the end of my first term, my friend the university president encouraged the Bede College captain of boats to try me out for the eight. After the trials, he called me to his room. 'I'm putting you in the boat,' he said. I was overjoyed.

In the first eight, we rowed the Thames Head of the River race before Easter, after which I went immediately into the second four for the inter-collegiate regatta, then, when our university oars were called to higher duties, into the first four. In the summer term, after a number of local regattas, we competed in the Lowe Bowl at Durham Regatta, a closed senior event for university colleges, Durham School and the university second four. Durham School invariably produced fast crews, the university seconds were strong and Bede didn't look likely winners. But we went through to the final and faced the School. They had just despatched the university four, in which our own captain of boats was rowing. He told us we could do it.

The waiting before a race was always appalling. We moped, sat around, felt sick and ill, weak as a flu patient, and made countless trips to the loo. When time came to lift the boat off the rack and walk it to the landing stage, I could hardly raise my arms, but, once clear of the staithe, the strength flowed back and the familiar sweep of the blades through the water reassured the mind that this was it, the final, and we *could* do it. Because racing in a shell requires total coordination and fluency of action, all four men in the crew moving as one, blades striking together, pulling together, extracting, feathering and angling back together, the level of concentration is almost mesmeric. Indeed, we frequently used to practise one-handedly, with our eyes shut, cultivating a fingertip balancing of the oars' looms, sensing the run of the boat, the consistency of the stroke, the harmony of our balanced moving up and down the slides, the total relaxation between strokes, complete force of work through the stroke. It was so much a combination of feel and power.

We sat on the stake boats, blades squared in the water at half-stroke, the School crew alongside, some three oars' length away. The start is an explosive sequence of short strokes, lengthening to full, accelerating to racing speed in as short a time as possible. It's nervy and alarmingly easy to tense up. The adrenalin pumps, but control is the essence. A racing shell is skittish, the slightest irregularity in displacing weight will tip it sideways. Each member of the crew has to be doing exactly the same as the others at every moment, and the motion forward and backward in the boat, the swing of outstretched arms moving the blade to the extreme of the arc at the catch then through to the finish and out again, has to be precisely measured, matched and managed. In the excited flurry of a start, that can easily be disrupted and the vital poise shot.

The umpire raises his flag. 'Get ready . . . GO!' and eight oars bite the water, spray flying, slides clunk to the back rest, the coxes roar. Half-stroke, three-quarters, three-quarters and full and the race is on, the water hissing down the smooth shiny varnish of the hull, blades sending away the puddles at the close of the stroke, faster and faster to flat out, every pull of the blade equivalent to lifting something like a 25kg sack of potatoes from floor to shoulder height.

I sit in the bow, the big men of the engine room, two Tims,

in front of me, Eric the stroke out of sight, Brian the cox evident only by his shouts of: 'Drive, Bede, let's take them, give me their stroke. I have stroke. Give me their three. Power on. You are going through. I have their three man. Give me their two man. I have their two man. You are doing very well – hard strokes, big finishes, clean at the catch, push through the water, push. I have their bow, I have their bow. Now, on the next stroke, give it ten, and . . . *drive* for one, *drive* for two, *drive* for three . . .'

And I see the School crew almost a length down on us even as we draw level with the College boathouse. An enormous roar goes up: 'BEEEEDE . . . BEEEEDE!' so loud it seems to whack the boat broadside and sock my midriff. We race on, our blades through air and water in metronomic good order, loose but tight, the synchronised weight of our combined strength thumping a fierce rhythm, the puddles where the oars lift at the end of the stroke swirling away, miniature whirlpools, spoiling the School's water. They hang on, but we are over halfway now, approaching the stone bridge at Elvet and, on our side, the tighter of the two arches. A steeper turn will take speed away from us, but so-called Easy Arch in Elvet Bridge (the other is Hard) adds a few feet of distance for our opponents, so the odds are equalled. This is a crucial test for the cox – the arches are narrow, there is scant leeway either side for the extended oars – but we are through, a perfect turn and into open water, our wake a smooth curve edged with bubbles. As we shoot the bridge, the School enter Easy. We have over a length, clear water and the boat is singing. I feel no physical stress at all, the sense of a coming victory dulls it. The School have no answer. We have them dead and the huge pleasure of watching them losing. It's the only sport where that is possible.

Brian our cox's calls are shot through with triumph now, the clamour for more work, higher rate – 'take it up, take it up to the finish' – laced with an irrepressible tone of congratulation, just to show them, to ram the win home, to savour the exorbitant thrill of our superiority this day. I see the trees bending over the riverbanks, the glorious sight of the trailing crew clawing at our water and we are there, across the line, first. The pain hits at once, the lungs gasping and every muscle in your body wrung with the agony of stopping the effort, but it doesn't last long this time. The jubilation of winning numbs any physical distress and we rap the sides of the boat in salute for the School crew. Brian: 'Three cheers for Durham, 'ray . . . 'ray . . . 'ray,' and they for us. Then we are turning round for the delicious languid row back home in triumph, as the beaten four paddle disconsolately across the river to their landing stage below the west end of the great Norman cathedral overhead on the peninsula.

There were other pots, but first pot is the sweetest. In my second year, the Cuthbert's Society four beat us narrowly the few times we met. In one race, they won by 2ft only, neck and neck the whole way – such a gut-wrenching effort it took me a week to recover.

The Coventry Eagle never went to Durham, only the 11-plus machine, and it was stolen from the boathouse during one vacation. It occurred to me then to ask my father for the money I had accumulated all through primary school, buying savings certificates that I had handed over to him for safe keeping. 'I bought your bike with them,' he said. It wouldn't surprise me if he'd got someone to steal it for resale.

The annual trike race happened in Rag Week, round the quadrangled road on Palace Green, past the cathedral, the castle, the university library and a block of fusty old lecture rooms, locus of disquisitions on theology, Latin and Greek grammar and literature for centuries.

Most colleges entered the standard kid's tricycle that the letter – and spirit – of the rules demanded. One college boasted a large number of men in the university cycle club, and they souped up their machines with extended seat pillars, drop-handled bars, toe-clipped pedals and fancy wheels, hubs and chains. This not only gave them gross extra speed but the advantage of comfort too. Riding a small trike, cramped over its tiny frame, is horribly punishing on the thigh muscles. I could manage no more than about ten circuits before my legs seized up, whereat I handed over the relay to another member of our team, while the club men hardly needed relays. I did, however, have the experience of those early days: I could corner faster and tighter than anyone in the race and, resentful of the unfair mechanical edge the club men enjoyed over the hoi polloi, exacted symbolic revenge on one of them. Coming up on his wheel as we headed for the right-hand right-angled bend, I accelerated and slipped inside as he moved wider and tried to steer across the crown. I held my line to manoeuvre him out of space. He lost control and careered off the course through the crowd, who opened a gap to let him through, and came off in a heap. A massive cheer went up – the professionals, as in 'professional foul', weren't popular – and I hurtled on, unscratched. It is and will remain the only time I have ever delighted in a cyclist's coming to grief.

It occurs to me that the closest I have since come to the excitement and cohesion of rowing at near perfect balance and speed is the joy of cycling in a big bunch, which I get to do only rarely. There is, however, a similar physical and, yes, emotional harmony.

Between river and road
Why on earth I bought such a sorry piece of bric-à-brac I can't explain: a bile-green Raleigh with the charm of a derelict cooker and the mechanical efficiency of a bent screwdriver. Between leaving Durham and taking up my second job, as

head of classics at Gresham's School in Norfolk (my first was head of classics at Rossall Junior School in Lancashire), I lost touch with rivers, because there were no rivers near me, and played rugby. The cranky old bike ferried me the seven miles between my house and school and the cabinetmaker's workshop where I made furniture in every spare moment I had. It got stolen by one of the boys and returned anonymously on an offer of amnesty, but it stirred no affection in me. I did not even think of it as contributing to my fitness. Returning from a harvest supper in Corpusty, some distance from where I lived in Norfolk, the back tyre went flat. I was too tired to bother and rode on. It didn't make that much difference to the feel of the bloody thing. Eventually the back wheel seized up and locked solid. I got off and, in the dim light of a pale moon shining high above the deserted tract of land in which I stood, made out, just, that the inner tube had gradually oozed its way out from the tyre cover, snaked round the hub and tightened itself into an obdurately unpickable knot. Startled by a pheasant ockle-ockle-ockling across the road from the hedgerow, I began to fiddle at the vindictive oversized condom and, having finally got it free, remounted and rode home on the squelching tyre. I had no spare tube, anyway. That about sums up my feelings on the fossil.

One day, returning from the afternoon's rugby coaching to the school sanatorium, where I habitually changed and took a shower, the nurse, who had been awaiting my arrival, told me that I had to report to the local hospital next morning, urgently. I was given no further explanation.

Kelling Hospital, set in pine woods near Holt, had been built for the treatment of tubercular patients when the affliction, often called the disease of the poor, was rife, in the 1920s. The consultant who confronted me when I was called for examination was a pulmonary specialist. He snapped the X-rays taken at a routine check-up onto the viewing screen and said: 'On the evidence of these shadows across your lungs, you shouldn't even have the strength to stand up for very long – the effort would place too excessive a strain on you – let alone run around a rugby pitch. We need to do some tests. You were told to bring pyjamas, wash bag, books, etc., were you?'

I nodded. 'How long is it going to take?' I asked.

'I don't know. Ten days, two weeks?'

Two weeks' skiving through an unnecessary convalescence when I was a kid to skip school exams was one thing, playing hookey now that I had professional responsibilities on the other side of the desk was something else, but for nearly a fortnight in Kelling that's how it felt. I lolled about, underwent various tests, was told next to nothing, occasionally had visitors, read a lot and suffered intermittent pangs of extreme conscience at this buckshee fraudulent holiday. One morning, the consultant arrived and asked me how I was feeling. I told him I was tip-top, rude health, raring to go, and he, perhaps to teach me a lesson, announced that I would be having a bronchoscopy next day, general anaesthetic, no food after six in the evening. The suspicion was that the shadows on my lungs were scarring from an attack of sarcoidosis, possibly malign, where itinerant alien spores in search of grazing land on human flesh munch it for a while and, replete, lift off again. They leave scars. These scars were the blotches on the X-rays.

Next morning, I was wheeled, semi-comatose with the pre-med opium injection, into the theatre, and, while I was off dancing cheek to cheek with the sleep fairies, a robot camera roamed the canals and tubes of my chest cavity, bouncing off the walls like a racing bobsleigh. When it had taken its quota of pictures of the remote landscapes of my thorax, it tugged on the line and was jerked and hauled back up the shafts by the production crew waiting on the surface. I think, perversely, of the 12 midgets hired to publicise an opening of a Disney film in Manhattan from a rooftop. Someone incautiously sent up some whisky, the midgets got roaring drunk and had to be lowered back to the pavement in instalments in a large laundry basket.

I woke up feeling completely flattened, pummelled, hoarse, sick and faint. Not dissimilar to the wait for a race.

The consultant walked in. 'You're fine,' he said in that breezy way the medics have when they think they're in control because they've got the readout. 'You can go home.'

Fine, I thought, pondering the infelicity. If you say so, mate. He then dilated on the results of the bronchoscopy. Luckily, the sarcoidosis had been benign, but the scars on the lung tissue would diminish my intake of oxygen and radically impair my physical capacity. 'You won't be able to push yourself so hard,' he said. 'There will be, I am afraid, a gradual slowing down.'

This wasn't a death sentence. It wasn't even a very well constructed sentence. Nevertheless, slowing down wasn't in my vocabulary then or since, and, given that he had just told me I was fine when I knew I wasn't, equally I would choose to ignore his prognostications about my slowing down. To hell with that. I was 26 years old. Time for some new wheels.

It wasn't hard to ditch the fossil. (It might have come out of that bike shop in Finchley whose floor was knee-deep in tangled up bits and pieces of bike over which the owner had to clamber to serve at the counter. What on earth he sold in there I can't recall, but it was the biggest installation of metallic rubbish I have ever seen outside some of the whackier exhibits in Tate Modern.) On it, I rode home from supper one night in Norfolk, fairly drunk, having regaled the company with vapourings about how excess of alcohol doesn't make too much difference to riding a bike. In the pitch black, my front lamp shining not even as brightly as a good deed in a naughty world, I came off four times, and, finally, in a ditch, fuddled, far gone and quite flummoxed as to which parts of this densely knit congeries of assorted matter were me, which were the bike and which were the hedge I had steered into, I truly thought I was going to have to stay there and sleep it off. I did finally manage to get me to my feet and the bike upright and both of us home, but it was a close call, and the lacerations on my face, arms and legs next day bore disgraceful witness to my swinish overindulgence.

Out shopping in Holt one Saturday, I met Alison, a friend who worked at J.M. Dent. She was editing the new *Everyman's Encyclopaedia* and asked me if I happened to know a man whose name I have now forgotten. I asked why. She said she needed someone to write the entry on cycling as a sport. I told her I could do that and got the job. Being the first piece I ever wrote on cycling remains perhaps its only distinction.

Three

Tour de France and Cowshit Corner

The advertisement in the local paper read 'For sale: racing bicycle'. I don't remember the price, but the seller lived in North Walsham, some distance from Lower Gresham, where I lived. During the war, all the road signs in Norfolk were taken down to confuse any enemy who contrived to get ashore. After the war, the task of relocating them was obviously parcelled out to teams of goofs with no sense of direction, scant grip of place names and quaint ideas of what is funny. Finding the way through the back roads and byroads of deepest Norfolk in the inspissated gloom of unillumined night can be a trial. You follow signs to Barningham, say, arrive at a T-junction within a mile or so of the place, it's pitch black, not a light to be seen anywhere, and the only sign indicates some town 15 miles distant, nary a mention of Barningham. I did see Barningham once, briefly, on a bike ride. Next time I went, it had been moved. That or it was actually Bessingham, after all.

I eventually found the house and, inside, the bike. I took one look and knew it had to be mine – a mass-produced machine inscribed with a one-off name: Eddy Merckx.

I had, by now, become a devotee of the Tour de France, and that was, in part, because of Laurence.

Having been a live-in house tutor at Gresham's for two years,

I'd decided to swap free subsistence for independence, rented a horribly damp house on a farm estate and moved in at the beginning of the summer holidays. Then, almost immediately, I bought 'Middle House' in Lower Gresham. That summer, I'd started making furniture at Rob Corbett's workshop. He taught part-time at the school. I asked him if I could come to learn cabinetmaking and he agreed. He didn't hesitate. He loved making furniture and was ready to help anyone who shared the passion. That he took me on without a clue as to whether I had any flair or ability was remarkable. He took me on no more than trust.

And it was not as if trust had always paid off for Rob. He had been in the navy and, going back from leave, had discreetly trailed another rating with the same ship's name on his cap stop to stop on the London Underground because he didn't know the way. When they both alighted at Ealing, the end of the line, Rob finally asked the other sailor the way, because he was following him. 'I don't know,' said the other man. 'I've been following *you*.'

The gift of trust is beyond price, the offer of it, an incalculable generosity. The writer Jean Cocteau, in disconsolate mood, once groaned that he was getting no encouragement in his work. This was an expression of a darker, more profound problem, his own lost confidence, and his friend, Sergei Diaghilev, the great Russian impresario and latter-day Maecenas, saw it. He also saw the talent and said: '*Etonnez-moi . . . je vous attends.*' (Astonish me, I'll wait.) Astonish me because I know you *can*. It was gentle, it was tough.

The first morning Rob had me manhandling large heavy baulks of elm through the power cross-cut saw and stacking the pieces in stick, that is on slivers of wood to allow air to circulate. 'I'll soon cure you of this bugger,' he said, with a smile, 'this bugger' being the maggot in my head about learning how to make furniture. I ran with sweat, my arms ached, I was coated with a layer of evil-smelling elm sawdust – it encrusted my lips and eyes – the high-pitched whine of the electric motor and the bite of the teeth in the wood was vile, my concentration was fevered by a constant fear that one of my hands would slide off the timber into the spinning blade, but I resolutely refused to be cured of *this bugger*. Next morning, Rob greeted me at the workshop door and said: 'OK, we're going to make thirteen chairs, and two will be for you.' I hadn't expected any payment: this was largesse indeed. We set to.

At the mortise machine: a fairly straightforward task, lowering the bit onto the marked square, except that on one marked square I got the piece of wood the wrong way round. In went the bit, realisation struck like a wasp at my neck and my brain got the shakes. I stumbled across the workshop floor, clasping the ruined wood as if it must be the rod for my miscreant wrists. Rob, hunched over his bench, peering through glasses held together with Sellotape, the lenses screened with dust and impastoed with fingerprints where he'd tried desultorily to clean them, looked up and beamed. 'Cock-up?' he said. I couldn't speak. I mumbled some miserable syllable of apology and nodded. 'We always expect a cock-up,' he said. 'It's a bonus when it goes right.'

One long hot afternoon of that long hot summer, a middle-aged woman walked into the workshop and stood in the doorway. She had a girl with her. Rob's assistant Smithy and I stood behind our benches and looked down the workshop towards the nimbus of bright sunshine spilling in through the doorway and the two women caught in its light. 'Hello, Joyce,' said Rob.

'Hello, Rob,' she replied. 'This is Laurence, from Paris. I'm showing her round the village.'

'You've come to the right place, then,' he said. 'Do you want a cup of tea?'

They demurred, stood awhile longer, staring round at the

workshop, the machines, us – Smithy and me behind our benches, idle, out of courtesy – then said goodbye.

Over our cup of tea, which came almost immediately, Smithy chortled and said: 'I wouldn't mind taking her out.'

'Who, Joyce?' said Rob.

'Fuck off. The French girl.'

I liked Smithy. He was about my age, around 25, down to earth, faintly amused that a bookworm should be wanting to learn how to make furniture – he'd been put to that by his pushy mum when his yen had been to follow his father and work on the land. He mocked my hay fever, for instance – 'Hay fever? Middle-class disease. Little old farm boys can't afford no hay fever' – but was endlessly patient with my questions and uncertainty about what to do next. (In Norfolk parlance, 'little old' is a stock epithet, hence a 'little old baby' in a cot or a 'little old labourer' of 70 summers.) Smithy was engaged on what used to be called self-improvement, i.e. learning to cook. Example, on a piece of paper left in the well of his bench: 'Recipe for boiled potatoes.' *Recipe* may be a bit strong, but if you've never boiled a potato, you need a method, obviously.

Now, if anyone was going to take that French girl out, it was going to be me, I thought, and after work I cycled straight up to Joyce's house. Rob and I had set a large gatepost at the top of their drive a few weeks before.

I knocked at the door. Laurence answered, a wide-eyed girl of 17 with chestnut-brown hair, a gap in her teeth, a glint in her eyes and a winsome grin. In the scraps of French still left over from school days, like discarded lists in a pocket, I asked her if she'd like to come out for a drink with me that evening. She smiled indulgently, said yes and, at 7.30, I returned in my old Rover and knocked once more at the door. This time Jean's husband Bill, whom I had never met, answered. 'I've come for Laurence,' I said.

'The French girl?' he said, and I wondered how many other teenaged female foreign nationals they were boarding for the summer.

'Yes,' I said. And so we went out.

Next morning, a Saturday, I arrived at the workshop and Rob gave me a twinkling smile, lips pursed on the buttons of a laugh. 'Bill phoned me last night. For a reference.'

'Oh, yes,' I said. 'What did you say?'

'I lied,' he blurted, and the laughter popped its lendings and burst forth.

So began a friendship and then love affair with Laurence which endured for many years. On one visit to Paris, I discovered the cycling monthly *Miroir du Cyclisme*, superior in every way to the cycling journalism available in England. *Cycling Weekly*, 'the comic', wasn't much better than a parish magazine in my opinion and its forays across the Channel to the real home of professional bike racing were infrequent and half-hearted. The *Miroir* put me in touch with the great tradition of Continental racing, and I was enthralled. I am sometimes asked how long it took me to write my book about the Tour de France. In simple terms, that's easy to answer, but in fact it took me some 20-odd years of study and enthusiasm – OK, obsession.

From a bookshop en route from the metro station to the apartment where Laurence lived with her mother and two sisters, I bought Marcel Bidot's *L'Epopée du Tour de France*, the 'epic', from the Greek *epos*: a word, then the great tapestry that words weave into an epic poem. Already I was becoming acquainted with the sense that the Tour was rather more than just a bike race. Desgrange's vision made of it something central to the French national psyche, hence his passionate belief that the 1919 Tour was integral to post-war recovery. The very first time the *Grande Boucle* strayed beyond the frontiers of the hexagon it was into Alsace, German-occupied territory, in 1905. The insinuation was pointed. During the Second World War, the race director who succeeded Desgrange (he died, aged 75, in 1939, 17 days after the Tour reached Paris), Jacques Goddet, was approached by the German occupying administration. They wanted him to organise a Tour de France to show that the country was in good shape, morale high, enjoying life. He refused point-blank: the Tour was not going to be made into an enemy propagandist's cat's paw.

One of Smithy's cousins, Roy Wyman, came frequently to Norfolk visiting the family. A brilliant mechanic – he built wheels for Alan Shorter in his spare time – he worked in the Vauxhall factory at Luton. He'd wanted to be a gamekeeper, but marriage had ended that. (Perhaps he was better out of it. I knew one Norfolk gamekeeper whose penchant was for rogering a goose whilst wringing its neck for the oven.) Roy was a talented rider, rode a lot of races, including the Tour of Scotland with the army team some time in the '60s, and was my first contact with the world of real cycling as opposed to the kind of dossing to which I was accustomed. Roy had raced a lot in Belge, as he calls it, knew many men of Flanders, the hard-nut kermesse riders, the old stars of track and one-day who ran bars in and around the famous towns and circuits, the coming generation of cyclo-cross and road specialists, like the de Vlaemincks, as well as the mechanics, the fans. We got on well. He has a wry sense of humour, an easy manner and a knack with stories. We rode together whenever we could. A favourite route was the Cowshit Corner run, starting at Binham, where we picked up Richard Wood, the school doctor. Cowshit Corner, my coinage, was on the cusp of a bend outside Richard's house, opposite a cattleyard.

Richard had never ridden a bike before I met him. He was a first-rate doctor with a louche contempt for most of the medical profession, a man of easy charm and darker loathings. His book (with Peter Turner) on the celebrated Norfolk photographer Peter Henry Emerson appeared in 1974, but he was, characteristically, dismissive of it. Educated at Harrow, he had that disdainful feigned superiority to anything so vulgar as being good at anything or showing away about it. He was, though, very witty, amusing, irreverent, bright and wonderfully good company. His enthusiasm for cycling went from total ignorance to absolute addiction in about the time it took to buy a racing machine and bring it home.

Roy, Richard and I coursed the lanes of Norfolk, bantered and laughed, Roy calling the sprints, me haring out to what I thought was the finish, Roy sailing past off my wheel with a mocking cry: 'Wrong line.' He arrived one day with three slivers of aluminium cut from discarded Campagnolo chain sets: one for each of us and Smithy. (Smithy did not ride, although he did have a growing collection of oldish machines which, in the Norfolk idiom, he was 'tricolating up' as his fleet of bikes for hire.) Thus, for the first and only time since the Bede College Boat Club, I became a member of an unofficial masonry: the Campagnolo Key-ring Club. I kept my curved fragment of the holy metal blessed by the sacred name on a loop of leather lace, to which I also attached the front-door key of Middle House, a handsome mortise number with a shapely elliptical hanger.

The Merckx bike had brought me on. The to and fro to Gresham's was flat out in the mornings, because I was always short on time, and a tired but grateful escape from school in the evenings. I not infrequently mounted the machine very late on a Saturday night, having taken a party of boys to the theatre in Norwich, for example. Sundays I kept sacrosanct, for myself, no intrusion of classroom or extracurriculum. I made it a rule never to take marking home – I shifted that at school. Most of my colleagues (as they styled themselves) in the common room went into a sort of state of suspended animation during the holidays, all purpose for their being in abeyance till term started again. They moaned and snapped peevishly on the first day of term – bloody this and bloody that – but it was quite obvious that they relished being back, being schoolmasters, fulfilling their life's true function, like the prefects they had once been but with added clout and status. They had had their own apogee as public schoolboys – names on the honours boards, first XI or XV colours, the cynosure of every eye in big school or chapel – a brief sortie into the otherworld beyond the alma mater, where they shone less brightly, university being a forum rather more taxing on particular distinction, and so once more to the home patch, possessed now of a degree and possibly the coveted Blue, home to the familiar scene, the worn vocabulary and the same old shtick as masters reminiscing on the glory departed, *o tempora, o mores* the ceaseless burthen of their irascible lament. Schoolmasters sighing for the glory departed.

For me, life was what happened outside school, and I was ever reluctant to quit it. My tardiness was all part of that – like Shakespeare's 'whining schoolboy, with his satchel/And shining morning face, creeping like a snail/Unwillingly to school'. Occasionally I got a timely lift from a local copper – he was an acquaintance, bundled the bike into the patrol car and whisked me in – but more generally I was a disgracefully bad timekeeper. There was, too, *always* a headwind. Halfway along my journey, past the ruined workhouse Beckham Palace, the road turned sharp right in a dog-leg, but that malevolent observer, the Demon of the Gales, watching me execute the 90° bend through his lunar quartz eyeglass, alerted his minions and the evil gremlin crew swung the celestial turbines round on their mountings to drive the wind full into my face, still.

One morning when I walked into my classroom – part of the Thatched Buildings, as insalubrious as an abandoned games hut redolent of unwashed bodies, desiccated floorboards and damp paper – the boys of the fifth-form Latin set stood to greet me, chairs scraping, an unmelodious chant of 'Good morning, sir' followed by a suggestive silence, broken by one of them, who asked: 'Is your clock right, sir?' I looked at the clock. I was early. Cheeky urchin.

Gresham's was a fairly happy school, relatively undistinguished intellectually, but, as in so many public schools of the day, the prefects had too much power and abused it. One punishment required a boy to run round each of the five boarding houses and get a note signed by the duty prefect. The Old School House, of which I was tutor, is in the nearby town of Holt, so the run took time. One of our boys, an inoffensive, not very good-looking (that signified) dimwit, a gangly, unhygienic boy with no athleticism in him (that also signified), thus a prime bullying target, was given a round-the-houses run. The prefects at the farmost house refused to sign his chitty until he had run up a flight of concrete steps, backwards, a few times and they were satisfied. He ran, they were not satisfied, he kept running and, finally, they broke him, physically, psychologically. He wept uncontrollably, but, such was his sense of alienation, I suppose, he did not report what had happened either to me or the housemaster. I found out – the rumour telegraph – got the story from him and, next morning, asked the headmaster for a meeting with the housemasters. That nasty bit of teenage sadism was eradicated.

The Merckx machine had kindled a new desire for speedier riding on a more extreme bike. Tapping his contacts, Roy got me a second-hand royal-blue Alan Shorter hand-built frame and a pair of Shorter wheels. I added Weinmann brakes, Stronglight chainset and bars named for the Giro di Sicilia – one of the few races Merckx didn't win. He was, though, my inspiration, and the fact that he used Campagnolo componentry in my view merely confirmed his lofty brilliance – for that name, Campag to the aficionado, had something of the Grail about it and still does.

It was the way the Campag rear mech, apparently made of goblin silver, was so compact, instantly recognisable from the ubiquitous Huret, and the elegant slim tongue-shaped levers, speckle-edged with tiny embossed detail, shimmering with the kind of classy superfluity that whispered excellence. The lustrous Campag chainwheels had the filigree refinement of a brooch fashioned by the great Renaissance craftsman Benvenuto Cellini. Even the specialised Campagnolo toolkit, costing at least a junior prince's ransom, had the glitter and finesse of a casket of jewels. When it came to components, I badly wanted something Campag on it, anything Campag on it, but had not the money. From the very start, the stuff was expensive, three or four times the price of the alternatives. For Campagnolo had only ever used the best steel and alloys, and where other early chainwheels, pedal cranks held in with cotter pins, rarely held true, the cotterless Campag item always ran straight. And the cantilever of his rear mech could withstand rough handling. Where a Simplex gear buckled if the bike fell over, the Campag parallelogram absorbed the impact and sprang back into position. But I could not afford the Campag and reluctantly sank to Simplex. Yet, aching for the exorbitantly priced former, I had an idea: the bolt that holds the seat pin in the frame. Campag made one – twice if not three times the price of a common-or-garden bolt – but I shelled out, and Shorter got the holy touch, albeit small: the blessing of Campagnolo.

On the Shorter, I rode my first, and last, time-trial, on a road south of Norwich. I turned up one evening and was allowed to ride with one of the local clubs. So long used to riding by myself or with my pals, yet conscious of wanting to find out how fast I was, not just how fast I felt, I decided it was time for a showing. So much for that. I was overtaken by my minute man, trailed in with a sense of 'what's all this about?' and went home, neither disappointed nor giving up.

This was decidedly not my scene. My instinct was for road-racing, and it was, too, the clubbiness of the meeting which put me off. I didn't want to be part of that. I'm not a joiner, I'm a stripper. Flogging up and down a designated piece of road didn't appeal, and one taste was enough. I renounced on it. Trimming seconds off times didn't interest me. I was as fast as I was, and who cared how fast. I covered the distances I covered as hard as I could. I knew how to push myself to the limit, and, conscious of that doctor's commination, push myself I would. I did, however, note my ignorance, my lack of experience, nous, cunning. That's what Roy had, from his years of racing. Me? Brute force and absolutely no application of the bonce.

It must be said, too, that in those days there was not the opening for road-races that there is today. Even so, my approach tends to be all or nothing, and I would simply not have wanted to devote the time to racing unless I was as well prepared as I could be.

Yearning for a skill had taken me to Rob's workshop, and I remain convinced that skills are a vital part of education. For sure, I had linguistic skills, which I had not put to much use as yet, but I had not really been aware of acquiring them. Words had always come easily. I adored Latin and Greek literature and grammar, and thanks to Laurence my French was improving. She told me, early on, with a gleeful smile: '*Tu parles Français comme une vache Espagnole.*' (You speak French like a Spanish cow.) Had she wanted to be really acerbic, the cow would have been Basque. About a year later, however, in one of her letters – she wrote in French, I in English, we conversed in a fluent swap of both languages – she wrote: '*La vache Espagnole est morte.*' (The Spanish cow is dead.) It was a great accolade.

Through Rob, I not only acquired a skill almost from scratch. In the painstaking process of acquiring it, I learnt what a skill was. In his workshop, I learnt more about writing, my life's work, than ever I got from books or study: about starting a job and seeing it through, about keeping one's nerve, about the mystery of construction and the risk of stretching, always stretching, preconceived, even predetermined, limits. The Spanish windlass, for instance – a nautical contrivance.

I was mending a governness's cart for a friend. One of the door posts had broken in half and the top had sprung out, taking a section of the side with it. I made a new post, fastened it to the loose flap and now addressed the task of seating it in position with the lower part of the cart's side securely housed. To bend the assembly into place, I bound a length of stout rope round the whole cart, loosely enough to allow a loop into which I inserted a timber baton. Twisting this tightened the girdle and steadily drew the flap of the side back to where it should be: the Spanish windlass. Rob supervised the operation, and, as I drew the rope tighter and tighter, the cart squeaked and squealed ominously. The gap closed steadily to begin with, but the closer the door post got to its correct position, the harder the twisting became, the more shrill the complaints of the tormented wood. (Torment, torque and torture all come from the Latin word for twist, as on the rack.)

The post seemed to be there, the rope seemed to be as tight as it could get, the job seemed to be done, but no, look closely and there was just a shaving of a gap. The post *wasn't* quite home, and home was where it had to be. 'Give it another turn,' said Rob. My hands were sweating. I could just imagine a turn too far and the entire trap imploding and slumping to the floor, matchwood, firewood, broken lumber, no longer the cart I had undertaken to repair.

I grasped the handle and, heaving at the weight, slowly wound it a single revolution, the yelps of the wood hideous to the ear, the rope strained to its limit, my nerves going the same way, but, as the tension racked up, the tiny gap closed and the post went in sweetly. 'Done it,' said Rob, with evident relief. He'd been as apprehensive as I, and that was always the phrase: 'You've done it, then?'

In learning even the rudiments of a cabinetmaker's trade, I began another trade, that of writing. There was an element of wanting to test myself, too. As a schoolmaster, I was, effectively, asking and answering the same questions that had been the pabulum of my intellectual life since I began at primary school and all the way through to university. Most of the schoolmasters I encountered hadn't even got a teaching qualification. They had spent almost their entire lives in school, as amateurs and then professionals. What, in short, had they ever done outside a classroom? Not much.

In my first year out of teaching, I worked as a self-employed builder. I had to start from the very bottom, as it were, and the learning curve was horribly steep, but I was earning money by my own skill and wits. That, I observe, is not so different from the trade of a racing cyclist. They call it the *métier* in French, from the Latin word *ministerium*, which means the office of a priestly attendant and then work, labour, employment. Simply put, that entails learning what to do and how to do it most efficiently. The task requires both physical and intellectual adaptation.

There was never a time when I did not want to be a writer, just as most racing professionals never wanted to do anything but ride a bike. I came late to the practice of the calling, stalled by immaturity and a naive amateurism. I could write, I reckoned, but there were, I told myself in excuse, plenty of people who could write, so why should I? Like quitting the schoolmaster's life, writing has to be *done*. As Anthony Burgess put it, when he got going, 'there was a job to be done', and that is the way I see it, inspiration and inner compulsion to boot. There is another factor, and that is the sense that whether you can or cannot do something well, if it is something only you can do, some unique bit of human activity or enterprise, then you must do it or waste a gift, however slender the gift is. When Brian Robinson spoke so casually of all it took to get him from Yorkshire to the Continent and earn his bread as a professional bike-rider as 'learning the trade', my heart warmed. That is on the button. We talk on the phone now and then, and, in the course of one conversation, he expressed what I take to be the nub of the true professional attitude: 'You care but you don't worry.' Every time a piece of my work is rejected, by publisher, magazine editor, potential agent, BBC commissioning editor, the disappointment is keen. Every time. But a setback merely stiffens the resolve. For, as Mark Twain put it, 'A man ought not to get depressed by setbacks, he should make up his mind to get even.'

One Easter, Laurence's middle sister Sylvie asked me a favour. She made the request in her formal lopsided Anglopoise: 'I would very much prefer to pass this summer in England with the aim to improve my English. This would be a nice exploit, I believe.' I said of course I would help. She added: 'Perhaps it would therefore be possible, if you advice, hrchm, advise me to procure an employment on my behalf and also a friend of mine, a girl, who is very nice and entertains a similar intention.' They'd stay in Middle House with Laurence and me, of course. I got the two of them jobs as waitresses/housemaids at the Grand Hotel in Cromer, once a favoured venue for the toffs from London – Oscar Wilde and the racy set were habitués – now a rather seedy relic of its former fashionable heyday. Smithy rented me two of his bikes so they could get around.

Four

Very Flat? Norfolk?

In the weeks before they arrived, I took to the roads. In Noël Coward's *Private Lives*, Elyot and Amanda, a divorced couple, meet by chance, each on honeymoon with their new spouses. The exchanges are acid:

> AMANDA: Where did you meet her?
> ELYOT: At a house party in Norfolk.
> AMANDA: [Pause.] Very flat, Norfolk.

It's not true. Bits of it are flat, mainly in the south and west, but the bit where I lived was far from flat. In fact, Ron Hill, the long-distance runner, described the Norfolk marathon course (which I ran twice) as one of the hardest he knew.

The Cromer Ridge, southernmost extremity of the Ice Age glacial sheet, turns the north Norfolk coast road into a big dipper: sharp hills, curvaceous meanders, snaps of gradient that deliver constant change of rhythm and make it a perfect training ride. Some of the climbs inland are pretty tough – Bard's Hill out of Salthouse, the winding ascent up to the Roman Camp from West Runton, the final hoist into Holt – and there are a few stinkers in the hinterland, where the landscape is pitted with dells and hollows and the geology squirms as if wrestling against that silly slur, that canard, 'flat'. I rode in all directions from Middle House: down Sustead Lane past the clumps of wild orchid, the banks of wild honeysuckle beloved of flocks of goldfinches and out along the extensive perimeter brick wall of the Felbrigg estate – that wall I used to clamber over in winter to scrump fallen beechwood for my open fire. In the opposite direction, the lanes round the far distant Holkham estate, home of the mad Earl of Leicester, were very different in character: lined with hedges or winding through broad open fields like irrigation channels. I thought nothing of 30- and 40-mile round trips for a swim off the sandy shore at Wells or Burnham or the nearer shingle beach at Cley-next-the-Sea, where I still bathe whenever I am there. Along those cross-country byroads, not so long ago, I was struck by lightning. Belting back to my friend's house in a thunderstorm, I felt a smart slap on my head as if from a fish slice. Lightning. Cleared my system out a treat.

Richard and I cycled the Peddar's Way one weekend. Originally a Roman road – it runs straight as a beeline across the Brecks to the farmlands – it was tramped by pedlars (i.e. peddars) in the Middle Ages and runs some 93 miles from Knettisham Heath, east of Thetford, through Thetford Chase, a vast acreage of woodland once a hunting park, north-west to the coast at Holme next the Sea. We met at Castle Acre on Saturday morning, rode up the unmade trail, stopped at a pub and saw the ten minutes' worth of Tour de France coverage that was our weekly staple in 1975, the year Merckx got beaten. Wanting him to win so badly, did I bring him bad luck? Silly. Thévenet's victory was masterful. I met Thévenet years later, for an interview, and we have since become friends. That time at the Hotel Ibis by Charles de Gaulle airport, we talked for about three-quarters of an hour. I recorded the conversation, which I never do with an English speaker. Listening and talking in French, however, I am always undecided in what language to scribble frantic notes. I finally switched off the machine, asked him if he'd like a beer, and we talked on. When it came time to leave, I said that in winning the Tour he had beaten my hero. He smiled broadly, gave a slight shrug and said: '*Désolé.*' (Sorry.)

The Peddar's Way climbs up and skitters down humps on an earthen then sandy track. Near Heacham, we beheld the wide purple and lilac spread of the lavender fields like a royal carpet. At Hunstanton, a Victorian seaside town and beach resort – Sunny Hunny – with famous stripy cliffs, we swam and cycled on to the hotel at Thornham. Next day, we rode east through the narrow roads which criss-cross the broader highways to Warham Camp, near where Richard lived, for a last can of beer, under Norfolk's big sky. He later moved to Staithes near Whitby and I encountered, for the first time, the extortionate percentage rates of the steep Yorkshire banks.

Riding the lanes of Norfolk now, some 30 years on, their familiarity rises on the yeast of memory. Recently, from Bale, famous for its sacred grove of *ilex*, or holm oaks, a very pagan site cheek by jowl with the church, to Corpusty for lunch with Rob and his wife Mary, I powered through Sharrington, Brinton and Stody, near the farm estate where I'd briefly rented that house. From Hunworth Green, the back road narrows, and suddenly I recalled the ford round the corner, and there it was. The round flint tower of Edgfield Church stands a mile from the village it once served, and the road climbs through trees to a slight crest from where it zips down to the track following the course of the Bure to Corpusty. It flips over an old railway bridge, below it a disused railway line, closed by Dr Beeching in that pernicious vandalism of the nation's railways.

I still love Norfolk: the good times as well as the bad have no hold over me now. They are past and we move on. Revisiting a place need not entail reliving what happened there, and of that I am glad. We are an amalgam of all that has happened to us, but we need not make that amalgam a sort of filler with which to plug the gaps in our happiness or understanding. Keep nothing shut. Keep, rather, an open mind, an open heart and open eyes. Rob once came across a man digging a narrow hole in a field with a spit spade. Holes fascinate Rob: the technology, the bodily contortions of getting earth to the surface. He asked the man what the hole was for. The man stood up and replied that he was 'mortising the globe'. Not a bad metaphor for the thirst for experience and the wisdom it imparts: mortising the globe.

I drove to meet the three young Frenchwomen, Laurence, her sister and her friend, at Norwich station. Sylvie I knew, of course, Françoise I knew not at all and, within a few days of their arrival, did not wish to know any better. She took the house over. She struck me as being vain, showy, loud, fragile, neurotic, childish and spoilt. She had sex spilling out of her and feigned not to notice. It was a relief when they set off for the day's skivvying, but, their first Saturday night, they were still not home at past eleven o'clock, after an afternoon shift. I had no phone and found myself in the unwelcome position of fretting grown-up *in loco parentis*. Laurence fretted at my anxiety and remained silent. We went to bed.

Some time after midnight, car lights blazed up the lonely road on which stood my house, the middle of a terrace of three. Car doors opened, shrieks of laughter and loud raucous cries. I went down to see Sylvie and Françoise joshing merrily with two guys, one of whom was heaving their bikes out of the boot into which they had been crammed like junk. Françoise was playing hostess: 'Come in for a drink, come on.'

'Forget that,' I said. 'Where have you been?'

'Out. What's wrong with that?'

There wasn't anything wrong with that. What could be wrong with that? They were grown up too, except that it was my house and I had to go on living there after the rowdy irruption of Parisian nightlife into the bucolic tranquillity. I saw the Lotharios off into the night, and the atmosphere in the house went from uneasy to fraught.

They gave up waitressing, where their English might have been improved, and instead went strawberry picking, which paid better but where their English would founder in the wash of local dialect and pronunciation. Françoise was staying a fortnight, and, one morning shortly before she was due to leave, she came down to breakfast and stared wildly at me. Her face was pale and drawn. Dramatic pause. Then, like the tragic Mrs Siddons as Lady Macbeth, she pointed to two large bruises at the base of her neck. '*Someone* has tried to strangle me during the night,' she declaimed, eyes ablaze. No guesses as to who she thought the culprit must be.

We took her, at last, to the station and saw her onto the train, she protesting lachrymose gratitude and what a lovely time she had had and how I must visit her in Paris because it had been such fun and she would miss us terribly, and mad twitterings of that ilk.

Two mornings later, I got up early to make a cup of tea, went downstairs and looked out through the part-glazed front door, which opened directly onto the road. On the bank directly opposite sat a young man with a sallow complexion, dark sunken eyes, elbows on knees and a small attaché case beside him. He wore a trilby hat, grey Maigret mackintosh and was staring fixedly at Middle House. I went into the kitchen thinking: 'Whoever he is, he's come here, and I do not want to know.' He looked like a hitman sent by Françoise.

I took a cup of tea back to bed. Laurence slumbered on. I read and, when she woke, went down to make more tea, remarking casually that there was a strange man outside, apparently casing the house. She leant across the bed, looked down and cried out: '*Mais, c'est Pierre-Maurice. Sylvie . . .*

Sylvie.' She ran next door to where Sylvie was sleeping. 'Mouton [the nickname], *c'est* Pierre-Mo-mo.'

Right. They knew him. Of course they knew him. How could I even begin to think they didn't know him?

Thus Pierre-Maurice joined the ménage and moved in with Mouton (sheep), so-called because of her frizzy hair. Laurence they called Pic, woodpecker, except that I had christened her Coucou because, like the French word (for cuckoo, cuckoo clock, post-chaise, cowslip, peep-bo . . .), she was many things. The English sense of cuckoo, crazy, does not exist in French, but that, alas, was to come with the onset of her porphyria. Me they called Graphonio, from some mishearing of gramophone in the French way – Grahm – of saying my name.

Pierre-Maurice and Sylvie were studying at the same *école normale supérieure* in Paris. He was one of a number of aspirant lovers – she was flirting with them all, surrendering to none. Pierre-Maurice, with admirable dash, had decided to pursue her to the summer hideaway and, as they say in Norfolk, pin her. I was immensely impressed. Most of my friends either complained that Norfolk wasn't on the way anywhere – implying that I was not worth a detour – or that they didn't know, or couldn't work out, where I lived. Pierre-Maurice had made his way from Mulhouse, in Alsace, by train, ferry and train to Norwich and on to Sheringham, then by foot to Middle House, and all he'd had was an address and that most pressing of motives: sex. Gonads are go.

Middle House became francophone. The four of us got on well, but life in that tiny establishment was very crowded. Laurence, in particular, suffered because of it and retreated inside herself. When they all went home, there arose an unwonted coolness between us. The intrusions had been too febrile, we had spent little time together on our own and it had almost been a relief when they'd left and I'd had the house back to myself. I took to the roads again, cycling harder, further, faster every day as if to aerate the suffocations of that bizarre summer. By the end of August, as the start of another term began to fill its buckets with cold water ready for the Calvinistic dowsing of my libertarian spirit, the ache for Laurence became acute, and I decided I must see her. I would, of course, cycle.

Her mother's family house was in Vouvray, on the banks of Le Loir (a minor stream not to be confused with La Loire), a hamlet outside Châteaudun in Eure-et-Loir, some 240km south of Dieppe. I fitted a bag to the rear carrier on the Merckx, caught a train to London, stayed with friends overnight and got up at three in the morning to cycle to Victoria for the first train to Brighton. From Brighton, I cycled along the coast to Newhaven in the gloaming of dawn and caught the ferry. I booked a cabin but slept not a wink. Rolling up the ramp onto the quayside in Dieppe, my front tyre punctured.

The day was hot. Through Rouen and into the wheat bowl of northern France, long straight highways which occasionally shimmied into gentle curves slicing across open grain prairies, pale silver-gold in the August sun. I remember the approach to Chartres especially: the cathedral and surrounding town perched up on their mound way, way in the distance, the only high place in the rolling landscape. This is how cities must have loomed out of the largely unhoused countryside in the past – empty expanses of land dotted with trees in clumps, spinneys and forests, and on the skyline, the profile of urban wealth: spired church for the overarching presence of God, high surrounding walls like a temporal version both of the fear he engendered and the security he promised.

I was, by now, beginning to tire and had a raging thirst. Water bottle? The idea. It was Jacques Anquetil who said that 'driest is fastest', and hadn't Lawrence of Arabia trained himself to do without liquids? Good enough for me, in principle, but I was as dry as harvested chaff and overheating like an empty car radiator, my throat and chest scorched.

Panting for drink as my loins yearned for Laurence, I stopped at a bar and drank four cool lemonades, the sides of the chilled glass pilling sweat beads. The first and second went down straight. The third and fourth I took more slowly, my sips of the sweet tart zing punctuated by gaseous belches. That lemonade was pure ecstasy, and sitting in the sun outside the roadside bar a time-stopped interlude of that perfect relaxation which is the ephemeral Nowhere between when the suffering stops and when thinking about it having to start again filters in. For the moment, I slouched like a sybarite in the luxurious relief of cool succulence. I think I ate a sandwich too, the only food I took all day.

Beyond Chartres, the pain began to worsen, not in my legs, but in my arms. I tried the temporary relief of riding without hands on the bars but was too tired to risk much of that. Daytime began to file away its hours of light ready for the late-shift handover. Evening checked the blackout curtains and long before I got to Châteaudun had pulled them tight along the louvres of the horizon. I had, of course, no lamps, and between the sullen bone-deep nagging ache in my arms, the strain on my eyes and the near delirium of actually getting closer, I was rolling on no more than a stubborn refusal to stop.

Out of Châteaudun's penumbral glare of sodium street lamps and amber and neon from bars and cafés into the pitch dark of the byways towards Saint-Denis-les-Ponts. I knew the road but could see only sketchy traces of it in the blur of night's cross-hatching. The house was lit by an outside lamp. I saw it in the distance through the trees, drawing me on the final metres. I cycled up, turned into the drive, crunched over the gravel and nearly collided with Laurence's grandmother as she came round the side of the building. Startled, she hollered wildly. I staggered off the bike to apologise and said: '*Je suis cuit.*' (I'm cooked, worn out.)

'*D'alcool?*' she whooped in a Sybil Thorndike rising glissando. *Cuit* also means drunk. Behind her came Anie, Laurence's mother, and Laurence herself.

Joy had sat on my wheel the whole way and moved in with us when we went to bed – joy, the one long-term guest we had unwittingly excluded from my house in favour of the interlopers that July. Fatigue I left outside, with the Merckx, to which it properly belonged: they could exchange tired mutual satisfaction and compare bruises. Laurence and I made love, blissful sex. We were together again.

Next morning, after breakfast, we cycled into Châteaudun and, a couple of kilometres up the road, my right crank fell off. The holding bolt had snapped clean through. It must have been hanging on by a mere scurf of metal to get me to Laurence's – as indeed I was hanging on by a fuse wire of willpower. The task accomplished, it yielded to physics. I rode on one-leggedly.

The family knew the bike-shop man, of course – small community, few secrets, local contacts – and next day, Sunday, we took my bike round in the car to his house. He said he'd fit a new crank and it would be ready by Monday. We returned to the Paris apartment later that afternoon. I caught the train to Châteaudun first thing in the morning and went straight to the bike shop to announce my presence. The man greeted me warmly and said he'd already done the repair – the bike was waiting for me at the house of two of Laurence's elderly maiden aunts. He charged me a pittance, I thanked him heartily, collected the bike and, by about midday, was on the road heading for Paris, hard as I could go.

It was one of the most exhilarating rides of my life, where everything clicked – effort, strength, rhythm, exuberance – 80km of sheer pleasure masking any stress I may have felt. At one point, close to the Massy apartment, I found myself on a motorway slip road. Don't know what happened, missed a turn, what the hell. Not far to go, couldn't be bothered to ramble about looking for the right way, put my nose into the handlebars and hit the gas. Suddenly, I was conscious of a man on the far carriageway gesticulating and blowing a whistle. A traffic cop. Fortunately, he didn't pull out his service *flingot* for a pot shot. I decided to ignore him, pushed even harder and, within a kilometre or so, was flying up another slip road away from the shooting range. I rolled up to the foot of the tall apartment block in a lather of sweat and a brisk tremor of satisfaction. It had taken me just shy of two hours.

Inevitably, on the 170km of the return trip to Dieppe some days later, I had rather less vim in my legs and an extra kilo or two of goodbye sorrow weighing me down.

Of the week we spent cycling round Vouvray one Easter, there were only two extravagantly memorable incidents: the loss of the bikes going and the loss of the bikes coming back. We travelled in my green Morris Minor with a friend, our bikes strapped to a roof rack whose fastenings, with clamps in the gutters, were flimsy. We made it to Paris in good shape and set off for the country next morning. As we drove onto the motorway, I heard a faint whisk of noise overhead above the distinctive baritone of the Cowley engine. I wound down the window and reached up to the roof. There was no rack. I glanced in the rear-view mirror and saw, in a heap on the inside lane of the autoroute, our bikes and the roof rack like a heap of scrap. Luckily, there was very little traffic about. I reversed up the hard shoulder, retrieved the truant fardel and secured – ah, flip word, *secured* – the whole gubbins (one bike, not mine, a bit mangled) to the roof and, for added safety, lashed it fore and aft to the bumpers with rope. Approaching Calais on the return trip, the bloody thing went AWOL again, to the consternation of Mamie, Laurence's grandmother, who was travelling with us. But I was a practised hand at retrieving aberrant roof racks from the road by this time, and the recovery took no time at all.

The week was fun, more of a lark than any great distances. Coming back wet and chilled through from one ride, Laurence and I commandeered the shower together to save water, as her youngest sister Agnès, aka Bilou, stood outside the cubicle, stark naked, shivering, remonstrating with her callous sibling: 'Lau-ren-ce, *t'es dé-geu-lasse.*' (Laurence, you're disgusting.) With me, it seems, she had no quarrel.

Laurence was diagnosed with porphyria, the disease from which mad George III suffered, an extremely rare illness, caused by an excess of porphyrins, the colourant in red corpuscles. (*Porphyreos* is Greek for purple, dark red.) The resulting imbalance causes intermittent nervous tension, convulsions, acute depression and anxiety, disorientation and pronounced irrational behaviour, rapid and extreme emotional shifts, even personality changes, turbulent personality changes. And, during an attack, the most severe pain. A number of things may trigger an onslaught, and I have never witnessed such physical and emotional distress as when Laurence was being clawed to bits by that terrible affliction. Pregnancy would have been life-threatening, and oral contraceptives were out of the question.

She eventually came to live with me in Middle House. I had already put it on the market, thinking that we ought to start in a place that was ours, that we had chosen together, not mine.

One afternoon before she arrived, Richard and I cycled back from Holt to find my father ensconced. He had broken in and was sitting there waiting for me, as if it were his house. He and my mother were in the throes of splitting up – it never happened – and his view of things, always solipsistic, cast me in the role of sympathiser on his side. That I had to broker negotiations between them was, in itself, repugnant. This intrusion on my life – he was obviously spoiling for a fight, in ambush of my space – infuriated me. Whilst Richard waited outside, tight-lipped, I went inside, got changed, re-emerged with the Shorter and told my father, brusquely, that I didn't expect to find him there when we came back. We rode off, and Richard's good humour and the calm of the Norfolk countryside, my favourite cycling miles at the time, gradually quelled my rage. There was also something new in this putting as much distance between my father and me as I could. I wasn't escaping. This was my territory and he had invaded it. A month or so later, I came back one Sunday morning having stayed overnight with friends on the coast, to find him once more in my house, this time with my mother. She was upstairs, weeping, he downstairs, already broaching my sherry. I opened the front door, walked into the room as he came across towards me. I recognised the twisted grimace on his face, flushed and repellent, and thought: 'Migod, he's going to hit me.' Instead, he looked at me pitiably and said: 'How do you feel about my being in your house?' Then I realised: all those years of clumping me round the head, he had been scared of me. It was pathetic.

Laurence moved in with me in late August. We got a buyer for Middle House and, one Saturday afternoon of the Michaelmas term, I came home from rugby training (I was now coaching the First XV – for the first time in the history of the school, they went unbeaten, and I was accused of being professional) – with a decision. I sat on the settee next to Laurence and said: 'That's it, I am going to leave teaching.' I had asked the headmaster if I might work part-time so that I could go more frequently to the workshop, but he declined. I had always known I did not want to be a schoolmaster for the rest of my life, and that meant stopping. Now was the moment, I was convinced, totally certain and, although that was the start of the insomnia – what was I going to do, how was I going to make a living – I never once felt a single tremor of doubt. The confidence was invigorating. When, some time after I had left, I met two of my erstwhile colleagues, one of them, speaking for both, said: 'We wish we had had your courage.' That was woefully sad. Courage? It didn't take courage. All it took was conviction.

A few weeks later, Laurence went home to Paris, summoned by her father, and I knew it was over. There had been many vicissitudes, recount of which has no place here, but the hurt of that summons and her submission before it was complete. I packed up all her things, and her aunt, who lived in Norfolk, collected them, including the bike she had brought with her. I handed in my notice and packed up Middle House, furniture, books, chattels, and rented a room in a friend's house. I left Middle House for the last time, the rooms piled with cardboard boxes containing all my possessions, on a dark November evening in 1977 and went for supper with Laurence's aunt and uncle. When I arrived, Nicole looked at me and asked if I had heard from Laurence. Something in her voice told me instantly: she was pregnant. I phoned the apartment. She came to the phone. She had just come out of hospital having had an abortion. At either end of the phone, there was such dreadful, such immeasurable grief. 'I am full of tears,' I said. How we ever said goodbye I do not know, but the phone went dead eventually – as dead as I felt.

Lost and gone: job, house, lover, unborn child.

Without the propulsion of many things, I might have sunk. Friends, work, all that I was and wanted to be somehow kept me moving. She wrote to me: 'Our love is sacred. I want to be married to you even if we do not live together.' It didn't end there, but, for the moment, I did not have it in me to do much more than turn the pedals, as it were, heading in some direction of where I could not determine.

That afternoon before I drove away, a young farm labourer who was a bit light in the head, tricked out in military uniform, stalked across the shorn field opposite Middle House in the sunset-red flare of a line of stubble fires. He stopped, raised a bugle to his lips and let forth a tuneless blast of brazen sound – a salutation of the dying day, perhaps, a call to some spirits in the wandering of his mind, or nothing at all, just the noise. As the echo died, he stalked on and out of sight.

A friend with whom I occasionally slept said, one morning early in our affair, that she had been badly alarmed lying close to me after we had made love. 'Your heart keeps stopping and starting,' she said. 'It goes be-bop ba-boom and then a long silence and blurp . . . blurp . . . blurp and more inertia.'

'Inertia,' I said, 'that's it. Inertia. Actually, I have a syncopated cardiac rhythm, a dicky ticker. Not that I come and go, blow hot and cold, go off people then come on strong. It's just my innate way of flexing, keeping in time with the unpredictable jerkiness, the jazz, the flic flac of the contradictions.'

She shook her head. 'You talk too much. Come here.'

'It will take time to adjust to it,' I went on. 'You may come to find it rather soothing. At least you'll know it's me.'

'Quiet. Come here.'

Jane and I got married in January 1980, but our first holiday together, at Easter the year before, had been a five-day cycle ride from Corner House, where she lived, to Suffolk and back. On the Saturday, as we rode across a bit of common land near the coast along from Aldeburgh, I heard a dull clunking from somewhere on the Merckx. Couldn't see what caused it straight away, then I noticed the down tube oscillating above the bottom bracket. It had sheared through at the base. We rode on into Leiston, and, as we went past a garage, I noticed, in the open workshop, a blue propane gas bottle. Aha. Welding. We stopped, found the mechanic and asked if he could braze my frame. He mended the fracture with a handsome bronze collar of weld, like an ornamental torque, and said it ought to get me home. In fact, it lasted for another ten years before the seam cracked and sagged beyond repair. I replaced the frame with a second-hand nondescript, but the bike was never the same, and I eventually bought one of my friend John's machines and use it still.

The last big ride I made on the Merckx was in 1985 with Lucy, our daughter, then aged four. We went by train to the Dordogne, to stay with friends, and cycled around, her perched on a seat fastened to the crossbar, feet on steps fitted either side of the head tube and her hands gripping the bars. That was so much better than one of those rear-mounted seats. She could see something more interesting than my back and, sheltered by my arms and upper body, she was, I felt, more secure. On the way to Bergerac and the museum of automata, on a baking day, I rode our combined weight, me, Merckx and her, up a long sapping hill without bends, steep and ugly. Halfway up, Lucy announced: 'I'm all hot and bothered.'

'*That*,' sweetheart, I thought but did not say, 'barely even scratches what I feel right now,' but it spurred me on, somehow, and here we are at the pavement café, all thoughts of climbing off, *ever*, put aside.

Five

The Outer Circle

Riding with my friend Simon along the B482 west of Marlow, past Lane End, Bolter End and Cadmore End towards his house in Skirmett, in the Thames Valley, a sunny Sunday afternoon in May, blue skies, no traffic, easy pedalling, I was perplexed to see a cycle lane, 30m of it, in open country, no houses within earshot of the strangled cry of a lone cyclist hitting the deck, no patent reason for its being there at all. I wondered if the local council had apprenticeship schemes for cycle-lane painters. A delicate business, after all, scrawling white lines on municipal property. Can't just send a bloke out with a specialised contrivance and expect instant perfection on his first attempt. Certainly the variety of stencils used for the representation of the beautiful machine in white daub on tarmac is wide in form and, in many of the dippier samplings, not altogether plausible. But this? Had some novice bicycle-lane artist been out sketching, practising for his first big assignment in a town somewhere, despatched by the old lag in the highways department?

'Listen, lad, we need a meaningless show of random civic spirit here, an outreach to the barmy brigade, the do-as-you-like wallahs.'

'Are we talking, er, cyclists, sir?'

'Keep your voice down. We're talking cyclists, exactly. Do-as-you-like, bike. Certifiable chronic stutters.'

'Chronic stutters, sir?'

'Nutters. We need to top up our quota, so get out on a deserted stretch of the B482 and show us your mettle. I leave the siting to you. That's part of the test. Give me a pointless stretch of lane we can boast about, no concessions to use or function, none, some extra metres we can make an authorised claim for, and there's a boiled egg and soldiers for your tea if you get back without being spotted. OK, off you go.'

I was amazed that, in this conscience-free corner of Oxfordshire (or is it Royal Berkshire? Who cares?), any members of the indigenous saloon, SUV, Land Rover and people-carrier community even acknowledged the existence of the bicycle per se bicycle as a viable mode of transport let alone made cursory provision for the sad-sack down-at-heel unwashed grovelling minority who actually chose (or were, poor lumpkins, forced by penury) to ride them.

Having been born in London, and having grown up in its northern outer fringes and then the southern fringes of Hertfordshire, I visited real London only on excursions, mainly for the theatre. Going to live in the capital's heart, the Circus Maximus of homicidal fury on four wheels, came as a bit of a facer. Initially, I contemplated with some dismay the gladiatorial combat of car versus bike, the risible paucity of cycle lanes and the way they lead you on, like an arse-wiggling vamp with a lickproof cleavage and thighs bare to her knickers, to the promise of a real up-and-under good time, only to dump you on the limits of perdition with the words 'Welcome to the Euston Road. Call it Hell'. And the bicycle messengers. What a singular breed they were, are: wild-eyed urban lone stars zipping through the choking compress of cars on the brink of common sense, charged with bravado, brothers and sisters in a peculiar adversity, high on carbon-monoxide fumes, indifferent to abuse, kerbstones and one-way signs. Commendable cool.

After nearly eight years together, Jane and I split up. For the second, but not the last, time all my possessions went into storage.

In the summer of 1987, I spent a month in Greece, rowing on the inaugural sea trials of the reconstructed Athenian trireme. I also made a radio programme about the adventure. Beforehand, I got reacquainted with small boats, cycling into Norwich to take out a sculling shell from one of the boat clubs, up and down the River Yare, occasionally strafed by an angry pen swan coming in low, wings spread and beak trained on my head. I also rode down into Suffolk to see my mother: Strumpshaw, Limpenhoe, Reedham Ferry, Maypole Green, Uggeshall, Wangford, Blythburgh, Westleton to the house in Aldringham Common by the heath. At Blythburgh one Saturday, I met up with a bunch of other singers, many of whom I knew from the days when I sang with the Aldeburgh Festival Singers, to rehearse and sing Thomas Tallis's 40-part motet *Spem in Alium*. From the ceiling beams of the church gaze down the famous wooden angels. Cromwell's iconoclast troopers spurred their big cavalry mounts into the nave and shied bricks at the angels to break or bring them down but failed. The flagstones of the floor are dinted with the rearing horses' hooves.

We rehearsed for two hours, had tea – Lucy had come with me, playing in the village hall with the other kids who had come – and then went back into the church to sing the piece. It lasts for ten minutes. We were high with excitement, we sang well and, even as the echo died and we shivered with the electric thrill of what we had just accomplished, someone whispered: 'What do we do now?'

I said: 'Why don't we sing it again?' and we did – not so

accurately, the seat-of-the-pants brilliance had gone, but it was fine.

As for Wangford, it's near the home of whacky Hank of that stage name, the country-and-western-singing 'Jogging for Jesus' gynaecologist, though, of course, 'right under the X of Texas' is where he'd *rather* be.

In Greece, I met a bunch of men from the Durham Amateur Rowing Club and, at their invitation, joined them to row the Boston Marathon that autumn – 30 miles from Lincoln to Boston – and, once more against all expectation, found myself training in an eight on the River Wear, contemplating the silhouette of the great Norman cathedral caught in the stain of a scarlet sunset one evening in September.

That autumn I lived on the fifth floor of an Elizabethan beacon tower outside Melton Constable, not far from the house I'd shared with Jane. The mad mother of the owner was a bit of a trial. Crazy old lady number one. 'All this and heaven too,' she wittered, over and over, again and again, with an inane glassy grin, or else: 'This is where my daughter lives. What are you doing here?' Well she might ask. I passed her once on the long track leading away from the big gazebo, one of many built to relay the fire messages across England warning of the Armada. Stopped and asked where she was going – she was forever wandering off. 'Melton Constable,' she said.

'You mean the tower?' I said.

'That's it.'

'I'll give you a lift, then.'

She got into the car, I turned round and drove her back.

As I sat working one day, a man materialised in my room, clumped past my desk – there was no door – and up the short flight of steps to the lantern on the roof. Festooned with carabiners and a coil of rope, he didn't say a word, didn't even acknowledge my presence. About 20 minutes later, he came back down and vanished soundlessly on soft-sole boots down the stairwell. I asked the owner of the place later who he was. 'He's a cat burglar,' she said. 'He does roof jobs without scaffolding – much cheaper. Very handy.' She also had a tap on various car thieves – useful for the times when she locked herself out of the motor. Possibly.

The big gale of 1987 had lost its primal power by the time it reached Norfolk from Kent, where I now live, but I woke up that October night to the scream of the wind and the whole tower shaking with its onslaught. There were other tensions abroad, too. I'd lived in Norwich for a year after our separation, and my return to the area wasn't welcome in some quarters. Having got the equivalent of old-style rough music from a number of former so-called friends anxious to drive out the prodigal, in late December I loaded my travelling kit into the car – a small selection of clothes, typewriter and paper, reference books – and drove to Aldringham to live with my mother for a while.

I wrote, cycled out west past Saxmundham and Framlingham, back through Tunstall and Snape, ran over the Common to the sea and along the beach to Aldeburgh, ate too many puddings and was, generally, in a limbo. I had no plans other than to continue work on a novel about the Battle of Marathon, Philippides the runner and the true origin of the marathon race. (The story generally accepted is a romantic fiction.) I had very little money. For more than a year I had been principal reviewer for a local paper, reading, and reporting on, up to five books a week – I went into the office and took my pick, pressing for more to do. I also reviewed concerts, plays, recitals and wrote the occasional article – a write-up of the Tallis spree, for example. I was eventually sacked for filing a withering notice of a wretched play at the Theatre Royal, Norwich. 'It wasn't,' I said, 'acted badly. It wasn't acted at all.' The lead actor made a hoity-toity, swingeing, self-regarding attack on me in the paper. I was summoned by the literary editor, who had asked me to do the job at the last minute because he couldn't or didn't want the assignment. (Perhaps he sniffed trouble.) Needlessly obsequious, he couldn't actually bring himself to say I was getting the bullet, but when he oozed: 'You're an errant genius and some of your contributions have been exceptional, every one of them of high quality, however . . .' it's clear I was. His Uriah Heep-like hand-wringing was laughable, and, since he had recently mislaid a notice I'd written about a concert at the Snape Maltings, including the world premier of Hans Werner Henze's 'Tango', I couldn't take the dismissal too seriously. However, the loss of even that paltry income was a blow.

Then my father came back from Tenerife, where he now lived. Finding me in the house, he went off like a burst waste pipe, a torrent of vituperation, insult and contempt, plus a couple of expressions I didn't immediately recognise . . . always a problem with his truncated vocabulary, the subtext. I got the incoherent message – 'Absquatulate, mister, you hear?' – immediately packed my bags and the box of books while he rammed a brace of cartridges into his shotgun and stomped off gardenwards to vent his rage – his own default setting – on the wildlife.

A Jesuit, apparently, must always be ready to leave for an indeterminate length of time to another posting in 45 minutes. I could trim that by half.

And so to London.

Alison of *Everyman's Encyclopaedia* knew someone who had spent a number of years living in London without a permanent address. He had a large circle of complaisant friends with whom he stayed a night or two. In one house, his berth was a capacious cupboard. He had a full-time job but no full-time inclination to settle in one place. I have known two men with a similar dislike of home as a concept. They travelled about, did occasional work, had minimal luggage, read voraciously but carried only one book at a time. This they swapped for another book when they had finished with it. In the nearly three wearisome years that I had no fixed abode, *home* assumed a near mystic appeal.

Whilst I was living at my ma's, I met an actress who lived locally and kept a flat in London. This, for two months at the beginning of my peregrinations in the smoke, I borrowed. We didn't become lovers – she had an unidentified vaginal infection when we first started seeing each other and the bloke, an aspirant writer, with whom she did and did not live, either eventually cheered up or cut up rough. From Tufnell Park to Streatham Hill, mad old lady number two and the first corpse I have ever seen.

The house belonged to a musician friend, Peter Jarvis, with whom I later wrote two operas. He and his wife Jane spent much of their time down in France, renovating a tumbledown fortified manor house in the Dordogne. Peter said I could stay in Killisier Avenue and play guardian to his mother.

Dibby wasn't completely harpic ('clean round the bend') but she was close, and the fact that behind the pottiness lurked an intelligence not altogether off its gimbals made her sudden appearance in my bedroom with a frozen chicken for my supper (for instance) even more unsettling than if she'd been just plain daft. 'I thought you lived here,' she said once.

'I'm trying to,' I replied.

An elderly couple occupied a flat at the top of the house. Jim had been a rear gunner in bombers, a 'tail-end Charlie', and gone through the entire war unscathed. Since the casualty rate among the guys isolated at the aft tip of the fuselage was higher even than the average very high rate among aircrew, this was miraculous. I asked him if I could shake his hand and hope a bit of his luck rubbed off. He chuckled and said: 'Funny, a lot of people ask that.'

But I hated Streatham: its dingy streets, its low-grade shops, its location halfway between London and Croydon, which is a fair working definition of nowhere anyone would opt to go on pain of a million quid. I loathed everything about it. A minicab driver who worked at the firm round the corner got into an altercation with a couple of his hires. They hared off to wherever it was they kept the armoury, came back with a shooter and zotzed him. I happened to be walking past shortly after the murder and saw his corpse sprawled in the gutter, and a small crowd of bystanders not, I think, mumbling prayers for his departed soul.

The vitriolic woman striding up the crowded High Street one Saturday morning might have been voicing the dejection that seemed to permeate the place. She had a square of net-curtain material tied round her head and chin, a leaf-green coat slightly too small for her, fawn woollen socks pulled up to her knees, carpet slippers. Staring straight ahead, apparently oblivious of anyone, she was pushing a shopping trolley at arm's length, as if it contained something nasty, and haranguing the world whether the world was listening or not. 'I told them, I told them I wasn't going to take that shit any more, I wasn't going to take that shit any more, no, not any more, not that shit, I wasn't going to take that shit and I told them, I told them straight out, no more, no more shit . . .' Ranting on and on and on. I sympathised in an abstract sort of way.

Every Wednesday evening and Sunday morning, I cycled from Streatham to Putney for a row in the London Boat Club occasional eight on the Thames, where I had trained and rowed with my college, and one Sunday all the way from Putney to Eel Pie Island for lunch at the Twickenham Boat Club, through the first lock of the non-tidal upper river at Richmond. The Rolling Stones played at the Eel Pie Island Hotel, I think, but the more outré and seductive aspects of the '60s – which my father called the most morally degenerate and reprehensible epoch in the history of civilisation – rather passed me by. I say passed me by: in truth, I wasn't even in the vicinity. I was too busy shying away from the raunchier aspects, torments and temptations of pullulating adolescence. Love had its handbooks, Keats and Gerard Manley Hopkins. Sex was masturbation.

Coming back from Putney one evening, I passed a herbal clinic in Balham, memorised the number and phoned for an appointment. I had for a long time been prey to a murderous itching in my anus. The chronic irritation coupled with the agony of frenzied scratching at the raw flesh often brought me close to tears. I'd had a haemorrhoidectomy, anal dilation and applied a number of creams and salves. Nothing I tried had calmed the torment for any length of time, and riding a bike can't have helped. I even tried psychotherapy but lasted only five sessions: I had got so adept at fooling myself that fooling a complete stranger didn't seem a clever option, especially not having to pay for it. The herbal clinic combined teaching of students with treatment. The earnest apprentices sat in a semicircle in front of me for the diagnostic interrogation. Amongst the long series of questions: 'Is the discomfort worse when you are under stress?'

I answered (get this): 'I don't really believe in stress.' Stress was for the weaklings, the saps, the tins of milk, the namby-pambies. No one with any moral strength or backbone got *stress*. This was (ah, but you guessed) my father speaking in me, insidious claptrap from an emotional cripple. They might have given me a gentle talking to on the matter of egotism, macho folly and stunted inner perception but, instead, prescribed a herbal ointment, a herbal tea, a herbal lotion with which to bathe my poor victimised bum. For a brief interlude, it worked. The itching went. I hardly dared think I was cured, but the treatment was, demonstrably, working. Then it stopped working and the misery, after the uneasy lull, redoubled.

I was missing Lucy horribly, had no idea what was going on in my life or what I was doing with it, playing at, imagining I might do. Halfway through that day when the nervous crisis blew, I had managed to produce only five lines. The usual output was around 2,000 words. Then Jane phoned to talk about a man she'd met on a plane and fallen for. She was really keen to find him, hadn't got his address, didn't know how to trace him. Could I help her? He was a freelance cameraman but worked periodically for the BBC, and perhaps with my contacts there . . . The lovelorn monologue went on, uninterrupted. Finally, I said I would do what I could and put the phone down. In a welter of loneliness, self-pity and unspeakable anguish, my ego collapsed. I broke down utterly and cried and sobbed.

(I did find the man.)

Next day, I went in for my appointment at the clinic, looked round the half-circle of young men and women staring back at me impassively like inquisitors and said: 'I think I believe in stress. I want everything: comfort, massage, sex . . .'

They got part of the message: I got the massage. From one of the men. None of the women responded to my newly acquired relaxed candour, which I thought a bit mean. But that admission to stress, what I had always reckoned to be a weakness, was one of the most empowering leaps of self-knowledge and understanding I had ever made. It was like dismissing the secret policeman in my head. The terrible itching did not go away for a long time even after that, but it went in the end (from my end) and if it came for no other reason than to teach me that salutary lesson about real strength and apparent feebleness then every demented clawing of my nails had purpose after all. For we need to be kind to ourselves, not too stern with our failings, tolerant of mistakes. We all need all the help we can get. Full stop. My old friend George Francis, about whom I wrote a book, used to say 'the people who take kindness for weakness are the weakest kind of people'.

Poor George, in an ultimate act of sickening despair, killed himself. It was an unkind end for a man of great sensitivity. Asked to speak at a memorial to him, I said that I could have trusted George with anything, and it was true. Sadly, it turned out, not with his own life.

From Streatham to Barnes, where I began work on a two-part dramatised biography of Antonio Vivaldi for Radio 4. For a whole month, I cycled to and from the Gramophone Library (now defunct) near Broadcasting House in Portland Place. I flashed past lines of jammed cars, happily leapfrogged motorbikes, often for miles, when even they got stuck in traffic through which I on my bike could find gaps. From nine to five, I sat in a room or lay on the floor listening to every bit of Vivaldi's music available on vinyl or CD. I recorded much of it, too, so that I could listen again when I got back to my temporary home. The more I heard his music, the more I loved it. Every day, I cycled into town, from where I lived in an upstairs room of my friends Adrian and Mary's house. Residence, too, of crazy old lady number three. She opened one of my letters containing a cheque from the BBC and banked it with a building society. I retrieved the money and, so far, (*absit omen*) no other crazy old ladies have materialised to add to that disparate trio of weird sisters, like a watered-down, picaresque version of Clotho, Lachesis and Atropos, the blind Fates of classical antiquity.

Initially, I enjoyed my sorties on the bike in London and got to know the great city sprawl very well: the short cuts, the through routes, the dodges, the actual layout, which the diagrammatic plan of the Underground, till then my template, could not supply. I got to relish the combat too: racing the traffic, cutting through gaps, surfing the stop–start stream, going hard over the lumps and bumps, taking the traffic on with demonic exuberant energy, flashing past slower cyclists. I even rode through the Blackwall Tunnels, there and back, one evening when I joined friends for supper in Blackheath. The noise was appalling, the millrace of cars and lorries breaking past me terrifying, but there was an idiotic thrill in it too.

One day, however, I came out of my listening room, where I had just spent a tantalising half an hour with luscious voluptuous Becky the PA, instead of Vivaldi's sumptuous sexy Gloria, looked at the lines of cars, their tailpipes squirting noxious chemical halitosis into the balmy evening air, and shuddered. I was tired out anyway, but the sight of the traffic queuing up to block me in, to run me off the road, to chase me down, to screech across my front wheel, to asphyxiate my lungs, suddenly appalled me. The war out there wasn't fun or even a challenge, it was lunacy. I had, quite suddenly and sensibly, lost my nerve for it and, that evening, listless and at half-speed, I picked up with a bike messenger round Vauxhall. We rode some way together until he peeled off near Brixton. 'Thing is about this game,' he said, 'it's so fucking tiring and non-stop, you don't like taking days off, 'cause when you do, your system closes down with the relief of not OD'ing on the fumes. And when you aren't sucking them in, you get headaches. Plus you lose your edge with the cars, and the more you think about it, the dafter it feels. It's a fucking treadmill, mate. I wouldn't recommend it.'

Visiting other friends in Barnes, as we left the house one morning, the phone rang. 'Get that, Graeme, would you?' said Miranda.

I picked up the receiver and a woman's voice said: 'Is that Graeme?' (Maybe it was 'Graham'.)

'Yes,' I said.

'Hi, just phoning to see how you are.'

I said: 'I'm fine. Who . . .?' but the voice continued.

'Are you, you know, still doing stuff?'

What stuff, I thought. Drugs? Bondage? Group sex? 'I think you must have the wrong number,' I said and put the phone down. Another missed opportunity.

Over the next ten months, I lived (and worked) at nine other addresses in London, including two spooky weeks in an empty house near Holloway – bare floorboards, mattress, one plug-in lamp – vacated by the previous occupants, who had sold it and moved to the country. During a three-week sojourn in a flat in King's Cross, I wrote to a friend in Norfolk appending the address, not so that she could reply but 'to reassure you that I am not living in a cardboard box. *Out of* a cardboard box but not *in* one.' A PA of one of the producers for whom I did a lot of work at the BBC showed me the full list of my accumulated postcodes in her address book once: I might have been a champion moonlighter, an obsessive flitter, except that all I was seeking to evade in those days as a reluctant nomad was the stress of being a reluctant nomad. Jerry Lee Lewis said that the three virtues which kept him going through all the vicissitudes of life on the road were Tenacity, Dignity and Arrogance. I'm not sure about the Arrogance, though it does take a certain solidity of purpose and resolve to carry on working in such circumstances. Perhaps more an echo of the character in Ralph Ellison's *The Invisible Man*: 'You need three things to get by in this here city [New York], Shit, Grit and Mother Wit and, man, I was born with all three.'

For five weeks in September of that first year in London, I occupied neighbouring houses in Kentish Town successively while the owners were away on holiday. When I moved sideways on changeover day for the second stint, I met Lindy. She had called to see Vicki, the mutual friend for whom I was going to house-sit. By the time Vicki came home from Aegina, Lindy and I had begun our relationship. My itinerancy continued, but in June of the following year, after more traipsing around

– another venue in Holloway, Greenwich, Blackheath, Wales, Northumberland – I moved into the flat she owned, but didn't inhabit, at the top end of Camden Town. My furniture, books, clothes and bikes (I was riding a borrowed bike in London) arrived from storage in Norfolk and I had a home – not mine, but a door to which I had the key, rooms where I could live and work undisturbed. The Merckx lived outside, the Shorter next to my work table, inside.

The support and forbearance of my friends in that time of wandering saved me from going under. Some debts of kindness, love, magnanimity we cannot repay, except by lavishing them on others in our turn.

From St Augustine's Road, I cycled up the longish steeps of Highgate West Hill – included in the last stage of the 2006 Tour of Britain – to Lindy's house, to stay with her, or else to head on north through Whetstone, Barnet and Potters Bar, the cycle routes of my teenage years, to the quieter roads of Hertfordshire. The dreary haul out through the suburbs was never much fun, though, and an hour or two round Cuffley, Essendon, Letty Green on my own was always partly degraded, alas, by the thankless prospect of the dreary haul back.

Setting out that way to drive in Lindy's Porsche to Newcastle, where Lucy and Jane now lived, I hit the first massive traffic snarl-up near Newark. An hour later, swinging blithely off the lip of the roundabout onto the Doncaster bypass and too late to carry on round the roundabout, I plunged head first into the second monumental jam. I saw cars . . . cars . . . cars, all the way to Aberdeen, stationary vehicles. I sat there for long enough to know I had to get out of there. The early focus-training kicked in. As sporadic quivers of movement convulsed the constipated tarmac bowel and gaps teased open, I manoeuvred my way slantwise through them from the outside lane to the inside lane and onto the hard shoulder. Into reverse, back I go, 200 yards up the free road to where the hard shoulder shunted into a kerbstone like a bolt on a cell door and I was locked in again, yards from freedom. OK: the central reservation it had to be. I drifted back across towards the outside lane again till I was nearly there, when a lorry lurched to a stop behind me with a massive exhalation of air brakes. I could see the driver's face in the rear-view mirror, screaming at me to get moving, get out of the fucking way, let him through – where to? – hammering the horn, rocking the cab backwards and forwards on the dip of his brakes. I refused to move. Then, there it was, the last gap into the outside lane. I swung into it, up the kerb onto the spline between me and the far side, a spin of the wheel, I'm down and round and off south again, on open road.

Even as I turned onto the A614 to Bawtry – where the bloody hell is Bawtry? I didn't care, Bawtry looked clear ahead to me – I thought: 'There's a play here.' I wrote it, a two-hander called *JAM*, which played in Edinburgh and various other venues.

An exchange:

> SHE (miming on a bike): The thing is, on a pushbike you keep going, not very fast, perhaps, but where all the cars grind to a halt, you keep going. You know the story of the tortoise and the hare? That's it: slow but steady gets there in the end, and more haste less speed. Never truer than today. I've always favoured a bike, myself. There ought to be more bike lanes, of course, little relaxing air lanes, like country paths, to ease the cardiac cramps of the poor old Environment. 'Go to work on a bike' . . . it could be a slogan, if there were any work still to go to. A bike is not only efficient and cheap – it uses up the same fuel as a spare tyre – it's clean. It doesn't emit emissions, apart from a bead of sweat, and it's jolly healthy exercise, apart from

the emissions everyone else emits. Safe, apart from the intermittent maimings. We were, I do believe, a happier nation when everybody, de rigueur, wore hats and most of the population pedalled their way.

HE (driver, arriving in an office swivel chair): Bloody velocipedes, get everywhere, like grit in oil, wobbling about all over the place, stick their hand out and expect the car behind to screech to a halt while they pirouette on the white line. Oy, get out of it.

SHE: What do you think you're playing at?

HE: Fuck off.

SHE: You nearly knocked me off.

HE: Well, I didn't, then.

SHE: What's your problem?

HE: You. What's yours?

SHE: You're in a van.

HE: You're in the way.

SHE: I've got as much right to be on the road as you.

HE: Take it then.

SHE: How can I if you're running me over?

HE: Who's running you over?

SHE: You.

HE: Have you been run over?

SHE: You bloody nearly did.

HE: So I bloody nearly didn't.

SHE: It makes no difference.

HE: Not to me, it doesn't.

SHE: What?

HE: Fuck off.

SHE: You were driving like a maniac.

HE: I've got a dustcart up my arse, a boss on my back and *you* are getting up my nose.

SHE: We are all road users.

HE: No. I am a road user. You are litter.

SHE: The Highway Code makes provision for pushbikes the same as motors.

HE: Does it also make provision for Zimmer frames? I tell you what, the world'd be a lot safer place it if wasn't for pushbikes.

SHE: Who for?

HE: [Pause] Fuck off.

An apoplectic motorist did actually shout that line about the world being a safer place without bikes at me.

A while ago, driving down to St Ives in Cornwall in early July, the only distraction in over six hours of bypass crawling the hundred miles or so from an overnight in Bristol at Lucy's house, was the picture book which a little girl looking out of the back window of the minibus in front of me obligingly flicked through for my diversion. The road did eventually clear but, three miles from my destination, the queue reformed, this time behind a council dustcart and a hearse. Appropriate, somehow.

Six

Why Ever Would I Miss London?

The pavement area at the top of St Augustine's Road, where another cranky old lady, the bead of whose glittering eye I always studiously avoided, doled out food supplements to bloated pigeons and squirrels, served as a dump and collection point for discarded televisions, ironing boards, the odd suitcase of used hypodermic syringes and, one day, a pair of elbow crutches. I pictured the scene: the lame man (or woman) hobbles up to the corner, stumbles into a cone of white light emanating from heaven, gazes up and it's Jesus, of course. Halt individual cries hallelujah, the angel chorus chimes in with loud hosanna, down go the crutches and the invalid skips off jubilantly.

A screech of tyres as I round that very corner past the latest bargain on offer, a Parker Knoll settee, upholstery somewhat distressed. A black guy in a mauve Vauxhall leans out of the window and calls across: 'Hey, man, you want to buy some jewellery?'

'No, thanks,' I say, and he hits the accelerator and tears off.

Once I saw, in a skip outside the flat, a sheet of cardboard on which someone had written: 'Good morning my love and welcome to a new day in the Reich of God.' It patently hadn't made the impression it was supposed to make, to have been rejected thus. And the two messages on my answerphone – message 1, a woman's sultry voice saying: 'I really miss you, it's been so long, miss you really badly.' Message 2, the same sultry woman: 'You probably realised I got a wrong number. Sorry.'

A man stands outside a pub in Kentish Town at eight o'clock in the morning, swaying like a palm tree in a wind, one hand gripping a can of lager. He stares uncomprehendingly at the small bit of the world onto which his eyes can latch some focus and, with a dry bark, vomits onto the pavement.

No one ever need ask if I miss London.

For the ten years I lived in the flat, I swam at the Highgate Men's Pond all year round. I'd swum there desultorily in spring and summer, but the winter dips didn't appeal. Then a leather-bound spheroid intervened.

I cycled down to Gloucestershire for a cricket match. I love the adventure of the journey, the contented solitude, the prospect of arriving, the last miles – Lechlade, the limit of navigation for powered craft on the Thames, to Cirencester and on into the narrow, placid, wooded lanes and bosky hollows by way of Sapperton and Waterlane till the road tops out above the deep valley in which sits Bisley and my destination.

A sleepless night of unlooked for but extremely enjoyable carnal exchange left me blissfully content but with the torpid reactions of a zombie. Phil Adler's XI versus the Bisley cricket club, for whom he played, comprised a few other of his friends, regular batsmen and bowlers, and a talentless extra, me. Out in the deep field, I saw the ball lofted my way, went for it, caught it, slipped, fell onto the hard, hard ground and dropped it. A wicked sharp spasm shot through my shoulder. Phil called out: 'Are you all right?'

'No, I don't think I am,' I said, chucking the miscreant leather back with my serviceable right hand.

'Go into the slips, then,' he yelled, even as a man hurried across the pitch to where I stood, taut with pain. It was Leo Cooper, husband of Jilly. He took me off to hospital, a friendship began, and it was through him, some 14 years later, that I was introduced to the publisher who commissioned my book about the French revolutionary Terror. This was hardly suffering for Art but close enough.

As soon as the collarbone had knitted, I started to swim, expressly to strengthen the atrophied muscles, and decided I would go on for as long as I felt comfortable. I did not want to get caught in a fetish. September went into October, the temperature slowly declined but my tolerance of the cold rose and I was hooked.

A woman who swam in the Men's when the Ladies' was shut (we had a reciprocal arrangement) said that it was 'like swimming in the sky', and I loved the silky feel of the fresh water, observing the natural world, coots, grebes, moorhens, even a rare kingfisher, from surface level, watching the turn of the leaves as the acids of autumn flooded their veins and the burst of the variable greens in spring. I revelled in the glint of the morning sun on the eddies and ripples spreading in front of my breaststroking arms. I enjoyed the banter in the changing area, the warm greeting on the cold days when Geoff the keeper strolled in to warn us 'Very strong wind-chill factor today', the repartee – me doing my stretching exercises, letting go a deep yawn, Eddy the brickie saying: 'Are we keeping you up?' – but above all the ecstatic sensation of acclimatising in the cold water, resisting the penetrating chill, the intense satisfaction of staying in what was a near out-of-body state for up to 20 minutes, even when there was ice on the surface. I have no natural resistance to cold. My endurance – and I stayed in far longer than anyone else – was largely psychological. I was cold but didn't feel cold. Sometimes, when the water was choppy with fast-running small waves that slapped me in the face, I felt like the Good Ship Lollipop out there, and Terry, the head keeper, invariably got a bit fidgety when I disappeared from view behind a thick bank of morning mist. I did take it too far sometimes – a hard ride back to the flat when I must have been teetering on the verge of hypothermia gave me worrying palpitations one morning.

Lucy and I travelled much. I saw her as often as I could – I went up to Newcastle upon Tyne to look after her when Jane was away in New York at a clothes show, always for the weekend of her birthday and for parents' evenings at school. We went skiing in the Alps, visited the trireme in Poros, camped in Scotland, stayed with friends here and there, made a trip up the Thames, from Cookham to Oxford, another on the Wey Navigation in a Thames skiff – a boat with a sweet blade action. Iron hoops set into the sides for the canvas tilt and, bingo, a floating tent. And two cycling holidays.

I caught the train to Norwich, sat in the guard's van and trued my back wheel, which had sprung a wobble, then went into the carriage and learnt some basic Dutch for the circuit of Holland in July 1993. Lucy was at the station with Jane, and we caught another train to Harwich, from there by overnight ferry to Hoek van Holland and set out at seven o'clock in search of *koffie en gebak*, hot coffee and warm sponge. It was Sunday. There was no cake, no coffee, no café. Protestant Holland was shut. We headed north up the coast and eventually, around nine o'clock, to Scheveningen, where I asked at a hotel if they could possibly give us some food and drink. The waiter went into the kitchen. A young Englishman came out and said they couldn't help. I applied the pressure – starving daughter, long bike ride – and he yielded: a cold collation of cheese, ham, salami. Lucy has always liked savoury, so this was fine. (When she was about two, we took her to Alison's wedding and I caught glimpses of her cheeks getting fatter and fatter, swelling like a hamster's. I asked her what she was eating. She gave me a gnomic stare. I gently parted her lips and looked into the cavity of her mouth: it was completely stuffed with unmasticated black olives – stoneless, luckily.) When I asked for the bill, the man shook his head – 'No, that's all right' – and gave us two Mars bars to help us on our way.

The cycle track over the dunes soon began to fill with Sunday cyclists – a few racing bikes but the great preponderance large-framed, comfortable Dutch machines favoured by young and old alike. Whole families were out – kids in rear- or front-mounted seats – bowling along the roller coaster of the littoral path in the August sunshine. *Bromfietsen*, too, mopeds, so called because they make a *broom broom* noise – we'd say vroom. Confronted by so many ups and not taking the consequent downs as any kind of reasonable compensation for them, Lucy got quite tetchy: 'I thought you said Holland was flat?'

'Most of it is,' I said, and she went quiet. Her silence was eloquent: I'd plainly been making up that bit about flat and there was no excuse, so don't even *try*. Plus there was a needlessly interfering pesky offshore sea breeze.

From Zaandvoort, our first stop – a swim in the sea and supper in a restaurant by a sun-kissed beach – we rode next day east to Amsterdam, hoping to see the Rijksmuseum. It was shut. We did see the famous omnigatherums of bicycles everywhere, mighty indabas of two-wheelers, bikes painted garish hues with cabbalistic patterns chained to the canalside railings, parked by trees and lamp posts, leaning one against the other like courting couples, like commiserating drunks, like art installations . . . In late afternoon, we rode onto one of the motorised pontoons (no fee) which serve as moving bridges across the Amstel inlet of the Markermeer and headed north through countryside and prim bungalows with manicured lawns and regimented gardens. Holland's horticultural mini-acres are improbably neat, dinky and colour-coded, from the domestic beds to the large front lawn we saw, its width and depth entirely occupied, apart from three miniature windmills, by a small army of painted garden gnomes, staring balefully at the back of a sign reading 'NIET VOOR DE VERKOOP' (Not for Sale). They'd obviously been stuck there for years, those sullen gnomes, stir-crazy, desperate to flee, longing to be sold to a more expansive owner, and they'd had those three miniature fucking twee windmills up to the tops of their varnished pointy hats and back again.

Lucy took a spill and grazed her knee, but we got to Volendam in time for a chemist who supplied iodine-impregnated plasters. Then a *logie mit onbijt* (bed and breakfast) for a comforting shower. The sky next morning was filled with huge Dutch School banks of billowing cloud highlit by a hidden sun, slate grey and kohl black with inset enamel medallions of bluebell blue and hyacinth. Long straight tree-lined roads took us via Edam – cart-loads of red-waxed cheeses in the square – up the west coast of the inland sea, Ijsselmeer, against a headwind 50km to Enkhuisen. From there, the ferry across the water and road again to Lemmer. Everywhere, cycle lanes. Holland is comparative bicycling paradise. Cars give way, by and large, as the law says they must.

The woman at the guest house in Lemmer showed us to our room and disappeared. In it, one single bed. I went out to look for our hostess, but she really had disappeared. I wrote a note, in Dutch, asking for a larger room or two beds, and we went out for supper. When we came back, the woman beamed at me: 'You speak very good Dutch,' she said, in English, and lo, there were two beds in our room. Nowhere did we encounter anyone who didn't speak serviceable English, and my sallies into Dutch were hardly necessary, except by way of courtesy, making an effort as a traveller and a guest in their country. Such efforts, sometimes comic in their stilted hesitation and garble, are never wasted.

Shortly after we set out next morning, the rain started and persisted nearly all day – rain and wind together, a dreary slog along a dyke, the wind hammering at us all the way, Lucy kvetching, as well she might. Giethoorn – named for a vast hoard of goats' horns buried there, possibly a herd drowned in a prehistoric flood – is known as the Dutch Venice, originally settled in the thirteenth century by an extreme sect of self-flagellants escaping persecution. Since they were already flogging merry hell out of themselves, perhaps the persecution they fled was kindness. They dug peat in lieu of rent for the land. The pits and channels which yielded the peat filled with water and made a lattice of canals interlinking small lakes. At our lunch stop, I pulled out my wallet – even the paper money was wet. I said to Lucy: 'Thing is, once you're wet, you can't get any wetter' – which isn't strictly true. You can get wetter. There are, surprisingly perhaps, degrees of saturation. But one thing is irrefutably true: the one place you mustn't get wet is inside your head. Once the moisture creeps in there, you're done for.

Giethoorn must be a charming place under fair skies and a cheery zephyr: that day it was no better than a large muddy water cistern filled to overflowing from the nozzles of an enormous sprinkler system.

We rode on.

'Which would you get rid of if you had the choice,' I asked Lucy, 'wind or rain?'

'Rain,' she said, her face circled with the hood of her waterproof, the expression set resignedly. I'd have chosen wind, but maybe she was right, and the wind would have dried us out.

For the last 20km to Elburg, the rain got heavier. The cycle path wound through a roadside copse, which acted as a natural wind tunnel, the gale blasting at us. I grabbed Lucy's saddle with my right hand and drove our side-by-side tandem along as hard as I could. We emerged from the trees onto a long causeway, 4km from a swing bridge over the canal. The rain and wind ratcheted up in order to make us swear, sit up, give in, slow down, but no chance: grimly, we forged on. At last, we reached the bridge, and the rain stopped as if in applause. Elburg, an ancient walled town, was another extreme fundamentalist centre of what they call 'black tights religion'. We booked into a hotel. I washed our gear, switched on the radiators to dry it out and the TV to watch the first Alpine stage of that year's Tour and cracked open some beer.

Outside Utrecht, I came off on a wooden bridge slick with rain and grazed my hip. That night, Lucy insisted I take the first shower and laid out my clean clothes for me – sweet girl. In the drizzle by the Oude Gracht, the Old Canal, we'd cast around for our directions to the hotel and a young man had ridden up on a bike, umbrella in hand. 'I can see you are not sure where to go,' he said. 'May I help?' He took us most of the way, pointed up Biltstraat and waved goodbye.

The stand-in concierge at the hotel was decidedly less helpful next morning. We'd put our bikes on the balcony overnight, as requested, but he wouldn't allow us to bring them in through the breakfast room before ten o'clock. Since there was only one other guest in the breakfast room, staring sleepily into a cup of coffee, this stricture was unreasonable. The jobsworth wouldn't budge. It was 9.40. We retired to the room, willed some acceleration out of the clock and went back to exert some moral pressure. The petty keyholder relented, unlocked the balcony door, and we were on our way to The Hague. We arrived as the working population was streaming home towards us along the cycle/pedestrian path. They simply kept walking, parted and let us through. Warm smiles. No antagonism. No jostling for place.

Jake and Victoria gave us pasta, salad and Dutch apple cake for supper en route to the ferry. I'd taught Jake at Gresham's and he was now teaching architecture in his native Holland.

I told Lucy we needed to do the final 25km as fast as we could. She nodded and off we went. We did it in an hour – not yet 13 years old and she rode like a champion. 'I really hated that last ride,' she said afterwards, largely for fear of not making it to the ferry. We did make it, with ample time in hand.

In 1995 – earlier in the year of my first ever ride up a Tour de France col – we rode along the coast of northern France from Calais to Cherbourg. The big dipper of the Caps road west of Calais was not the best way to bed Lucy's legs in: wide swooping descents which taxed her nerves and long climbs up which she struggled. I rode with her, for encouragement, but the 40+km to Cap Gris Nez, where we stayed the first night, was very hard. Through Boulogne and Le Touquet, gracious boulevards and swaying palms, we reached Stella Plage, a seedy little seaside town which offered no rooms anywhere. I knew we hadn't many more kilometres in us that day and was not wholly sanguine about finding a bed within any short distance. On a whim, I suggested we investigate a complex of brick buildings and outhouses near the beach – Stella Maris (sobriquet of the Virgin Mary), a Polish-Catholic Centre des Vacances. The man in the *accueil* not only said we could have a room, for a risible sum of money, but he sold me a couple of bottles of beer for next to nothing and told us that dinner was at seven o'clock in the dining hall. This turned out to be a room the size of a hangar, teeming with Polish-Catholic holidaymakers. The babble of hundreds of voices was jolly, the food was wholesome and we, the irreligious interlopers, were in clover.

Berck means 'yuk' in French, but whether the seaside town of that name through which we cycled deserves the association, I cannot recall. It is, however, known for sanatoria devoted to diseases of the bones. The waters of the Bay of the Somme, a few kilometres south, were shallow, brackish and cloyingly warm. I tried to beg a refill of a water bottle from a woman in a house near the beach but she refused. I asked another and she also refused. A man overheard the rebuffs and rather shyly opened his ice box and held out a chilled litre bottle of Evian with a benevolent smile. We downed it and rode on feeling slightly less poached and salted.

That night, we stayed in what has become almost a ghost town, Onival Ault. Grand houses with lofty gables and high balconies, decorated with tiling friezes and nameplates – e.g. *Sans Gêne* (Free and Easy), *Au Clair de Lune* (By the Light of the Moon), *Bluette* (Spark) and one extravagantly art deco'd edifice called *Tourbillon* (Whirlwind) – stood, most of them, empty with a sort of plague notice hanging from or nailed to their once elegant facades: A VENDRE (For Sale). The prices in the *immobilier* windows reflected the decrepitude, the forsaken air. Onival Ault was one of those towns on this Côte d'Opale frequented by English gamblers in search of casinos when they were illegal in the UK. (The nearest casino is actually in Ault, a kilometre further on.) Le Touquet was posh, Ault and its satellite rather less so, and while Le Touquet continues to thrive, Onival Ault is run-down, emptying, forlorn. Just north is the beach from which Duke William's invasion fleet embarked for England.

A heavy day along the coast road – long sapping climbs which tuckered Lucy out. By Sotteville-sur-Mer, we needed to find a lodging and went past an enticing sign for *chambres d'hôtes* which, for some reason, I resisted. We rode on another 3.5km, could find no rooms in an overcrowded and unsupplied little town and headed back to the sign we'd ignored, through fields of flax, the stalks laid out to dry. Up a track to an old Norman farmhouse where the woman at the door, in answer to my request for a room, said she had none. She must have caught the disappointment in my eyes, or else Lucy's tiredness, because almost at once she added that she did, however, have a tent. I said we had no sleeping bags. She said that there were sleeping bags in the tent. Hurray. We had our home for the night and one of the best meals that whole trip: everything home-cooked and home-made, cider kir (with strawberry syrop) as an aperitif, farm Calvados as digestif, and, for breakfast, sponge cake (at last), fruit compôte, delicious fresh-ground and fresh-brewed coffee.

We made friends with a charming young Dutch couple in a camper van next to our little green tent, and it was with some misgiving that I said we should leave our patch in the sun and head off again.

Lucy was knackered. It was a bad, bad morning for her and steamy hot to boot. I nursed and comforted her as best I could, but all at once she came to a dead stop and burst into tears, a combination of physical weariness, not being sure of where we were going to stay and homesickness. Instead of continuing round the coast through Fécamp and its Benedictine abbey, I decided we should cut across country through Cany-Barville to Saint-Romain-de-Colbosc near Le Havre, also that I would call at a tourist office and ring ahead for a room. I told the woman who promised accommodation that we would arrive some time between five and six. 'I am counting on you,' she said and rang off.

A long lazy lunch in a grove of lime trees near the seventeenth-century château of Cany restored Lucy, and she was back in chirrupy good spirits, chattering as fast as she turned the pedals into rural peace away from the conveyor-belt main roads.

We got to our booking – a large, decrepit three-storied farmhouse out in the country – at 5.35 in the evening. It was deserted. The garden was a mess, scattered with tipped-over vegetal-green-slime-stained plastic chairs, bits of machinery, boxes, crates and *crottes* of dogshit. The dog which must have dumped them barked inside the house when I rang the bell but with no great enthusiasm and soon gave up.

We pedalled further down into the tiny hamlet to a sign offering *accueil paysan*. The peasant of the promised welcome answered the bell. He had a single, thick black eyebrow connecting one ear to the other, like a headband, straw in his hair and dust caking his flared nostrils. His wife wasn't at home, he mumbled. She handled the domestic arrangements, though, by the evidence of what we saw when he took us inside, the domestic arrangements weren't taking up a great deal of either her time or her energy. The man opened a door and pointed to a poky cluttered room in which stood an unmade metre-wide truckle-bed with a goitred mattress and a gumboiled duvet.

'This is deep Hicksville,' I whispered to Lucy. 'Let's get out of here before he locks us in the cellar.' I smiled at the lummox and off we went, back to the first place. We set up chairs and waited for half an hour, drinking the beer and Orangina we'd bought in town. No one came.

Thus, an hour after we'd arrived, we rode back into Saint-Romain, checked into a friendly little cheap hotel and watched French *It's a Knockout* over a set menu for a fiver. The French *It's a Knockout* seemed to work on the basic premise that violent mistreatment and/or ritual unspeakable humiliation of the contestants offered prime entertainment value . . . this long before the advent of *Big Brother*.

Next day, my birthday, we cycled over the new Pont de Normandie, in the tyre tracks of that year's Tour. Lucy took one look at its long steep ramp and said: 'I'm not going to be able to get up there,' but I said just to take it steady, she'd be fine, and so she was. Along the Côte Fleurie (Floral Coast), through the little port at Honfleur, Deauville, which Lucy christened the Nice of the north, and on to the famous Pegasus Bridge across the Caen Canal south of Ouistreham on the Côte de Nacre, where we stopped for a drink at the first house to be liberated in the invasion – by British paratroopers, before midnight of 5 June 1944.

In Caen, we visited the exquisite Abbaye des Dames, the local honey-coloured stone as pristine inside as if it were newly built. In Bayeux, I translated the Latin for Lucy as we walked slowly round the tapestry. In Arromanches, we toured the museum of the D-Day landings. Omaha beach is an eerie place. I have swum there once and it is undeniably haunted. The presence of those countless ghosts is palpable. Pointe du Hoc, a short way along, where the US Rangers scaled the cliffs, is just one of the many names which resonate from those climactic months of the invasion of and battle for Normandy. We passed others up the Cotentin peninsula to Cherbourg, through the massy hedgerows of the bocage through which the Tiger tanks crashed in the bloody fighting that summer of 1944.

The all-night cabaret and disco halls aboard the late ferry from Cherbourg on Sunday were doing lively business, but we watched a film in the deserted ship's cinema before going to the cabin. As the ferry docked early next day, we discerned a certain crapulous reluctance in the queues of passengers shuffling towards the car decks to grapple with sunlight. We, by contrast, pedalled off in offensively bright spirits, breakfasted in Portsmouth and so home.

Seven

Gnat's Piss and Grand Cru

The Col du Galibier, at 2,642m, most often forms 'the roof of the Tour', i.e. its highest climb. First included in 1911, it appeared on every subsequent Tour de France until 1949 and quite regularly since then. (Only the six-times included Iseran, 2,720m, and the Col de la Bonnette-Restefond, 2,802m, thrice, top it.) It was the Galibier that drew me to the Alps in the first place, the mountain whose name symbolised all that was most heroic in the Tour, the quintessence of its epic tradition. Ride up the Galibier, I thought, and you will have been to the heart of the mystery of the great bike race. Maybe. Well, that's the dream we all nurse, isn't it? Going up there on the bike, converting the celluloid gloss of the magazine pictures, the seductive image of the television coverage, mountain slopes crowded with fans, the gaudy fiesta of the Tour spectacular paying court to the very public suffering of the riders themselves, converting all that into the hard tarmac, the distance, the punishment of the gradient, swapping the romance for the solid truth of the real thing?

The French call the Galibier 'the Giant of the Alps', 'a sacred monster', except that *sacré* can also mean 'unholy'. The ambiguity is telling: the Galibier is, in the rank of myth and natural wonder, magnificent, sublime, but it can also be a pig. It's not unique in that, of course, but the myth counts for a bit extra.

My frank obsession with the race, reading about it though not yet writing about it, finally impelled me to make a decision that, it's no exaggeration to say, changed my life. In the winter of 1994, I suggested to my friend John that we go to the Alps and ride them. He and his then wife Angela were redoubtable cycling tourists. The idea appealed. We were on.

I had, of course, cycled in France but never for any protracted length of time. Possibly the yearning to do so was first prompted by the account a girlfriend's mother related of a cycling holiday she'd enjoyed in France between the wars. She and a friend simply crossed the Channel and headed off into the Mademoiselle from Armentières *parlez-vous* countryside with their bikes, bowled along wherever the fancy took them, called at farmhouses on spec seeking board and lodging, were never turned away and had a wonderful time. Those were the days when hearty types trumpeted the benefits of the Great Outdoors, the heyday of the Clarion Fellowship – radical socialism, class equality and cycling all in one, wanderlust brought on by the smile of Lady Freedom. I don't like hearty types myself – a matter of style . . . in their case, none – but I do like some of the activities they bang on about.

Whenever I mount the bike, whether for the drudgery of food shopping or a ride out into the lanes of Kent, five minutes away from home, I enjoy and cherish a liberty uniquely associated with the beautiful machine. Now I was heading for something else, too: to touch, even vicariously, the reality of what I had only ever, so far, dreamed about – the Tour de France.

Training for the adventure was something of a problem. I got a pair of rollers and endured the protracted ennui of home-training. An actress, with whom I have worked a number of times, reads her day's pabulum of lines as she pedals the exercise bike in the mornings, but that's more book than bike, and I never warmed to the reduced domestic version of the beautiful machine: it does a job, that's all. My pal Simon was in the steam bath at the RAC Club in London having just completed a ride across America, west to east, when a man came in, flopped down on the bench, pooped out, and said: 'They've got a great new exercise bike in the gym – you should give it a try.' Simon didn't respond.

To supplement the longer forays into Hertfordshire, I used the Outer Circle round Regent's Park as a training piste – there's only one traffic light, so, with luck, I could develop a good speed and sustain it at tempo for a couple of hours in the quieter times of a Saturday afternoon. Circuit after circuit, the lights were with me, and then, racing at near maximum towards the intersection, I saw the lights change to amber. In the split second between seeing the red and judging the distance to the other side, I make the moronic decision to risk the crossing. I jumped the short line of cars which had halted and, stranded in the open middle of the junction, caught sight of the yellow sports car revving hard, headed straight for me, Death in a canary Lotus. This was it. I was a goner. Yet, somehow, the driver managed heroically to brake and swerve so that he no more than clipped my front wheel and shunted the fallen heap – me and bike – a yard or two into the gutter. A small knot of people immediately gathered round, including the driver, who got out of the car in obvious consternation. By some amiable fortune that I certainly did not deserve, I was not only still whole and breathing but had drawn to my aid a floating cell of London's ancillary services: an off-duty nurse, ambulance driver, policeman and a woman with a mobile phone, probably an accident-trauma counsellor. They swung into action even as the police sergeant poled up.

He asked me if I was all right, which, apart from shock, a torn hand and abrasions to my legs, I was. I immediately told him that the accident was my fault entirely, that the driver was in no way to blame, by brisk reactions he had saved me from far worse injuries. 'What happened, then?' the copper asked.

'I'm in training. I jumped the light. I was speed-pissed.'

'You were what?' he asked, presumably thinking I was bug-eyed on amphetamines.

'I was racing flat out . . . didn't think. Stupid.'

To the driver's solicitude, I could only apologise profusely. His unfeigned concern for my safety and absence of any aggression or rebuke shamed and embarrassed me. Having managed to wheedle his name and address out of the police after I had given a statement (they weren't keen), I later sent him, in gratitude, a bottle of champagne and what could only be a banal explanation of why I had so thoughtlessly risked his car, his peace of mind and my life. He wrote back to thank me, to say that he was simply glad that I had not been badly hurt and to wish me well in the Alps. He pressed no charges. It was noble indeed.

On the way to St Mary's Hospital in Paddington, the carnelian and silver ring I had had made for me, crushed in the accident, removed from my finger and put in a back pocket, went missing. (I got a near duplicate made.) The bike suffered only a smashed front wheel and, when the hospital had done all they could to mend me, I wheeled it, and me, both hobbling, home.

John, Angela and I met at the famous South Mimms service station, once a big rallying point for amateur racing cyclists, to catch the Bike Express coach – down through France to Valence, where it stopped in a motorway lay-by to let us out.

10 September 1995, 4.30 a.m.
In my saddlebag: two pairs of underpants – one silk, one

thermal – hat and gloves, slip-on shoes, shorts and shirt, spare handkerchief, warm top, waterproof, washing kit, repair kit, Virgil's *Aeneid IV,* Patrick O'Brian's *Clarissa Oakes* and C.S. Lewis's *The Problem of Pain.* I was, you note, going to give the experience of these mountains close philosophical as well as physical scrutiny.

This being a Sunday, the local men were gathering early for some Sabbath hunting, so the café in Thodure was open and crowded. We drank reviving coffee and rode on into an ashen pewter dawn, the sombre outline of the Col des Limouches and Col de la Bataille backlit by the rising sun. I found myself sweating even in the slight chill of early day, grunting with effort on a slope that looked no worse than the long drag up to the Pond past Parliament Hill. All my flap-doodle about establishing a smooth flow? Laughable. But, we'd been cooped in a coach for about 17 hours, it was cold, I was nervous at the start of the trip, and warming the motor, getting into what the French call 'a good carburation', takes time. Still, first lesson: what a gradient looks like very often has not much to do with what a gradient is. The true measure of gradient is what it does to you and what you have to contrive to do back to it.

The serpentine lifts of the long Gorges de la Bourne road were my first real taste of Alpine climbing and, as the warmth of the day and the exercise coursed through my muscles, I did begin to feel something recognisable as a rhythm connecting legs and breathing. I went ahead, stopped to wait for the others, propped Shorter then myself against a parapet wall. An old lady emerged from the adjacent house. I said good morning. She asked if I was tired. *'Non, il y a du soleil.'*

'Dieu merci.'

Agreeably sane, that old lady.

From there, up the climb to the heights above Grenoble and the sweeping hairpins down into the Isère valley. As we rode south towards Vizille, the sense of entering a grand, a daunting mountainscape on frail human-sized machines filtered in. Twelve hours and some 128km after we left the coach, we were looking ahead at the outline of the ultra-high ranges caught in the haze and warm sunglow of early evening . . . the Alps. As yet, excitement far outweighed any foreboding. That would come.

The first close sight of the mountains always inspires awe. 'Awesome' gets bandied about much these days: it originally referred to holy dread, specifically the mortal terror occasioned by contemplation of God's divine majesty, its 'awful purity'. Such fear is what makes the Quivering Brethren in *Cold Comfort Farm* tremble, and the Shakers in real life. Whatever your religious per- or dis-suasion, there is an element of divinity in mountains – that is, something beyond our comprehension and mortal power – else where did belief in the existence of gods come from? The Latin poet Ovid writes of a dark grove below the Aventine Hill in Rome 'in the deep shade of holm oaks. Just to see it elicits the response: "there is divine power here".' (*Fasti* III, 295.) When, in the film *The Greatest Story Ever Told*, John Wayne played the centurion at the foot of Christ's cross, he had to say the line: 'Surely this was the son of God.' The cameras rolled, Wayne stared up at the dying Jesus and said the line. The director gushed: 'Gee, John, that was so . . . so moving, just full of . . . you know, feeling? Could you just give it to us once more, with just a teeny weeny bit more *awe*?'

Take Two. Lights, sound, camera, action. Wayne squared up and drawled: 'Aw . . . surely this was the son of God.'

Of the first two alps I climbed, l'Alpe d'Huez and the Col du Glandon, I have written at some length in my book about the Tour de France. Riding the Alpe was a hell of an initiation, and, because it was one of the few climbs that I recognised from the television coverage, as I looked up at the last long zigzags above me that morning – the clutter of chalets and hotels at the top – I felt a very powerful affinity. This might have been a common or garden ski-station highway in winter, but, in another guise, it was also exclusive Tour de France territory. There was no territorial indicator, of course, just the familiarity of the upper reaches as the moto-cameramen tracked the leaders riding up the narrow corridor between the spectators towards the finish – that and the tarmac visitors' book across which your wheels passed, the names of the heroes, past and present. Yes, here was the road they rode and here was I riding it. Some presumption, but you have to get over that incongruity – *you* essaying the Tour route? – and, on the Glandon, I certainly got over it.

I had to talk myself through that one most of the way. Willpower found itself in alien domains, like a domestic cat in tiger country. Forget 'presumption', with its grandiose overtones, try the rather more mundane 'foolhardiness' for size. At our lunch stop in the village of Huez, halfway up the climb to the ski station, I looked at the map and recorded my assessment in the journal:

> From the map, the Col du Glandon presents little problem. A long drop into the valley at whose head the Glandon stands, then 29km from an altitude of 720m to 1,924m with a couple of steep sections. If not a breeze, at least manageable, rounded off with a 22km downhill glide into La Chambre – apt name for an overnight stop.

Sheer hubris. Hubris is giving V signs to Fate.

'Manageable'? On the bare evidence of a map, *that* was the intellectual equivalent of speed-pissed plus a bit, plus a bit more. The monstrous arrogance of it. But hey, I'd just ridden up l'Alpe d'Huez. I was a seasoned col-bagger. Bring the next one on. No fucking problem.

Simpleton. That 'manageable' clogged my gears, tightened the brake blocks on the rims, fouled my thought processes, saturated my muscles with quick-freeze and sat in my gut like cold suet.

The ride up the Glandon was a callous empirical demonstration of just how seductive and misleading bald statistics can be, if you accede to their blandishments. I was gaily passing off 51km and a socking great mountain as no more than an undemanding afternoon doddle to an easy pull-in for a sundowner on the terrace of a picturesque country inn – in other words, taking mountains for granted. Bad mistake. It isn't over till it's over. The Glandon took one look at me, cocksure, swaggering me, and on that punishing *post meridiem* of hard-rock experience set its implacable face against being over for a long, long time. It decided to squash me till I whimpered then toss the bits into a drainage culvert.

The first 15km ground on and on round slow bends screened by trees dripping with some distant cousin of rain and a cold sweat of apprehension. The sky was as wan as dough and damp as a fever patient's brow. And, when the first 15km was done, the road suddenly dropped into a deep defile, a large sack of precious metres won thrown to the winds, and the wicked gradient back up out of that black hole, the start of another 14km of torture, almost made me weep. I had to say to myself 'Remember, Graeme, you came here to enjoy yourself', as mad, as surreal as that notion seemed in this nadir of my emotions and physical strength. I said it over and over again until I had climbed up the ramp and far enough out of the dejection at least to keep going. I was, as it were, riding on the rim with a flattened spirit.

I had no map. Would a map have afforded any comfort? Was it better not to know how far I had still to go when there was so far still to go? I don't know. After years, now, of riding cols, I simply don't know. I can no longer penetrate that depth of inexperience and the ludicrous assumptions it engendered. The fact is I laid bare an important secret that day, a fairly banal secret, too – that however far it is to the top from wherever you are, that's how far you have to go, and there's nothing you can do about it. Sound idiotic, daft? It is absurd, but to the novice it can be a hard, hard truth to accept, like the admission of stress and embracing it instead of pretending it doesn't exist – a fundamental psychological shift. For there were times in the misery of that ride when I really thought that I was not going to make it.

Riding down from l'Alpe d'Huez, my spirits soaring, I'd passed a man and his teenage son, with whom I'd exchanged greetings on the way up. They'd stopped at a hairpin for another breather, taking it steady. As I went by, the man called out: 'You made it,' and I called out: 'You'll make it,' into the slipstream of the breeze. Not making it . . . getting off to walk . . . riding back down to the safe haven of Bourg d'Oisans . . . no manner of surrender was a viable option.

This is the bedrock of reality: however grim you feel physically, whatever defeatist temptation clouds your mind, giving up solves nothing. The kilometres ahead of you, the steepness of the road, the suffering, mental and physical, that it's going to take to surmount them: all that lies ahead of you and will not go away. The inclemency of the weather may change, granted, the geology will not and time ticks on. Thinking you won't make it is like worry – it changes nothing and merely adds the weight of anxiety to the problem. This you can do without, so shun it in favour of the reality: I can't go on, I must go on, I will go on. The formula may be simple: it most decidedly is not simplistic. It has to be earned and learnt from the inside out.

Inside out is certainly what I felt on the Glandon. And I was lucky – I got to the top, the uphill slog over, just as the clouds began to dump their mega-gallons of added persecution onto the blighted solitudes of the Glandon. Back down the ascent, John and Angela were going to cop the whole deluge while the top was still far off.

One of the Midwich Cuckoos, in John Wyndham's remarkable novel of that name, observes that 'humour and compassion are the most important of human inventions, but they are not very firmly established yet, though promising well'. On the Glandon, I lost track of both, to my incalculable detriment. Never so readily again.

In addition to being flattened psychologically in getting to the top, on the descent I got drenched, chilled to the bone, my hands numb and seized up with holding the brakes on, but I made it down from the col through the cascade of rain and the thick drapes of a murky dusk in fairly good order to the restaurant/hotel where I waited for John and Angela. They had a much more testing ordeal, having got stuck in a cattle byre, sheltering from an electric storm, finally nosing off into the night through sheeting rain.

I learnt two things that day: first about the inevitable dam wall of limitations which you hit when you have pushed as hard as you can and gone on pushing as hard as you can. I sometimes arrived at Lindy's white and over-strained with the effort of flogging myself up Highgate West Hill – it made her quite angry and upset. But, through the coughing fit and the lung seizure and the blurred vision, I rejoiced that I could still drive myself that furiously. I also learnt that admitting to a temporary loss of appetite for pushing to the limit is acceptable too. Not caving in, just not savouring the fight for a while. It's OK to gripe now and then. On the Glandon, I had to remind myself that I was there because I had chosen to be there. I'd come to the Alps to enjoy them. Well, there are textures of enjoyment to be unpicked. But, choosing to be somewhere doesn't also include choosing what you have no control over. Putting up with a bad time doesn't entail taking pleasure from it, unless you're a masochist, and I am certainly not that. We're talking satisfaction here, when the pain stops, not an addiction to pain itself, which is questionable sanity. Occasionally it's kosher to get pissed off and stay pissed off for a while. The ability to do that makes for healthy psychological balance.

When I got to the hotel/restaurant some 8km below the col, I parked the bike outside, sloshed and squelched into the clean dry bar and said to the woman standing behind it: 'Excuse me, madame, I am very, very wet.'

She was unfazed. 'It's raining,' she said, with a shrug of unconcern.

John and Angela arrived nearly two hours after me, swathed in waterproof capes, looming out of the darkness and the driving rain into the light of a single streetlamp. I had sat behind the glazed door in vigil, coffee and brandy to warm me up as I stared out into the Stygian gloom of the rain-soaked Glandon night.

Washed and dry-clad we sat to supper, the only guests in the place: large tureen of garbure, meat stew with mashed potatoes, cheese and pudding, lashings of red wine.

I didn't sleep a wink.

The Galibier came on day three of our trip. L'Alpe d'Huez is a comparatively new – and custom-built – road, supplying the ski station at altitude. The road over the Galibier is centuries old and a direct conduit of Tour legend. Until 1979, the mountain's altitude was given as 2,556m, the road cut through the uppermost boss of the mountain via a tunnel. When one of the big supporting archways collapsed, the tunnel was closed and the road was extended upwards over the shoulder of the massif, an added kilometre of around 10% to 2,645m from the original 2,556m. Lucien Van Impe was first over the new super Galibier.

This was the col which would be my true baptism into the compulsion that is cycling over mountains. Oh, others complicated the mystery, for sure, and if innocence went on the Glandon, the Galibier took me to a higher level yet. It didn't come with riding past the large stone cylindrical obelisk to 'Henri Desgrange, creator of the Tour de France' either: it was crossing that unmarked line on the summit, the near imperceptible kink in the shoulder of the col, one of those frontiers between not knowing about something and knowing it. 'Know thyself.' Easy to say, hard to do, but oh the jubilation *when* you begin.

Desgrange used to wait for 'his riders' next to the spot on which his memorial stands. He introduced the Galibier in the 1911 Tour as part of an attempt to eliminate the fraudulent practices of 1910, which had left such a bitter taste in his mouth. That year, first inclusion of the mighty Pyrenean cols, a number of riders had infringed his adamant rule that every man must ride alone. The ideal Tour, he said, was a Tour which only one rider could finish. That was, in effect, saying that it would be a challenge which could push most of the hardest men in cycling beyond their limits. A pretty shocking concept, and, to this day, abandoning the Tour, for whatever reason, is, to most professionals, the ultimate in humiliation and betrayal of self.

Halfway through the 1910 race, the eagle-eyed martinet Desgrange fell ill and was forced to return to Paris. When he heard how Van Hauwert and Gustave Garrigou had given the eventual winner, Octave Lapize, unblushing support on the road, he was livid. From now on, he would ensure that such flagrant, such shameless, breach of the etiquette of pure athleticism wouldn't happen. 'Do not imagine my attitude towards the riders is one of severity alone. I am attached to them by unbreakable ties of affection, most sincere and very deep, but I intend to love them on the following principle:

he who loves best, punishes best.' Right: send them over the Galibier.

The bikes weighed on average around 14 kilos (François Faber's weighed 16 kilos). Fixed wheels, large and small sprocket either side of the rear hub for climbing and downhill/ flat. (Stirred by Matt Seaton's wonderful paean to the fixed wheel in the first edition of *Rouleur* magazine, I recently bought a Condor Pista, a most beautiful machine. Do I deserve it? Probably not. But, riding it underlines what extraordinary strength and bike-handling those pioneering guys must have had, not only to ride up the cruel lumps of geology but to negotiate the treacherous descents reliant on a single bean-pod front brake without spinning themselves into humanoid turbines.)

Emile Georget had the legendary honour of crossing the massive Col du Galibier for the first time in the history of the Tour, midway through a 366km stage. Desgrange was up there, so too a gathering of other officials and spectators, when, along the road towards them, came Georget, on his own, hunched over his cowhorn handlebars, goggles up on his brow, white neckerchief tucked into his cap to protect his neck. The sun shone though it was bitterly cold at that altitude. From the base of the climb, the road was scored and pitted, horribly uneven, no better than a goat track, a far worse trial to ride than the smooth surface of today's Alpine roads. Desgrange wrote:

> When Georget stopped and put his victorious foot to the ground on the head of this monster, he was filthy dirty, his moustache clogged with snot and bits of food from the previous control, his jersey stained with mud from the last stream into which he'd pitched headlong. Looking a complete fright, but with the whey face of a clown, he came across [there was a control] and snapped: 'That's made you sit up.'

Georget gave his own wry take on the fearsome experience:

> The men who dug the tunnel at the top of the col
> might have driven it through at the bottom. It would
> have been a little bit longer, no doubt, but it would
> have spared us a matryrdom. Between the tunnel of
> the Métro and the summit of the Galibier, well, I still
> prefer the Métro.

But Desgrange was cock-a-hoop. 'Does not this ascent of the
Galibier on bicycles constitute the first triumph of mortal
intelligence over the laws of gravity?' And of the mountain
itself, the rhodomontade of his prose never stinting in the
rubrics of hyperbole, he rhapsodised:

> O, Sappey! O, Laffrey! O, Col de Bayard! O, Tourmalet!
> I would not be failing in my obligation to declare that,
> by comparison with the grand cru of the Galibier, you
> are but wishy-washy, common or garden gnat's piss:
> before this giant, one can but remove one's hat and
> bow very low.

(The Sappey, Laffrey and Bayard are relatively minor humps
in the Grand Chartreuse between Chambéry and Grenoble.)

Well, I knew the stories about the Galibier, and, since I
crossed it, I have recounted many of them. Having ridden
up there adds a frisson of exceptional pleasure, in some cases
a shudder to recall what a bleak and lonely place it can be.
Also, since then, I have twice been investigated by the Inland
Revenue – a hazard of being freelance. They can drive you
to drink, another tax trap. The inspectors did not question
my claim against the money which that trip to the Alps cost,
but, if they had, I would honestly have told them that the
investment was priceless. Incidentally, one of them (on the

second investigation), when I recounted what work I had done in the year whose accounts they were probing – a book, various magazine articles, a theatre show, several pieces for radio, a short film . . . – remarked, bemusedly: 'Oh, so it's a bit like a hobby.' I concluded that he couldn't really accommodate the idea of loving what you do for a living.

We rode the Galibier in the sort of weather that compelled the organisation to give it a miss two years later, 1996, when Bjarne Rijs won. We set out from Valloire (where Eddy Merckx crashed in the neutral zone in 1975, broke his jaw, yet rode on so as not to diminish Thévenet's momentous victory) into cold rain, skies as grey as dull unenamelled steel tubing. Lighter laden, I went ahead. Shorts. No tights. No overshoes. Hadn't yet heard of them. No gloves (keeping them dry for the downhill). Minimal waterproof. Seventeen kilometres to ride. The road up ahead marked ominously with double chevrons on the map.

The approach across the open ground towards Plan Lachat, at halfway, was about as unromantic as a freezing wet day in the high mountains could make it. I passed clumps of dishevelled farm buildings, which even the flower-spangled glory of a hot summer would hardly render handsome. They crouched, hunkered down, sodden and morose, in stagnant swamps of thick cowpat-brown mud. A knot of shuttered chalets. Bleak moorland. The waters of the Valloirette River course unseen. Wetness everywhere. To the west, a mighty wall of mountain, the Aigles d'Arve; to the east, another rampart, La Sétaz Vieille. Threatening banks of foul weather. Ahead looms the col, somewhere, overshadowed by two majestic steeples of rock marking the end of the two opposing ridges: the Grand Galibier and the Pic des Trois Evêchés. The road noses into a line of dripping trees – no shelter there – and out the other side.

Plan Lachat is a huddle of ugly wooden ski chalets in a

crook of the ranges. Beyond it, the meandering road swings abruptly right and steeply up – frighteningly steep – onto the first of the ramps, the real start of the climb, the proper testing stuff. Everything till now has been preamble, no great tax of gradient, yet I've been in my lowest gear since we set out, which means that the only gear I have left is out of the saddle. On that subject: always get into as low a gear as you need early on. This reduces strain on the legs, and pushing big gears is for the brainless proud. We've all done it.

From here on, the Galibier is horribly exposed and, on this day of slantwise rain-cum-sleet, wintry cold. The road breaks every vertebra in its spine with stress fracture on the bare rock. No trees occlude or shelter the way forward. I can see the next hairpin snapping back on itself overhead as the hairpin I am on unbends from its tight V. I'm riding very slowly. Pedal stroke by pedal stroke. Suddenly, being on the Galibier is very scary. Had I thought much about it beforehand? Well, I had, but here I am inhabiting the gap between the mental image and the reality, treading the gulf between what I had nursed as possibility across to the insuperable fact of my own limitations. This is a massive alp with a deserved reputation. I feel as if I'm gatecrashing the titans' training camp. Occasionally I stand up on the pedals to relieve the cricking ache in the small of my back, 80m or so, and then settle onto the seat again.

The rain turns inexorably to snow. Now, when I honk (get out of the saddle), the back wheel occasionally loses purchase on the settling slick and I have to plonk my bum down to counter the skid. A Dutch camper van shoots past in a vile, wet, freezing broadcast of slush and liquid and very nearly takes me out.

Not far from the top, I see a huge gully to my right, a funnel between two huge gaunt pillars of rock, a chasm plunging over a precipice, swirling with ghostly flurries of blinding white snow in chaotic spirals of wind. I am riding into the lost region of thin air where frost makes pastel rainbows and that legendary demon of misfortune, the Witch with Green Teeth, trails nets of ice-fibre mesh to trap the unwary lone rider and sweep him into the thrall of mechanical breakdown and punctures, if not to throw him off the machine altogether. This is the realm of Frost-Blink, and I am riding a glacial brook not a tarmac road. But I think of the men of 1911 and then cannot match this, any of this, to what they did on those machines, riding alone, unsupported, into the unknown, into the freezing fog, on unmade tracks littered with loose stones, slick with mud, awash with old snow and off-land drainage or crisp arid from heat.

I get nearer – how near? Never enquire, just stick with it – and the realisation that I am going to make it begins to break, but no: *absit omen*. It's never over till it's over. Then I see ten or so cars parked either side of the road, a snowplough beyond them on the left-hand verge. The car passengers stand around in fur coats, overcoats, muffled with scarves, hats, gloves, their breath pluming in the frosty thin air.

I stop, dismount and call out: 'Is this the col?'

It's the col, and, as I fumble woodenly with frozen fingers at the straps of my saddlebag to liberate my gloves and a thicker sweater, one of the two dungareed snowplough men calls over to me in a sullen tone: 'A car's slipped off the road. We need your help.'

Right. They need *my* help. They've been stooging around waiting for a bike-rider. They have the population of a small skiing chalet togged out in toasty warm clothes, standing around like tripe at fourpence, the driver of said car included, presumably, and they need *my* help. I reply, with some acid incredulity in my tone: 'I've just cycled up the Galibier and you want me to help you with a *car*?'

'*Ouais*,' he says (yup).

I clumped over in the cleats. The three of us clapped hands onto the car, heaved it back onto the road. I clumped back, retrieved the Shorter and, somewhat puzzled and distracted by having had to play at roadside rescue, set off downhill in search of a café where I could thaw out and await the others. None of the loiterers said a thing. Only a woman standing under a cascade of icicles fringing an overhang called out: '*Chapeau!*' (well done). And suddenly I did think: the Galibier. I just cycled the Galibier. Wow.

Briançon prides itself not only on being the highest town in Europe, at 1,350m, but also claims to be blessed with more than 300 days of sunshine per year. Pity we arrived on one of the unblessed 65. Further soaking on the long, long downhill when there was little chance of turning the pedals at any kind of rate to pump the heated blood round. Poor Angela was suffering dreadful gyp in her knee. By the time we got to the hotel, it was pretty well congealed, and we packed her off to the hot tub in the bathroom pronto.

The rain had gone first thing next morning, and we rode away from the hotel in search of the road to the Col d'Izoard. Rambling what seemed like aimlessly through the side streets, I said: 'It can't be this way, John. It's uphill.'

Thus a new familiarity with mountains makes blasé jokers of us all.

The rain soon crowded in again and, higher up, froze as snow. The new familiarity also makes veterans of us, not hardened, quite, but never again innocent or dismissive. A Jewish joke has a young man of high intelligence and extreme arrogance taunting his rabbi with the futility of all his book learning. 'Pointless,' he says, 'utterly pointless. What have all those years of study taught you?'

Gently, the rabbi, a man of deep knowledge and solid patience, replies: 'They have taught me, amongst other things, about God's unfaltering love of even the most recalcitrant of His children.'

'God?' scoffs the young prig. 'Pah, ridiculous, there's no God. Don't talk to me about God. I'm an atheist.'

The rabbi pauses before saying, quietly: 'No, it's not an atheist you are. You are an ignoramus.'

The encouraging thing about broaching the experience of mountains, if you are of a mind and temperament to be so encouraged, is that ignorance and its concomitant disrespect become not only impermissible forever after, they are simply not possible. Entry into the mediaeval artisans' guilds after a long apprenticeship involved passage into what was termed a mystery, a complex guarded secrecy combining knowledge of a craft and the proven skill to practise it. As I rode towards the Izoard, I felt as if I had been initiated into a similar, if not quite so far-reaching, mystery. The climb was hard, the unfolding of the approach quite as challenging as that of the Galibier and the Glandon, the conditions of the day as cold and uncomfortable, the surface of the road as treacherous, but now I had a precious advantage: I was mentally prepared for what was coming. Physically I was no further on than the day before – how could I be? – but, having conquered fear and uncertainty one day, I knew I had it in me to do so again. They say that a rider can never say he has beaten the Tour de France, only that the Tour de France has not beaten him. It is always all to do again. The same with mountains: the utmost you can ever say is that on such and such a day, the mountain did not beat you. This is humbling, rightly humbling.

A kilometre before the col on the western approach to the Izoard stands one of the network of refuges across the Alpine ranges constructed on the orders of the emperor Napoleon Bonaparte, partly as a string of military guard posts along the frontiers with neighbouring Italy. It was in the refuge that I would meet the others, but, even as I glanced up at the last zigzags of the hairpins leading to the summit, I determined to press on and ride to the top without stopping, just for the satisfaction of completing the whole climb in one. That was another consequence of being so blooded: I had no qualms about having to do the final kilometre twice. My intention, after all, had been to add the Col de la Croix de Fer to my ascent of the Glandon – another 2.5km and not much more, I reckoned, than the climb of Highgate West Hill. That, however, had proved beyond me – I was too rattled, too worn out. In a way, the Glandon had beaten me, even if I had ridden up it.

We finally tore ourselves away from the snug joviality of the refuge, the hot chocolate and warm apple cake, the heat of the open fire, the fug worked up by a crowd of walkers in thick woollen sweaters, to brave once more the insidious cold of the open mountain road. Alongside the col sign stands a memorial to the Tour de France. Angela and I posed in the light blizzard for the camera record that we had been there. We posed again in front of the memorial to Fausto Coppi and one of the many younger riders who idolised him, Louison Bobet. Below us reared the sinister orange rock stacks of the Casse Déserte, towering out of a bleached lunar wasteland of stones on the southern approach like a petrified mudslide to either side of the exposed corniche. The blizzard still blurred our view, the scene looked arctic, spectral. In summer, when the sun is full, its heat is merciless, its glare blinding. As the road twists through the parched gulch of the Broken Desert, the notch of the col cut into the bare shoulders of mountain appears impossibly far away, impossibly high up. The Izoard looks hard every inch of the way. It is hard, every inch of the way, one of the most intimidating climbs in the mythology.

Everyone who rides this colossus of a climb will retain an indelible memory of it. And, if the ghosts of the Tour gather routinely anywhere on the route, you feel it must be in the lonely canyon of the Casse Déserte, amid the avatar menhirs, under the blazing furnace of the Dog Star. (The Tour and the Giro tend not to see them under snow, of course.) Those rock stacks might be the natural statue embodiment of the implacable *juges de paix,* blind, anonymous, impersonal, the arbiters of human frailty who preside over the Tour, who punish the *jour sans* without pity, who oversee with a cold eye the terrible faltering and the superhuman acts of bravery, endurance and tenacity alike.

Eight

Big Mountains . . . Big Mushrooms

I wrote a long account of that trip to the Alps from the notes I took in my journal en route, into which I wove a few stories about the Tour. I later pruned the narrative of our ride and replaced the travelogue with more and more about the race. This material, the outcome of many years of study of *La Grande Boucle*, became the basis of *Tour de France: The History, the Legend, the Riders*. Four years and eight editions after it was first published, I met Bill Campbell, the director of Mainstream, for lunch at the Groucho Club in Soho. It was Trafalgar Day. He ordered me a gin and tonic and said: 'I'd just like to thank you for the Tour de France book.'

'Is this the moment to remind you that you turned it down?' I said. He laughed. But it was true: they hadn't even looked at what I had written, only rejected the outline.

Mainstream had published my ghosted autobiography of the boxing trainer George Francis, but it sold poorly. I say ghosted. In fact, I wrote every word in the book. I didn't record George as he talked, at high speed, for hours at a time. I scribbled notes, as fast as I could. My recall is pretty sharp, and I wrote up and expanded the notes into full narrative. These gobbets of George's life and recollection became the core and then the substance of the finished book. But having listened very closely to George for so long on so many occasions, and because of our deep natural rapport, I got so that I could write as if it were him talking. Indeed, people were amazed that it was *not* ghosted in the more commonly accepted sense.

A year after the rejection, when I was living in the French Pyrenees and extensively revising my original text, I wrote to Bill suggesting that he perhaps didn't appreciate what a big market there was for such a book, that the Tour de France was hugely popular, in no small part due to the brilliant coverage on Channel 4, now shamefully lost to satellite channels. It was a forceful letter. Mainstream, at the time, published no books about cycling. Bill responded thus:

> Dear Graeme,
> Many thanks indeed for your letter of 10 June, which has convinced me that we should take another look at your history of the Tour de France.
> I would be delighted to consider it if you would forward it for my attention together with a stamped addressed envelope for the eventuality of its return to you. It was good to hear from you again.

I sent him the new recension of the manuscript in mid-July. Some time in October, when I was once again living in temporary digs, he phoned me and, after a polite exchange of pleasantries, said: 'Graeme, when do you think we should publish the book?'

That's an agreeable way of doing business: no crap, cut to the chase. Let's go.

Bastille Day 1996. Venice

The poet Martial records how the whores in ancient Rome had *sequi me*, 'follow me', cut into the soles of their sandals like stencils. The tradition is revived by the airport jeeps which tag planes from the runway to the terminal-stand with 'FOLLOW ME' signs above the driver's cab. John and I share the pacing for the 20-odd kilometres to the hotel in Treviso. On the outskirts of town, whores with scant skirts hitched up round their visible panty lines and minimal boleros loiter under lamp posts and at bus stops. They do not need to say 'follow me' or imprint it in the soft earth. They are already there.

Out of Treviso next morning, the riverbanks lined with hydrangeas, we head for the Dolomites. They are named after one Déodat de Dolomieu, a French geologist who, on a field trip to the south Tyrol in north-eastern Italy, discovered a calcareous rock which, unlike limestone, does not effervesce in weak acid. He published his findings in 1791.

The temperature climbs to 32°C as we climb the Passo Santo Boldo, 6km to no great height but steep enough and under a broiling sun. A switchback of 18 *tornanti*, hairpins, with several long intermediate stretches of long sweeping curve, the last four bends kicking us through short, dark, damp tunnels. The heat is like a flat iron clamped to my back. Sweat coils and drips from every bare spread of flesh, pooling in my eyes so that they smart and blink and I can see the road only through a blur. It takes time, too, to find my legs, to settle into the rhythm.

On the last stretch of the downhill, a cold torrent of water spills down the mountain and gathers in the basin of a huge concrete portico at the side of the road. The inscription reads: 'VIS PRAECIPITIS AQUAE HUMANO INGENIO COACTA LUX VITAQUE FIT.' 'Human inventiveness turns the cascading force of water into light and life.' This is one of a number of huge fissures in the mountain wall cut by torrents which tumble, ledge by ledge, to a very tempting fall just below the level of the road. There's a delicious rush of cool air from the deep-rock refrigerators and sweet bouts of refreshment as we pass. Santo Boldo, a Spanish hermit, planted a dead friend's episcopal crozier, slogged up and down the most precipitous slopes of the mountain to fetch water from the torrents with which to irrigate it and, like Peter's stave outside Rome, it finally burst into flower. Boldo died in AD 602, and the ridge remained impassable until the road was built, in 100 days during the winter of 1917–18, by Russian prisoners of war and a gang of formidable brawny local women, under the direction of an Austrian engineer.

Agordo, fringed to the north by outcrops of jagged mountain, like shark's teeth, is bathed in a pale magenta light when we ride in at 6 p.m., some 130km under our wheels. By 8.30, when we stroll out of the *pensione* after supper into a silvery afterglow, mist hangs like gauzes of talcum and, behind opacities of cloud punctured with openings of duck-egg-blue sky, the pale dying sun mimics the sheen of the moon.

A sundial on the side of the church quotes from Virgil's *Georgics*: '*[Sed] fugit interea fugit irreparabile tempus*' (III, 284). ([But] time, meanwhile, time passed, passed irretrievably.)

Passo Duran, 13km and 1,000m up the valley from Agordo, flanked with pine and larch, the leas of emerald grass prinked with wild flowers, and I sit in lovely shade under pine trees to write up the notes. The only respite the Spartans ever got from training for war was in battle. After the longueurs of preparing for these kilometres, it is a relief indeed to be riding them. The entire prospect of the landscape is, so far, on a smaller scale, more intimate than that of the High Alps, the roads generally narrower, though on that climb to the Duran, one hideous ramp of concrete and stone stretched out straight and steep and scorching hot under my tyres. Cyclists fly past calling out '*Va be*' (go well), '*Corragio*' (courage), '*Ciao*' (hi). An old lady in a field makes the open–shut gesture with her palm and cries '*Forza*' (strength). And propelled by such goodwill, we climb the Staulenza, another 1,000m and 12.5km up from the valley partway through a cacophony of cowbells and on down through a village called Dont. Ah, but we do.

We find a clean cheap hotel with a wood-fired pizza oven in the restaurant in Arabba, a village overlooked by the mighty block of the Marmolada.

17 July 1996

We decide to book a second night so that we can ride a big loop without luggage.

At the foot of the Passo Fedaía, where the slope is gentle, a man across the road calls out to me: '*Avanti signora,*' then, as I draw alongside, perceiving that the length of my hair has misled him, he counters with a comic gulp and oops: '*O, è un uómo . . .*'

At the top, 2,239m, after 14km and 1,000m of height gain, earlier suspicion confirmed: it's a bastard. Around 5km of something like 1 in 6 reduced me to a crawl – not hard – with one exceedingly vicious section of straight road and a very nasty continuous steepness leading to a rather more welcoming twist and turn, which could not, however, soften the nastiness of the gradient much. A car passed and the driver sang out cheerfully, 'One kilometre!' Hurray. Suddenly, I felt a renewed surge of power and flew at that last ugly slog with all I had, singing 'Reveille' on all my sleeping energy. I got to the crest coughing, spluttering, out of breath, but the road tipped over into a 150m downhill and a last brief rise to the pass. Hurray.

Through Canezei and the climb to the Passo di Sella, 2,244m, was a mild enough 6km followed by another 6km with all the ingratiating charm of a Spanish Inquisitor. At the top, I rode into a traffic jam. Building works allowed room for single file only and a non-stop sluggish haemorrhage of cars, camper vans, tourist buses, motorbikes and, like red corpuscles bearing the oxygen, cyclists. Internal combustive tourism in spasm. Drivers, oblivious to awe-inspiring vistas of mountains all round, leaning on the horn and overheating in overheated hooting automobiles.

Once through, we settled on the off-road grass verge for our second lunch: cheese and bread, peach, banana and yoghourt, fruit juice. Two blond Siegfrieds in shiny black matching walrus leathers, white silk scarves, aviator shades, moustaches, purred up on big BMWs and posed as if for glossy *Les Boys* magazine pics. The Marmolada stood high in the bright afternoon sun with snow on its chaps like splodges of shaving cream and, on the brow of the hill in front of where we lolled, a little girl, skinny and lithe, baseball cap back to front on her bobbed haircut, her arms flapping in the wind like tendrils, called out to another plumper little girl: '*Ah, meine liebste Schwester, was hast du?*' and then chattered on in German beyond me.

They might be junior Rhine Maidens, I think.

We rode down fast past a jade-green lake below the road, sunbathers scattered along its sand and shingle beach, on towards the Passo di Gardena, 2,121m. On a long battlement of Dolomite rock off to the right, two climbers perched up on the tiny holds, nearing the top, barely visible from the road but singled out by their white clothes and the binoculars of one car passenger lost in amazement at the audacity of it, picking their way all the way up from the foot of that rugged sheer precipice.

Near the top, rain splattered out of a darkening sky, and by the time I crossed the col it was pelting down. The following descent was dicey, cold crept into my legs and the climb to the Passo di Campolongo hammered most of any residual enthusiasm out of me. Like Fotherington-Thomas, I like to say 'Hello sky, hello clouds, hello little gentians, harebells, scabious, dandelions and lilies', but, at times of failing temper, a spirit of Molesworth shoves him bodily aside and crowds the pestilent hour with scowls and foul disposition.

Campolongo comes at last and the view unfolds, and there below us the road winding in broad serpentine sweeps back into Arabba at its foot, home for the second night. The sun comes out. Mr and Mrs Owner greet us at the entrance to the hotel like old friends. They see our delight – what a day and what a great feeling, yes. Perfect plenitude of being.

Ordinarily we never book, just arrive and take our luck. It's never failed us yet, and there is something undeniably anal about not being able to travel without making reservations ahead. As to my riding mostly on my own: John carried luggage for them both and Angela, though tough, is not quick. I went ahead and waited wherever seemed convenient.

The second day out of Arabba, we did a shorter loop over the Passo de Fedaía and the Pordoi once more. It felt like a day off, a treat, skiving, stolen time.

En route to Bolzano next day, we stopped by a lake, shellac greens and blues, limpid and sparkling at the edge. Irresistible. I stripped off and slipped into the luxurious chilly water. Angela followed. It was total contentment.

Two days later, the Passo di Tonale served up an ugly reminder of what contentment can cost. After a picnic in the glade of a pinewood below the Passo Mendola, we faced 72km to Ponte di Legno over the Passo di Tonale, 1,883m, a long undulating drag up the wooded Val Vermiglio to the foot of the climb. Those corrugations did for me. The heat was fearsome, the ups felt steeper and harder than they looked, the distance seemed never to diminish and my energy leaked away. At Fucine, 1,000m, there remained 15km still to ride and a further 883m to climb – more or less what we had done that morning when we were fresh. I was very soon riding on strength alone and little of that left. My knees ached horribly. It was sheer slog, not a modicum of joy, a salutary reminder of the misery that the beautiful machine has it in the flint-hearted angular side of its make-up to inflict. I went through a barrier of pain and rode on for around 5km in a benumbed, dreamy, Mogadon stupor but emerged and felt every worn and weary pang in my body. That morning, glorious views had beguiled the labour – a broad glacial valley, lake the colour of gooseberries, the baked-bean-red terracotta-tiled roofs of Bolzano glowing in the intense umber of the early sun. This road to Tonale was, save for the cluster of high peaks ahead – snow-streaked, swathed in eerie mist – virtually unloveable.

At last, at bloody last, the climb petered out and gave up. The wind howled across the exposed summit to replace the fugitive gradient, but there, 2km ahead, the ugly jumble of Tonale's shops, bazaars, hotels, garages, as if shunted onto either side of the road by bulldozers. The buildings stared sullenly across at each other as if at irreconcilable foes. I hated the whole place, its existence, its featureless anonymity. I was worn out, done, shivering with effort. Bought a drink, clambered back onto the bike and wheeled morosely away onto the relief of 10km downhill.

The others didn't get to Ponte di Legno until 9 p.m. I didn't believe they wouldn't make it, only feared they might not find the lowly hotel I'd checked into. I sat in the square until the light went then repaired back. But there are powerful impulses in friendship and camaraderie which can't be explained. By some force of mutual prepossession, they homed in as I had been willing them to home in.

We parted next morning, they heading north for the Passo di Gavia (and *not,* Angela said flatly, the Stelvio as well . . . enough is enough), I west, on the long road to Lake Como and thence Milan to catch the plane home.

Coming off the Passo di Aprica, I passed a string of people at the side of the road selling fungus. They had scoured the surrounding woods, no doubt, to trawl the edible mushrooms much sought by amateurs, *dilettanti* and restaurateurs. It's a serious game and well to remember that French *amateur* and Italian *dilettante*, at which we sneer in English, each signifies love and delight. No bad thing, even in a professional. The true mushroom hunter has to know exactly where to search, under this bush or that tree, and it's almost a psychological game of hide and seek they play, the fungi being so elusive. And what excitement when a real prize finally appears: the dark colour, the smell, the firm meat, the amanita known as Caesar's mushroom; the precious (and very expensive) Italian white truffle; the black and autumnal porcino ('piglet'), which is what Italians call the cep and we call penny bun. Finding a cache in forests of chestnut, oak, birch, beech (pines exude acids which the fungi shun), they will pick them and carry them off before cleaning them – any scrapings leave evidence of the treasure trove, and rivals must be decoyed. And they never, ever, reveal where the mushrooms come from.

One old lady sat impassively on a stool holding quite the largest cep I have ever seen, its cap about 27cm in diameter. She had no doubt weighed it and calculated how much culinary delight it would purvey and set a minimum price, hankering for a better offer.

The sun dried off the hanging damps both of the Aprica and my quailing spirits. Speed came out to meet and greet, and by the time I got to the lakeside I was racing mopeds, streaking along with joy in my heart and sanguine thoughts in my head. Life was good, even if the immediate circumstances of it, in this twelfth month of my fiftieth year, were problematic. Lindy and I were estranged, and the separation (temporary, I hoped) had made me tense and miserable. Such a mood does not conduce to agreement or understanding. I sought calm and confidence, not to override difficulties but to absorb and dissolve them. Haring along the banks of Lake Como that day, I began to feel a steadier purpose. Such feelings can the beautiful machine, in its supple frisky character, inspire.

A ferry plies the strait which marks where the right leg of Como, named the Lago di Lecco, joins the left, from Varenna to Bellagio, and, in a late afternoon sunshine bursting with colour,

I walked my bike on board. Aptly, perhaps, *lecco* means bait or inducement or titbit. It was quite the best way to approach the peninsula on which the lovely town stands, at the head of the Larian promontory.

On the rear of the promontory, a son of Como, the belletrist Pliny the Younger, had built Tragoedia, one of the two villas that he owned by the lake. One hopes he was happy in a house with so ominous a name. Rejecting the spiteful gossip and carping of the social round in Rome, in one letter from Como he writes:

> I hear nothing which it pains me to hear, say nothing it pains me to say. None of my acquaintance speaks slander of anyone else and I reprove no one, unless it be myself for writing shoddily. I am harassed by neither hope nor anxiety, troubled by no rumours. I converse only with myself and my books.

I felt, in Bellagio that lovely evening in July, some affinity with the man, at least in aspiration. Against an innate tendency to fight, I nursed a more accepting tenor of mind, in which adversity might be outmanoeuvred as well as faced and at less expenditure of soul and energy. In the cheapest hotel in town, I sat at a table wedged between glazed doors giving on to a tiny balcony and looked out across the crown of a fig tree, palm tree to one side, *ilex* to the other, and the higgledy-piggledy of houses which is Bellagio, and was at peace, with supper in prospect. Always a warming prospect, supper. Even the fact that the padrone had refused to let me bring my bike up to the room had not irked me, silly as I thought it. When I asked a concierge of a Barcelona hotel if they had a lock-up for my bike, he smiled and said: 'There's *lots* of space in your room.'

During the 1630 epidemic of plague, the Bellagio peninsula acted as a sort of quarantine and the local bakers made bread with uninfected corn for the people of Varenna. The loaves were left on a large boulder near the shore, later called the *sasso del pane* (the bread stone). The buyers took the bread and left money in a jar filled with vinegar, which acted as a disinfectant. The boulder was subsequently destroyed by a mine as a navigation hazard.

A morning swim in the lake clear of boulders and then I join the Sunday cyclists in crowds on the lakeshore road, most going in the opposite direction. The Duomo in Milan is closed. (By its west door, a memorial to Pliny the letter-writer.) Everything else seemed to be shut, too. Through the backways of the city, the empty streets, the shuttered houses of grandiose size, inhabitants all at lunch, and lunch was what I wanted. Out into country, an off-putting Sabbath day, quiet all round. I turn down a side road to a village: its restaurant is shut. However, a bar sports an open door. I ask if they are serving food. For how many, they ask and offer me pasta and cold beef with salad. I repair to a table on a side terrace in amiable shade, quaff a beer, contemplate a basket of bread, pitcher of wine. Joy. A sumptuous lunch when lunch had seemed out of reach, a snooze, a coffee and back on the road to Linate airport outside Milan.

That autumn, I conducted a conversation like Pliny's, with myself, and it occurs to me that such conversations precisely parallel the sort of mental journey we make when riding up mountains. The conversation was about funk. There is an old adage that any professional must be able to write – against deadline and block – as if there is a loaded gun pointed at his or her head. For a long time, I could imagine the gun all right, but not that it was loaded. Confidence had deserted me and answered no pleading calls to come back. At last I realised: the gun is *always* loaded . . . with an inexhaustible supply of time bullets, high-velocity slugs marked with date and hour, each and every one.

***

31 July 1997. Port de Salau, Franco-Spanish border
John, always in charge of the maps, kept very quiet about the
day's itinerary between Esterri d'Aneu at the foot of the Port
de la Bonaigua, which we crossed the day before, and Biert
in France, on the other side of the mountain chain. I was
always happy to surrender route-planning to him but had a
dark feeling that we were about to indulge his penchant for
off-road. I was overladen with dark feelings at the time. My
mother seemed to have gone to the brink of death and back
several times that year, and it had been a difficult decision to
go ahead with the Pyrenean venture. The riding was harder
because of a brooding unease. I hardly slept. The contradictions
warred within me.

Along the mild slope of the upper Noguera Pallaresa valley,
through a trio of hamlets to Sant Joan d'Isil then Isil itself and
finally the Lilliputian town of Alòs d'Isil, winding paved streets
barely wide enough for a be-panniered mule, where, by the
fountain outside the church, I sat in hot sunshine, reading, to
wait for the others. When they arrived, I suggested, grumpily,
that it was time for John to come clean.

Off-road it was.

The tarmac gave way to rough track. We picnicked by the
river and set off on the sinuous climb to the ridge. Rough track
gave way to grass, hairpins gave way to a narrow earth footpath.
Ill temper and deep introspection drove me ahead, and I
began to curse as soon as the footpath, just about rideable,
squeezed itself into the wiggly line of a sheep track and I was
forced to dismount. I stumbled along cholerically for some
distance in cleats, but, as the slope grew steeper and the track
wriggled ever more frequently round part-submerged boulders,
I changed into the soft slip-ons from the saddlebag.

The track, erupting in half-buried stones and boulders, inched
up towards the skyline, far above me. The effort of pushing the
bike, my shoes slipping on the grass, the foul mood and sense

of doom eroded all charity from me. By the time I got to the top, the mood had turned homicidal. A sizeable roofless stone ruin had been a border post and holding store for confiscated contraband. Beyond it, the mountain fell away like a precipice, to the right an enormous funnel deep into the bowels of the rock. I contemplated the descent only long enough to pick what looked like a feasible path and set off, cursing roundly, cursing every factor militating against my peace of heart and mind, yelling dark imprecation at the sky, the immutable powers, being stranded on the bare mountain.

A short way down, hefting the bike over rocks and troughs, I encountered three walkers and asked them where the road was. 'Oh, you have two, three hours' walking,' said the man. Fuck, I thought, that, and, hoisting the Shorter onto my shoulder with savage force, I began to run, as fast as the flimsy pumps would allow.

Some way along, I glanced across the widening split of the Salat valley, near its headwaters. On the opposite side of a deep ravine, a road. I was on the wrong side. My vile maledictions grew bitter and more tearful. But, even as I ploughed on down, into the trees lining the valley side, I saw that the path swung off onto a natural bridge. Within minutes, I was across and parking Shorter against a tree by the side of my escape route from this abomination of geology. My feet were sore and blistered, my breathing laboured, my head nearly splitting with wrath. Plated shoes on, I remounted and was away. I had no map, only the name of our destination – the Flanagans' lodge in Biert – and a town en route, Seix.

The bike leapt away on the tarmac like a greyhound off the leash. Demented anger loaned me speed, and there, ahead of me, a car swinging round the hairpins. I accelerated and rode up alongside the driver's window and tapped on it. Seeing me, she did an extravagant double-take and nervously wound down the window.

'Is this the way to Seix?' I asked, levelly.

She nodded.

I thanked her and dropped back behind.

An hour or so later, in hot early evening sunshine, I pulled up outside the home of Pyrenean Pursuits. Nick and Jan Flanagan were sitting with two others on the terrace in front of the lodge. Nick got up. 'You must be Graeme,' he said.

'I am.'

'We expected to see you an hour ago,' he said.

'You're lucky to see me at all.'

And so began a friendship and much else besides.

At four o'clock next morning, I bolted awake, fully rested, and decided I must wash everything in my saddlebag and the bag, too. Having laid the wet gear out on the terrace to dry, I went for a swim in the river across the road then wheeled out the bike and set off up the nearby Col du Serailler. Up through a friendly cover of trees to the col and on, down into the village of Comminac. Gradually, I felt a wonderful peace and serenity seeping into me. The morning was still and, apart from a dog barking, a rooster crowing, near silent. I rode back up to the col, down into the valley the long way round and once more to the lodge.

An hour later, as I sat, somewhat dislocated, at breakfast, the phone rang: it was Lindy to say that my mother had died the night before. That rage on the Salau had accompanied her last journey and the calm that crept up over me on the Serailler the ending of her pain in this world.

I commemorate her death with some sort of ride every 31 July, whether it be the foray of 60+ miles to my friends' vineyard at Breaky Bottom in a hollow of the Sussex Downs beyond Lewes or a symbolic doddle to a local pub.

Nine

To the Ends of the Earth

*Le mystère ne se voit pas, mes amis; il se sent. Il s'exprime
sans voix comme un sourd-muet.*
(You can't see mystery, my friends; you feel it. It
expresses itself without words, like a deaf-mute.)
    Albert Londres, French journalist (1884–1932)

My friend Simon was chairman of a big clothing manufacturing
company called Simon Jersey. Every year, he employed a
landscape photographer and my friend Richard, as designer,
to produce a company calendar of pictures taken in a Third
World country. In 1998, the destination was Timbuktu, in
Mali. Simon invited me to come along and make recordings
for a possible radio programme about the adventure. His son
Ben came too, and, the three of us being keen cyclists, we
would of course ride.

July 1998. Bamako airport, Mali
We walk across the tarmac in 28°C steamy heat to the ramshackle
airport-terminal buildings; various louche individuals in
creased uniforms lounge apathetically; a woman immigration
official sits at a rickety trestle table stamping passports. We
shuffle up and segue into the next queue: yellow inoculation

certificates. Neither Simon nor Ben, his son, has one. They're ushered into the medical centre, a dingy room where the doctor administers jabs to an unprotesting queue in between swigs of Coca-Cola from the open can he keeps in the same fridge as the vaccines, needles and syringes. One needle does a whole line. Ben protests: 'I'm not having a jab with that needle.'

'You can't come into Mali unless you have an injection against yellow fever.'

'I don't care: I'm not having a jab with that needle.'

'But you have to, unless you pay me $12.' (A week's subsistence in Mali.)

'What for?'

'A signature saying that you've paid $12.'

'And no jab?'

'No jab. It's a certificate.'

'A certificate that I haven't had the jab?'

'No, that you've paid $12.'

'All right, I'll pay $12.'

Simon stumps up too and they're through. Ben's bike has arrived – with a punctured front tyre and ruined inner tube – but none of his luggage. I join another chaotic queue crammed into the tiny *litiges* (legal claims) office to register the missing bags; another dingy room, with asthmatic air conditioner hanging wearily off the wall as if it's fixed there by force of habit only.

An official in a crumpled suit mechanically scribbles names and details on a page torn out of a notebook. To everyone reporting a loss, the same apathetic procedure. A woman from the south of France burbles about the way they do things properly on the Côte d'Azur. When I give the official Ben's name, a description of the missing luggage and the telephone number of our hotel, he tells me to phone next morning. I have no great confidence that anything will come of this.

Ben is patiently fixing his front tyre, running with sweat and good-humouredly cursing the airline. We discuss contingency plans. The absence of his cleated cycling shoes is the most pressing loss. Perhaps we can share out spare clothes, push on with our ride and, when the bags do arrive, get them sent on.

We roll the bikes past the inert form of the customs officer asleep on his bench and we're off. Tarmac road, green vegetation to either side. The rainy season has started – June to September. Clumps of trees, clutches of mud huts, a straggle of lean-tos and ho-downs, various items for sale – fruit, vegetables, domestic bric-a-brac, a tall oversized optic the size of a village handpump – a petrol station. A large ceremonial archway spanning the highway welcomes us to Bamako, capital of Mali.

The roads began to fill with mopeds and scooters – rider and pillion, sit-up-and-beg bikes – battered cars, bashed-up old minibuses painted dark green, the local bus-cum-taxis packed solid with passengers, mostly men, who spilt into the open doorway and hung out of embrasures cut in the solid sides. We stuck out in the melee: spotting us, kids went goggle-eyed, called out and waved frantically like village boys applauding a break of bike-racers in rural France.

The Hotel d'Amitié, built by the Soviets when the USSR was infiltrating Africa, is a massive sand-coloured concrete barracks of a building, 14 or 15 storeys of it, as ugly as any cheerless high-rise apartment block adrift in urban wasteland. The corridors reeked of damp carpet and cheap deodorant, but the rooms were as adequate as any we stayed in all trip and no cockroaches lurched out of the air-conditioning vents. Perhaps, I hoped, no worse creepy-crawlies would have made the long climb up to this eighth floor.

I was first down to breakfast. Since I had to make recordings, and because my French in this francophone country would be useful, I had a professional obligation, but this whole trip frightened me. I felt sick with dread. A long relationship had broken up, I had nowhere to live again, I was in a ragged state emotionally, and now . . . black Africa: so much that was unknown and unfamiliar exaggerating the uncertainties which already preyed on me.

Ben and Simon arrived, all smiles.

'Notice anything?' Ben said. 'It's your lucky day. We're off cycling.' He laughed and waggled his shoes. 'My luggage arrived last night. There was a knock on the door at midnight and a guy brought my bags in.'

My heart didn't sink; my heart was already long sunk.

We cycled out to the intersection with the main route traversing Bamako and, at a Ruritanian set of traffic lights, waited in the choked tide of cars *bachés* (converted minibuses) mopeds bikes lorries pedestrians.

At the side of the road, two women without legs, mounted like mantleshelf ornaments on flat hand-propelled trolleys on castors; lepers with stumps for hands; a young albino man, skin the colour of calf's liver, dappled with uneven, dark moles, a frizz of ginger hair, milky eyes staring hopelessly. The flotsam and jetsam of the Third World paraded in dumbshow as if on purpose to shame me. And where is the Second World? Is it a nebulous buffer state to separate and protect us, the developed, from the benighted undeveloped?

At 1.30 p.m., the heat closing in on us like unwanted attention, we stopped in a village called Kassela and went into a hovel on wooden poles, straw roof, packing-case walls, earth floor. A sign outside read: 'Restaurant Buvette' . . . the local eatery and bar. Inside, a young girl of about 13 tended a fire of split stakes lying between burnt-through fire-bricks, on which rested a large soot-caked cauldron. Squatting on a wobbly wooden stool at the far side of the fire, a young man. The girl ladled an amorphous mess of the grey-brown stew, meat and odds and ends, from the pot into a small saucepan, plus some dollops of rice from another pot she'd prepared earlier. The diner prodded the food mournfully with his fingers and ate it scoop by scoop, with no apparent relish. I asked the girl if there was any chance of heating some water for us. The girl told a tiny girl of about five – her sister, it must have been – to ferret out a portable double grate, into one side of which she shovelled some burning coals from the fire; on this went our little can of water. We sat on a low bench – plank slung on two stone blocks – to wait. The older girl whacked her sister from time to time, a routine reminder that she was in charge. The mite didn't even flinch, reacted not at all. She stared impassively at me. I smiled. She stared.

At 3 p.m., in broiling temperatures, we set out again along this soulless road, a paved strip blasted straight across an entirely featureless landscape – scrubland, sparse vegetation, lone trees bowed with aridity, dust and overweight branches. A string of goats straggled by. An enclave of mud huts; man with barebones ox; raised bed platforms under straw matting roofs, five or six people asleep. The road, the undulating concrete runway, went on and on and on through the barren sun-flayed wilderness. This riding had all the attractions of a turbo session in a sauna. The intense heat began to drill into my head. For a grim half-hour or so I lost power, as bad as the bonk. Ben was cooked and had to stop – he'd begun to feel chilly, a sure sign of heatstroke. He hadn't been on the bike for 12 months and was, so far, finding the pace a bit fast. I waited, then tried to relay him. He told me to go on, he'd be OK.

Simon had gone ahead. After an hour and a quarter, just as I came back up to him, he pulled off the road and dismounted, puce in the face, lay down under the shade of a tree. We drank the last of our water. Dehydration, more than being steamed in this solar pressure cooker, was doing for us. Ben came in and drank the last of his water. We'd set off far too late this morning. Half an hour and I felt recovered. I liberated the minidisc from the water- and sandproof canoe bag to record some songbirds tootling merrily in a copse.

We calculated – erroneously – that we had some 40km left to ride. A few kilometres on and we reached a village called Zantiguila. From the map, we'd ridden 75km, only a little more than halfway. No bottled water to be bought at the tiny kiosk selling drinks and assorted tins, bars, packets of this and that. We did have purifying tablets but they made water taste of swimming pool. We loaded up with Fanta, Schweppes tonic and Coca-Cola instead and pushed on.

Fifteen minutes later, the skies darkened, thunder growling across the flat earth. We were riding into a storm. Suddenly a savage buffet of wind punched us bodily off course and, with it, the rain slammed in. Jagged stabs of lightning ripped gashes in the lurid plum-black sky. Driving torrents of cool rain rebounded off the road surface as high as the pedals. The road was soon awash and sunk beneath swirling white spindrift like powdered snow emitting wafts of steamy mist. Riding ahead, I seemed, said the others, to be surfing a shallow river. The jolt of cold after the extreme heat was, for a while, uncomfortable, but cycling the storm was a blast of fun, a rapture of cool and wet, and the sky – mole grey with cockades of feathery white cloud filaments, fountains of white spray – a perfect chiaroscuro. When the rain stopped, a double rainbow blazed out across the pewter-grey heavens above the horizon.

Half an hour and we emerged on the other side of the deluge, drenched but giggling with silly exuberance. The storm show rolled on across the open stage behind us as we stopped for drink and energy bars. It was, by now, 6.30 p.m. The sun would set in an hour, and 40km lay between us and Fana. We hitched a short ride in a pickup, then rode on.

Pitch dark, lashing rain, vehicles roared up fearsomely out of the night behind us, torching us with halogen. We had no lights. We wobbled off the metalled road over ruts and ridges onto the earth verge to let them by and then regained the smoother surface. Occasional distant flashes of lightning illuminated the whole scene for two eerie seconds, and then blackness. I was off the front, putting the hammer down to get this ride done, nearly pitched head first into a couple of other unlit cyclists. Simon adjured me to slow down, for God's sake. In the scramble to avoid the crash, one of my pannier bags came off – the third time that day. Ahead, lit by flares, we discerned a barrier of oil drums strung across the road, a makeshift police checkpoint. We rode through without stopping and, at last, into Fana, where we found a sign for the recommended Hotel Mirador.

There were no rooms. I cycled off into the pitch dark in search of another hotel supposedly nearby. A dim glow way off from the road drew me, and I rode straight into a lake: the road had drowned. The dim glow was not a hotel. After an hour floundering around this misbegotten absence of anywhere, I rode back to find Simon standing next to a grinning black guy.

'This is Mohammed,' he said. 'He's a good man.'

Mohammed grinned wider. I looked at him and thought that, whatever else he was, he was emphatically not *a good man*. He was on the make, and Simon had bought it. Mohammed offered us his room at three times the price he was paying. 'That's fair?' he said, in a wheedling tone. Twenty pounds and forty pence for his single bed in a squalid concrete box: ridiculously exorbitant. We were a three-man inflation teredo boring ruinously into the local exchange rate. We supped on a chicken apiece, three of the scraggiest items of poultry that ever made it from egg to dinner plate.

Later, the whole place was buzzing – the locals packing in for a disco and, it was clear, pickups for an overnight shag-fest in the rooms kept empty: first come, first served.

Next morning, we rode on up the characterless road through the empty back of beyond, into a thick cloud of flies, which kept on coming for half an hour or more. From the faded French colonial bungalow-style hotel in Ségou, we put the word out that we were looking for a pinasse – a wooden, slab-sided, flat-bottomed boat – to take us downstream to within cycling distance of Timbuktu. Word flew ahead of us, and, at our next stop, in Mopti, the interested parties shimmered up and our Niger River trip was organised.

So far, the shock of the poverty, the forlorn aspect of almost every facet of life we observed from the road, had added to and intensified my sense of desolation. In Mopti, chief town of 'the land of shoe leather and stinking fish', as it's known, I watched the teeming populace as they flocked to the crowded strand of the River Niger: they drank the water, used it for cooking, washed pots, pans, their babies and themselves in it, they pissed and shat in it. The dry mud streets of what was an established *ville*, no shanty town, were littered with all manner of plastic and paper detritus, its buildings were gimcrack and dilapidated, its citizens milled about with no apparent direction or purpose. A market stall had racks of tatty shirts with Pierre Chardin (*sic*) labels. Wretched caricature. I felt profoundly uncomfortable, but so what? Like the Pharisee and the Levite on the road to Jericho, I was passing through.

We loaded our hired boat with the bikes, cases of beer and water, boxes of provisions and drums of 'fast' petrol – cheaper here than in Timbuktu, we were blithely informed by the boat's owner, a 21-year-old shyster to whom lying was a branch of grammar and reliability a matter only of dates. 'Trust me, trust me,' he kept saying, as if repeating it often enough would make it true, even to our wary ears.

Our three crew men boarded, Mahman, Djal and Lal, captain, cook and cook's mate, and we set off into the multi-channelled archipelago of the Niger.

***

The river bore us away into the Mali of the ancient continuum, what was there long before Mungo Park and the first explorers came and is still there 200 years later: the frying-pan flat ranges of dusty scrubland and semi-desert to either side, beyond the low banks where the stream ran sluggish slow and the higher mud ramparts opposite, where the quicker current chewed away at the compacted earth. Motor-driven boats, some as big as Thames riverboats, plied the river upstream and downstream, outracing the old tempo of man quanting the vessel along as we propelled the punts on the Wear, but this Mali had no clocks, and there was nothing to put a time on, anyway. The commerce was probably the same then as ever it was – wood and provisions, transport to and from one market or another. The hard-packed crust of Mali's earth spread endlessly below the big skies and wide to the sunblink where land and sky met. You could never call it scenery. People must have walked it once – the settlements which sprouted here and there suggested that walking it never had much appeal. All the villages, large and small, looked much the same, built as they've always been built, straggling lines of clay-brick houses, occasional angles of mud-brick wall, streets which were the empty bits between the rows. And to every village, its mosque – tall spire with prickling wood-beams like an anteater's bristly snout. In these villages, life went on, I imagined, as it had always done, and, if they persisted, would do forever: subsistence farming largely devoid of outside influence, our materialism. In one village we passed through on the way to Mopti, I observed a handsome young man in grubby shirt and frayed shorts, no shoes, sitting by the side of the road, his head in his hands, a look of penetrating sad vacancy in his eyes. Opposite him, a pink lottery booth. Painted on the side: 'At last a million in your hand'. It was empty.

Even to speculate on the crushing harshness of the life these River Niger villagers led would have been a sort of condescension. They grow what they can, barter with neighbours on the far bank of the river, bring home what they need in return for what they can do without. And they laugh. If nothing else, coming into contact with what I considered to be a bleak existence was a lesson in differences and acceptance. It was all beyond me to assess or even come to terms with. Islam drew them to and sustained them in a cohering faith. Wherever we went, the reedy voice of a muezzin pierced the air of the late dusk and the morning skies as night faded, summoning the faithful to prayer and reminding the infidel that '*Allahu akbar*', God is great, God is with us and God does not sleep.

> Awake! for morning, in the bowl of night
> Has cast the stone that puts the stars to flight.

Ben had a large-scale aeronautical map of the river between Mopti and the stretch just west of the dropping-off point for Timbuktu. He also had a GPS (Global Positioning System) instrument, that works through pinpointer messages beamed up to and back from satellites circling the earth. The *African Queen*, as we named the boat, had been instantly upgraded: a pattern of boat centuries old became as hi-tech in basic navigational equipment as it's possible to get.

As we pop-popped along, Djal would occasionally call out: '*Hippopotame*' and point to the bulbous snout of a river-horse protruding above the surface, apparently somnolent. They can be aggressive. In the 1940s, an entire flotilla of canoes bringing the faithful to prayers in Timbuktu was attacked by rampaging hippopotami. Two hundred people were drowned.

On the banks, women walked at a stately pace back to the village, a broad basket, a bucket or a laden plate seated on a cloth quoit on their crowns to keep the burden steady and upright. They seemed entirely unhurried. The work, the continuous work, imposes a non-stop, slow-pulse throb of toil on the day, one job leading to the next to the next to the next. Their straight-backed, tightrope-steady gait comes from what Victorian young ladies were made to do as exercises for posture. The men, by and large, slouch. The women care for them, and their offspring. They cook in the round-hut kitchens – no men allowed, by male law: demeaning for the warrior caste. The men sit around, waiting. Now that the warrior caste is only a folkloric souvenir and the spears are long rusted away, the men's main purpose in life is to impregnate the women and do the men's jobs, which don't take all day and leave time, ample time, for mooching. The women are permanently on duty, their lives paced to the minute by menial tasks, the incessant calls on their attention. It shows, too, in the unhurried self-contained way in which they carry themselves. They bear the life, they sustain the life, without giving any sign of being crushed by the unremitting labour of all they do, of all they have no choice but to do. Necessity has bred few inventions hereabouts. Ask any Malian woman pounding the millet in a tall wooden mortar what she would like, they say, and she will ask for a mechanical mill. There are no mechanical mills. Thus necessity is reduced to the most basic effort of ingenuity: to survive, day by long day.

   We pulled in to one village to buy fish. The settlement spread along the banks for about 100 yards, the beach sloping up quite sharply to a tiny escarpment where the houses were safer from flooding. There was no trash, no discarded packaging, no tins, no polythene bags, polystyrene bottles (they clamoured for ours), no boxes to litter their demesne. Beyond the back walls of this village perched on the banks of the Niger stretched empty wastes of sand, the Sahara, an unmarked chart of caravan routes. We stood on the beach, surrounded by a gaggle of children who ogled us, bickered good-humouredly as children anywhere.

They smiled, gawped and wondered. An elderly gent rode by on an ancient bicycle, an antiquated gun slung over his shoulder. What was he after, rabbits? They all seemed relaxed, content, at ease, but as we boarded again I offered some Bics, and a snakepit of hands was grasping for them, cheap plastic biros.

The boat pulled away. Simon said: 'What an existence. They've got nothing. They're not going to go anywhere. They're here for life. At least they seem to be happy with it, whatever little it is. The people in downtown Mopti had nothing in their eyes. A lot of them from places like this, probably; dumped there and they have to get on with it. Pretty desperate.'

Me: 'We arrive, linger a while, then leave. It's like a holiday job: you go in, do the work and fuck off. Birds of passage. No ties. Just visiting. Somewhere a lot better to go to.'

I think of the lines in Gray's 'Elegy in a Country Churchyard': 'Full many a flower is born to blush unseen/And waste its sweetness on the desert air.' Had I ever dreamed I would see the desert flower, wasted or not? Had I seen it now? As Henri de Montherlant says in *Les Jeunes Filles*, the one book I had with me which, for the most part, bored me rigid (my fault, probably): '*La terre promise vous entoure: vous ne le savez pas.*' (The promised land is all round you, did you but know it.)

Perhaps the feisty little boy who squared up to me by the side of the road, pointed at the bike and said: '*Donne-moi un VTT*' will go as far as Mali will permit him to go. 'Forget all that Bic crap,' he was saying, 'give me a mountain bike.'

As darkness came, the frogs struck up their croaking marsh jazz in the still air, carolling the advent of the nocturnal insects, their dinner, against a thrum of other night noises: cooing of a warm breeze, river burbling as a late pinasse worked its way to a mooring, our chatter, the lugubrious braying of a donkey. The stellar switchboard lit up, its twinkling radiance all but extinguishing the light of a crescent moon as it sank and finally set. The Tuareg caravans travel between dusk and dawn. Even in the cooler winter months, when they make the Azelai – the salt transport, 15 days' trek out from Timbuktu to the mines at Taoudenni, 15 days back – the desert sun blasts with concerted ferocity. It is friend to neither man nor beast in these regions. The nomads spread their tents and sleep until evening. When the moon goes, the constellations come into their dominion: they almost sizzle with white brilliance. We stared up to see a glittering algebra laid out across the indigo sky. Small wonder the Tuareg love silver far above gold: the kindly silver of the guiding North Star over a metal ladled from the molten sun's furious, unforgiving, relentless heat.

After the harrowing poverty, the filth and clutter of the towns, it was wonderfully peaceful on the river, to the accompanying slap of the sluice on the sides of the boat. Escape, for sure, but some kind of balancing context, too.

Ben pitches bivouac next to a dead cow, and Simon twits him for being soft and decamping. 'I'm not sleeping next to no dead corpse,' he says.

I point out that all corpses are dead.

'Not at Simon Jersey,' rejoins Simon.

A sandstorm blew all one night – no sleep and a sticky overall coating of silicate – and, every morning before dawn, the *capitaine* strolled back from his solitary devotions in the desert with the call to get going: '*C'est l'heure*', which sounded exactly like 'sailor'.

I recorded him, Djal and Lal each singing a different song as we cruised the river: they sang with unfeigned ease. Somewhere along the watercourse lay the turn-off to the fabled city, Timbuktu.

***

Morning. Fifth day

I sliced up a mango for the three of us, we breakfasted on tea and bread and, the motor of the boat putt-putting in the dawn quiet, we drew near to the stop-off at Diré and the road that went to Timbuktu. The sun was climbing at a steep angle remorselessly to its zenith in the joules-encrusted vault. We were all nervous. Simon chucked me his diary and asked me to write the names of the Timbuktu hotels in the back. I shot him a questioning look.

'It's all right,' he said, 'I'm not going to do a Captain Evans on you.'

'Oates,' I said. 'Captain Oates.'

'That's right . . . "I may be gone for some while" . . .'

'Well, make sure you leave us your water, will you?'

He didn't complain about it, but his back was hurting badly. Ben had to put his socks on for him.

In a brooding silence, we stripped unnecessary luggage out of the panniers – only basic requirements and a substantial litreage of water. We asked Djal to cook up a large helping of rice to fortify us for the desert ride: one of those meals you have neither stomach nor appetite for but spoon in, knowing it's sensible if not palatable.

Around 10 a.m., Diré hove into view on the north bank. Ben was busy with something in the boat. Simon, standing by the front of the canopy, beckoned to me. He passed over his journal, kept open at a page where he'd written a will. 'I don't want Ben to see, and it's just in case. Sign it, would you?' I signed it, thinking, suddenly, 'Fuck, this could be serious, what we're about to do.' It was, after all, the desert we were about to broach, the pitiless Sahara.

The boat pulled in, we unloaded the bikes and strapped on the panniers. Two-wheeled water bowsers they'd become. Ben said: 'I have to say I'm nervous about this ride. I don't think I've ever been so apprehensive about a bike ride in my life.'

'We all are,' I said.

We made a rendezvous to meet the pinasse five days hence, and Mahman, Djal and Lal watched as we rode off along the beach towards a gap in the houses fringing the higher shoreline – a road it must be, leading into town. What they were thinking, I can only guess at.

Ten

Pray to God

We rode up through the outskirts of Diré, round corners right and left, following our noses. There were no signposts. At one corner sat a camel chewing the cud, its legs tucked under it, a crimson-fringed halter round its neck. It turned its head as we rode by. It was the only camel we saw all trip, a surly-faced crittur, marked cynicism in that lingering glance it cast at us: 'Bicycles? *Bi*cycles? Pah.'

The buildings thinned out, and we were on the so-called good road. Most of the metalled surface was lost under layers of sand. The tarmac had been rutted along its length by heavy lorry wheels, broken up laterally by the ravages of rain and sun. The long furrows had filled with loose sand, the crosswise corrugations nagged the tyres angrily like rumble-strips. With momentum we would get through 20m or so of the lesser drifts, slipping and sliding as if on ice, till the sand grabbed at the wheels, momentum died and we'd come to an abrupt halt and have to push the dead weight of the loaded bike through a shallow dune. Occasionally, there'd be a level section of packed earth beside the road, 100m, maybe, of smoother riding and then back to the sand-swamped road. The wind was fierce, unrelenting, head-on, the heat in a dimension none of us had ever experienced:

cruel, indescribable and everywhere. We drank litres of water and sweated not a drop.

Out of the desolation of leprous light, turbulent wind, flying sand, appeared, like a hallucinatory vision, a man leading two donkeys. He was quite 16km from any fixed habitation. Where was he going? Where had he come from?

Incongruously, we passed a 'road narrows' sign, and the road did indeed shrink to half-width on a bridge over a dried-up stream bed. And in this gulch, dabbling in the minuscule puddle which was all the water left, a mother and four children. Supporting life in this wilderness, in these conditions? It beggared belief. We rode over the bridge, stared in wonder and passed on, rapidly boiling dry.

I found myself ahead and decided to hole up and wait in the minimal shade of an acacia bush, Moses's burning bush in the wilderness. Acacia thorns, thick as nails, up to 4in. long, can drive through heavy-gauge motor tyres. The branches screening me, just, from the direct blaze of the sun, I sat and pondered. Our chances of riding this piste were close to nil. We should retreat to Diré and find a boat to take us to Korioumé and from there ride into Timbuktu.

Still the others hadn't arrived. I remounted and rode back to find them under their own acacia. Simon's front tyre had punctured on a thorn. It had been the final straw – his back in considerable pain, aggravated by frequent tumbles off the bike, his strength worn down by the brutal conveyor belt of loose sand, ruts and ridges. Ben, suffering badly from the heat and dehydration – he'd had to stop to defecate – was changing the inner tube. He'd also concluded that we would be courting disaster to continue: we might easily not survive.

We sat under the tree to discuss what to do. None of us was a stranger to the overdrive of willpower. That we saw no surrender in this collective decision to quit says as much about the conditions out there as any elaborate description of them.

I hauled out the recording equipment, shielding it against sand and dust, and recorded our conversation.

'How hot is hot, men?'

'Oh, it's hot. You have to experience it to know. Nothing can give you any hint what it's like.'

'What luxury would you have if you could choose, here and now?' asked Simon.

Ben said: 'A Boeing ready to take off for England on a runway across the road.'

This Simon also goes for: 'I wouldn't even mind not having an aisle seat,' and laughs. 'I don't know, I'm changing my mind about twinning Timbuktu with Accrington. No wonder they call it inaccessible. It makes itself so. We're not even there.'

We chewed energy bars, drank and drank water. Simon suggested we wait there a while longer to recoup energy. Ben cautioned against sitting too long: the wind was drying us out and the heat would cook us whether we sat still or kept moving.

We decided to ride on towards Goundam, and, a mile short of what promised to be no more than an outcrop of nondescript buildings, I saw a large vehicle speeding towards us through clouds of dust and haze. No hesitation, I dismounted and flagged it down. A big, high-sided, open-backed lorry, three guys in the cab, a couple more hanging over the tailboard. I asked if they could give us a ride into Diré.

'Yes, OK. How much are you going to pay us?'

'How much do you want?'

'Five thousand CFA [£5] each.'

I beckoned to Ben as he rode in; we scrambled up over the sides – 3m high – into the back; the bikes were handed up to us and laid flat on a load of massive untrimmed stones that looked as dense as granite. We drove off to scoop up Simon and were heading back to Diré.

***

We perched on the roof of the cab, hanging on to the lip of the superstructure. The lorry, accelerator down, bucketed from side to side, leapt and caprioled over the humps in the road, bounced off the stonier ruts, jumped off its wheels and thumped sickeningly back onto them in the all-out assault on the sick scarred chine of this misnamed good road. The bikes slewed about on the scumble of stones. Plumes of dust belched out behind us, dust mingled with the diesel fog from the exhaust.

Suddenly, Ben spotted a small motorbike, driver and pillion, hurtling along a flat stretch of evidently solid desert floor away to the left, parallel to the road. 'Typical,' I said. 'Probably the only cycle path in Mali, and we missed it.'

Nearing Diré, we saw patches of startling emerald green along the roadside: burgeoning wheat, for the famous Timbuktu bread. This strip of land, between Diré and Goundam, is the only area in Mali where wheat is grown, cultivation of the crop facilitated by markedly cooler winter nights and more readily accessible irrigation, from the river itself and a healthy water table in this broad plain, the Niger's flood basin. But, these patches of green, cordoned off from the surrounding drab dun terrain, like mini oases, had a tentative experimental look about them. More like a test-bed of seed types, that strange lawn seemed to be. A lone figure prowled the lines of tender shoots: a devoted agronomist or a somewhat baffled slave to the force that through the green fuse drives the stalk? This field he patrolled was an orphan – 40 yards away, another small enclosure of growing shoots, another orphan. One wondered why this whole hinterland of Diré could not be wheatland, not a patchwork of experimental plots but a developed agriculture in the desert? Instead, it looked sadly hit and miss.

The lorry crashed its gears through the whole box, slowed down and grumbled into town, past the camel, to draw up in a small square outside Chez Djilli, a bar. We clambered stiffly back onto terra firma, the men in the back handed down our bikes and the driver stuck out his hand for the money. I peeled off the notes, passed them over and two of the others, who'd heaved the bikes over the side, stuck their hands out and said: 'What about the workers?'

I told them they were exaggerating – the French for 'Leave it out' – and added: 'Share. End.'

I joined the others in the bar, the cold beers already delivered to the table. Ice cold in Diré. *Dirus* is Latin for dreadful, awful, terrible, root of English 'dire'. These echoes began to resound louder and louder during our unscheduled stopover in Diré, perhaps unfairly: it's a sizeable town, positively grand and well organised compared with what we've met so far, a groomed centre of commerce and efficiency.

Djilli, who, hearing our English, preferred to be called Bill, wore the boubou – a loose knee-length embroidered shirt – over loose trousers the colour of chestnut purée. He was affable, relaxed, mine host, garrulous. He ran a clean, orderly, adult drinking hole. We'd parked our bikes by the closed wooden gate in the palisade which cordoned off the verandah around the bar. A shoal of small boys clustered around them, craning to peer into the bar's umbrageous interior for a sight of the bikes' owners. Bill shooed them away, flapping his fly whisk. They were leaning on his gate, blocking the customers' way, straining the hinges, spoiling the view, snotty boys, obnoxious species. Bill's place was exclusively for grown-ups; it was not a pop and peanuts joint, an ice-cream parlour, a Tango and Tizer servery for unwholesome ragamuffins off the street.

I told him what we were after, mentioned that we'd come by boat and that maybe it was still at the riverside. But of course he knew all about us.

'No,' he said, emphatically, 'it left this morning.'

We could have ridden down to the waterside to check but at this stage had no cause to doubt his word. The innate problem in a bargaining culture: you tend to be either too cynical or too credulous. I asked him to put the word out: we needed a boat or, better, a truck to get us the 130km to Timbuktu. The cold beer went down nicely. It was around 3 p.m.

A tall lanky guy in fawn chinos and a floral-patterned mustard-yellow shirt sloped into the bar, thick-framed spectacles, thin features, carrying a briefcase. He sat at the table on the other side of the room. Bill ambled over, they greeted each other, Bill sidled back into the room behind the bar and re-emerged with a glass and a can of lemonade. The guy poured himself a drink, sipped, listening to Bill, who'd slipped from French into Bambara. The guy addressed us, in French, about Timbuktu: there was another road besides the one we'd tried, he told us, much shorter, easier, in fact plane as a table. We could have been there in no time. The *goudron* – tarmac – between Diré and Goundam was a ruined cart-track by comparison.

This, verily, was startling information. It's always healthy to have contacts, but especially when contacts whistle up roads out of the desert. Local knowledge: you can't beat it. I asked the guy where to find it. On the other side of town, apparently – it's not marked on the maps because it disappears in winter; the river overflows its banks and whole tracts of dry land are lost under the water. But in summer, the exposed floodplain is a hard-baked mudflat. He reached into his briefcase and pulled out a surveyor's map. I went over and he pointed to the line, drawn in felt-tip pen, this unmetalled road he's talking about, clearly marked, leading pretty well straight from Diré to Timbuktu, past Kabara, the nearest landing for the city, where the river is, at this season, still too shallow to accommodate even pinasses. Seems we'd not only missed the cycle path, we'd missed the direct desert road. I reported back.

Ben was sceptical. I think he was wary of the gleam in my eye: he was anxious about my getting ideas of leaping on the bikes and pushing on, over this black squiggle on a hand-illuminated map. Where was the authority for its existence? Where was the backup, the chain of supplies, the points of contact with more than acacia trees and vagrant muleteers? We deliberated, ordered more beer, supped the cool fizz and pondered the fact that we had spent most of this day so far in the desert and . . . what now?

Suddenly, we were moving on: Lanky chipped in with an offer of a ride by this road. He had a vehicle, roomy enough for us and the bikes. I crossed the floor once again and bargaining began: Lanky, Bill and I in the negotiating ring; my prompters, like seconds, on the far side. Back and forth we slugged, trimming off pounds from either end of the offers. They started at £100. I stalled with the repeated dismissal: too much (thinking: £50). Eventually, Ben said: 'Offer them $80. They'll go for greenbacks.'

We added 100F to make up the £50, and I returned to the table and unrolled the wad of cash. Lanky whipped out a calculator. He wrote '750F' on a scrap of paper. I said nothing: they could refer to whatever exchange rate they favoured. Bill was hovering with a bit more purpose and input than stewardship of proceedings. He was definitely in for a cut here: his premises, his introduction, his new pals, us. So: they'd written £75; I'd tabled £50. The next move was theirs.

Ben and Simon went off on the prowl, leaving me to the wait, long or short. Flies swarmed round the open necks of the beer bottles; a transistor radio blared out African pop. Finally, attrition of patience won, the deal was struck, the cash accepted. I ignored the scrap of paper. We had, it seemed, a ride to Timbuktu. Timbuktu: savour the word, conjure up the idea, imagine the reality. It had faded a little in the white haze of the desert, evaporated somewhat in the heat, but we hadn't been badly disconcerted by the setback. Arriving in Diré for the second time that day, we'd refused to skulk. We'd decided to get to Timbuktu, and get there we would. And lo, in the bar we'd chanced to pitch into, here was resounding proof that a positive attitude worked. We'd needed a ride: a ride had materialised. Bill pocketed the moolah.

We waited for the vehicle to arrive. The loose hive of street urchins, undeterred by Bill's repelling tactics – lunging through the doorway to fling cups of cold water at them, no real punishment in this heat – swarmed around our bikes. I asked Bill when the truck was coming.

'*Toute à l'heure*,' (shortly) he says, without pause.

More waiting. Various small pickups came and went. We sallied out into town. I wandered off for a pee in a corner of two walls down a side street and then idled into the market, just round the corner from the bar; one stall with piles of what must have been sacred or learned texts – fascicles of ageing paper, furling at the edges, covered with close lines of handwritten Arabic script. The writing was too dense to be anything banal, surely – not laundry lists, catalogues of books. Numerous editions of the Qur'an, perhaps? And endless repetitions of that sublime evocation of human frailty in the divine scheme of things: *Allah kareem* (God wills it). 'If it is written,' they say, 'it is written.' The dogma of fatalism. Man must bear with equanimity what is and what will come. Allah's decrees are, at once, a reassurance of man's place in the cosmic plan and part of the armour of faith. It is a worrying creed. The fundamentalist sees in it a justification for, a validation of, any personal sacrifice. The simpler faithful take it as *causa causans* of natural disaster – flood, drought, famine, epidemic – and private grief: the death of a child, poverty, crippling illness, the tiny boy in Ségou, horribly crippled, who crawled across the ground like a crab, smiling . . . smiling. Against such an accepting *que sera sera* philosophy, practical rational science and technology can be powerless.

We'd eaten the last of our entirely succulent mangoes that morning; I purchased three replacements from an old lady guarding a small heap of the plump-fleshed fruit. She communicated the price by holding up fingers; I marked my agreement by flourishing the coins.

Into Bill's again. More waiting.

Finally, our hired Toyota 4 x 4 drove up, driver in the cab, two large lorry tyres in the open rear taking up an inordinate amount of the space into which we and our bikes had to fit. Simon's back was giving him sore distress. We installed him as comfortably as we could, propped up against the cab panel on a padded support. Bill looked on, proprietorial. Lanky strolled up; we loaded the bikes. Ben climbed aboard and, pushing through the crowd, came a stranger with a suitcase. He lobbed the case aboard and climbed in after it without a by your leave. Simon erupted: 'What's this bloke doing in our van? We've hired this for us. Tell him to get out. Get out.'

The interloper stared dumbly at us, sitting tight on what he perceived to be his rights: this was his ride as well as ours. Lanky smoothed his way into this overheating rumpus. I confronted him.

'What's going on here? This is not what we agreed.'

'What's the problem?'

'This other guy's the problem. We hired this van: what's he doing in the back?'

'You don't understand: he's the driver.'

'If he's the driver, why isn't he in the cab doing the driving?'

'He's the driver: you can see the tyres.'

I could see the tyres. Simon was saying: 'Tell him, either this geezer gets out or we do.'

The crowd was pressing in on us from all sides – a mood of disquiet rather than hostility, but I was concentrating on the diplomacy, if you can call it that. I wasn't gauging the menace, if menace there was, in the audience. I drew breath and squared up to Lanky for the next exchange without much enthusiasm.

My heart wasn't in it: frankly, I didn't give a worn-out inner tube for the whys and wherefores of this poxy argument. It was puerile. We were giving up our ride to Timbuktu here. I wanted to get there this day, the day we appointed for our arrival in Timbuktu. Blocked by the desert, I did not want to be swatted off by some futile debate about principle. However, my back wasn't screaming odds at me. I delivered the ultimatum. Lanky listened without flinching, merely repeating that this was the driver. I nodded at Simon and he heaved himself out. Ben and I shouldered the bikes over the side, the crowd seethed round us as we found parking space for them against Bill's fence, a disgruntled chirr, some voices raised in anger, discernible anger, now.

I marched up to Bill in the bar and said, quite cool: 'Our money, please.' He, full of 'I don't know what's going on and how could you possibly turn down such a fair deal', glumly handed over the cash. The 4 x 4 drove off, Lanky in the passenger seat as driver number two swung the wheel. Ben clicked furiously at the camera shutter to get the mugshot on film, and they were gone and we were, once more, stalled in Diré.

Things might have got ugly. We didn't stay to find out. We mounted the bikes and rode down to the beach, a faintly ignominious return journey to the bare strip of sand from where we'd started that morning. What was the plan? There was no plan. It was now 4.30, probably too late for a pinasse – the trip to Korioumé took five hours. We were, face it, in limbo. I hated being in limbo and decided I had to do something, anything, to salvage this day from the impasse it had slipped into. In my bag, I had a very high-sounding document of ambassadorial approval for our trip amiably provided by the Cultural Consul in Paris, whom I had visited some time before:

Un Peuple Un But Une Foi

AMBASSADE DE LA REPUBLIQUE DU MALI EN FRANCE

ATTESTATION

Nous, Service Culturel de l'Ambassade de la République du Mali à Paris . . .

We, the cultural service of the embassy of the Republic of Mali in Paris, declare that we have met Mr Graeme FIFE and discussed his projected visit to Mali in July–August 1998. It is our belief that the said project will contribute directly to the promotion of Mali as a destination for travellers. In confidence of which we provide him and his backers with this present approval of any lawful help and support which he may require.

I put this unlikely *passe-partout* in my back pocket and said: 'I'm off to find the mayor.' Ben was already setting up a temporary camp, unpacking the stove for some tea, the bivvy bag unrolled to sit on. A journalist in Paris had told me: 'Every town has a mayor, every village has a chief man: they're the people to apply to if you need help.'

I rode along the beach about a mile, passing lines of drawn-up pinasses and pirogues (fishing canoes), most unattended, some on the stocks, up into town, turned right along a wideish road flanked by larger buildings and saw, on the right, the police station. Riding past, I hesitated, but decided on a whim to ask. Even as I pulled up and dismounted, I knew I'd made a big mistake. I was voluntarily stepping over a frontier between a free domain and independent action into the domain of officialdom, fenced in by petty rules.

The police station was a two-storey building of drab concrete. Its outer wall formed a covered way round two sides of an interior courtyard, attached to the main block. Lounging on chairs in front of the open double portal at the front were about five men in threadbare, frayed, pale-green uniforms, berets, black leather belts, boots. Another man, corporal's stripes on his rolled-up sleeves and a look of undoubted amused malice on his face, leant like a hood's bodyguard against the door jamb. Getting involved with this crowd was definitely a miscalculation, but, whether from my impatience or our need, or both, I was stuck with it.

'I'm looking for the mayor,' I said, like Larry the Lamb.

There was no response. A crooked smile only, a leer of faint curiosity. He was wondering how to play this: I wasn't so much a catch as a clot handing himself in.

'I'm looking for the mayor, or the chief man here, please,' I repeated, as if this were the complaints counter at a Currys in Kent. No reaction. The corporal eyeballed me, I eyeballed him back. 'I know that every village and town in Mali has a mayor or a chief.'

This sounded impossibly British, stiff, haughty, out of touch, like that notorious headline in *The Times*: 'Fog in Channel, Europe Cut Off'. The corporal took his time, of which he had plenty, knowing, from my evident unease and impatience, that I had much less. 'Chief?' he drawled.

'Yes: chief. Can you tell me where to find the mayor or the chief, please?'

'The commissaire. You need to see the commissaire.' He paused. 'Your bike is blocking the entrance.'

I wheeled the bike through the portal into a lobby and parked it there in the covered way. The corporal led the way round a corner in the cloister to a door, above which hung a signboard: *Commissaire* (police superintendent). I waited outside; he talked to someone inside. I was ushered into a gloomy ill-lit room with jail-like bare unadorned walls and ceiling, furnished with a large wooden desk – nothing to speak of on it, no phone – and three chairs. On the chair behind the desk sat a man of about 35 years, sallow-skinned, tight-curled, short-cropped black hair, pinched features, scrawny build, avocado-green military-style uniform, clean and neatly ironed. On one of two chairs in front of the desk, another, slightly older, man in darker green uniform, brown skin, hooked nose, thick black hair and full moustache. I sat on the other chair in front of the desk. The atmosphere was not polite so much as expectant: they were waiting to hear what I had to say for myself. The man behind the desk looked misplaced, somehow, a man who knew what power was, as detailed in the book of regulations, but was a stranger to authority, that essential galvaniser of power. He was awkward. He sat inside his uniform but did not even half fill it. The other man, by contrast, appeared, or affected to be, entirely relaxed, comfortable. He was not in the hot seat, after all.

Addressing myself to the commissaire, I made formal greetings and showed him the attestation document. From the way he handled it, perused it, pored over it, from the puzzlement on his face, I was not convinced he could either place it or understand it. One thing was certain: he didn't know what to do. The fact was that courtesy, if not bye-law, required me, the stranger in town, to report to the local police – or the elusive mayor – say 'Bonjour, ça va?' and surrender a mandatory fee for passage or temporary residence. This I had manifestly not done – he might have already had wind of the near fracas down at Bill's. Instead, I was imperiously waving a piece of paper with a grand official seal stamped across an illegible signature. From Paris. Snotty foreigners. Did he know that I wasn't French? Possibly not. I was behaving, it must have been, in his perception, like one of that old breed of colonialists, like the Brit who takes as read Cecil Rhodes's pompous rejoinder to the apprentice imperialist: 'You must understand that, as an Englishman, you have already won first prize in the lottery of life.'

He lingered over the document. I waited for some response. There was none forthcoming. I explained why I was here.

'Why don't you take your boat?' he asked.

He was patently not listening. He didn't want to find himself wrong-footed. I'd already wrong-footed myself, with what consequence wasn't yet clear.

The other officer patiently repeated what I had explained about parting company with our pinasse. But no information going into the commissaire's head made any difference. He was plainly none too bright, and his mind was set on one thing only: the bureaucracy. He was the law thereabouts, and the law has its forms. First things first even in an emergency, especially in an emergency: attend to the paperwork, names in books, dates underlined, money paid. Nor was he in the least interested in bits of paper from far-off Paris. He wanted names of people he could see in front of his eyes, in his office, filled in on *his* official documents.

Finally he said: 'You will bring your companions here and complete the police forms for staying in Diré. If you did not stay here, it would not be necessary, but now it is necessary.'

No point in repeating that I was in his office precisely because we did not want to stay in Diré, that I'd actually come expressly to ask his help in getting out of Diré as soon as humanly possible.

I retrieved my scrap of paper, wheeled the bike out through the main doorway, past the sentries and the louche corporal, and set off back to the beach. Did we really have to go through this administrative charade? And what if we didn't comply? They were almost certainly too lazy to bother about pursuing us – except, I then reflected, for bribes.

I cycled back to the beach. Ben had set up a more established camp and he told me that Simon was off negotiating for a canoe-sized pirogue, without motor: two men punting us downriver.

ABOVE: Lucy, recovered from being 'all hot and bothered' after an ice cream, perches on the Merckx outside a café in Bergerac

LEFT: On the cycle path in Holland, Lucy stoking up with fizz

ABOVE: Galibier, outside the café with Angela (John on camera), replete with hot chocolate and cake, ready (maybe) for the ride down to Briançon

RIGHT: The unique pleasure of swimming in the sky: Highgate Men's Pond

ABOVE: Arriving at Roquefort after the long day's haul over the Pyrenees, May 1998

BELOW: Desolation, on the road in Mali

ABOVE: Bar Bouctou, evening, 30 July 1998 . . . the first beer

BELOW: Photocall, in the desert, Timbuktu. Simon to my left, Ben to my right

ABOVE: Setting off for the day's ride from the Pyrenean Pursuits lodge, Roquefort, in Biert. By the van, in a Bianchi Celeste top, Karen Purtill, her husband, Larry, to the left

BELOW: *Vin d'honneur* for André and Françoise Darrigade, Cerbère, 2005, Geoff Evans to my left

ABOVE: Before the start of the Raid Pyrénéen, 2005, with the Old Ports.
Dave Hickman, kneeling, far left, front row, Geoff Evans to my right
(no helmet) six from left, back row

RIGHT: On the Tourmalet,
my fifth crossing, partway
through the 2005 Raid

ABOVE: Phil and Friends: Phil and I at the front; Brian Robinson, in the shirt of his former team, Saint-Raphaël, bides his time behind Phil; beside him, his son-in-law Martyn (© Carlton Reid)

BELOW: With Luke, riding the Kentish hills, he resplendent in Sydenham colours, I on the splendid Condor Pista, my favoured winter training machine

RIGHT: The *patronne* of the bar/bread depot took a while to grasp the concept of what the English language sees as the pun in pain. Was it worth the effort? Probably not

BELOW: With Patrick Sercu, 'The Flemish Arrow', at trackside, Bremen Six Day, 2007. One of the great pleasures and privileges of the work: friendly, wide-ranging conversation with one of the greats of cycling
(© Camille John McMillan)

'That's preposterous,' I said, 'it'd take two days at the very least.'

'Well, you'd better get over there because Dad's pretty keen.'

Simon and the two young guys were, even as we spoke, walking towards us. I went out to meet them and, without ado, said: 'Sorry, but we've got to have a motor. Kind offer, much appreciated, but we're short of time.'

They seemed to take it in good part, and, almost simultaneously, one of the two young men spotted a large crowded pinasse steaming down the river towards us, about half a mile away. Maybe if our two boatmen could get near enough to hail it, we could hop passage. The three of us raced down to the water's edge and got aboard the slim canoe. The man at the stern pushed it nose-first into the skirting of reeds as I scrambled in amidships and the front man started digging in with the pole. We eased sluggishly out into the stream, then it was a race for the interception: the pinasse was moving far too quickly, we'd never make it, even though the quant-man was working hard, the canoe rocking with his effort, water gurgling under the bottom. The pinasse steamed on, aloof to any intervention of small fry, its coalie black bows breasting a flowing scarf of white foam and spindrift, its deck packed with passengers. Within hailing distance, my two ferrymen shouted and gesticulated. No reply. They repeated, a pause, and then a voice sang out from on board the pinasse. The news was bad: they were stopping in Diré. A fair shot, didn't come off. We span round and skidded back to shore.

One of the guys knew someone with a motorised pinasse in Diré. He suggested trying him. I agreed.

A motorised pinasse, I pondered . . . another day lost. Couldn't be helped. The two young boatmen and I walked down the beach back into town. We talked as we went:

they were cousins, mid-20s, handsome, soft-spoken, easy-going, amiable, keen to join in the excitement of getting us a ride.

At the entrance to the road into town, one cousin went off to find the boat-owner, leaving the other with me. The two of us waited and waited and waited. The sun had long sunk and the last light of this unfulfilled day was failing. A crowd of kids gathered, and the litany began: '*Donne-moi un cadeau. Donne-moi un cadeau.*' (Give me a present.)

Yet, even when given the biro – I had no Bics left – there was no palpable joy in the gift. They smiled, sure, but they always smiled. Mali was *La Terre d'Accueil* (The Land of Welcome). Their capacity to grin amid such poverty, such privation, was truly humbling. But there was no grace, quite the opposite, in snatching the present. Offer the gift to a press of children and the first and strongest hand will grab as many as are grabbable. And never a thank you, that sweet oil of *politesse*. Yet, if we had cheap pens to spare, it was because we had far more to spare than they could ever dream of owning. Why should they have thanked us? 'Property is theft,' said the early socialist Pierre-Joseph Proudhon, and in the case of Africa it's hard to argue the biting truth of that. Of the first missionaries, someone said: 'They gave us Bibles, told us to close our eyes and pray, and when we opened our eyes, we had the Bible and they had the land.'

After about 20 minutes, I'd had enough of the mithering clamour and wandered off down the beach alone. Dusk crept up like disappointment. Still we waited.

Finally, they arrived: cousin number one accompanied by five other men. I asked which was our man, and one spoke up. I addressed him.

'We're looking for a motorised boat to take us to Korioumé. I'm told you have one.'

'Yes.'

'How much are you asking?'

'150,000 CFA.' (£150)

'You're joking.'

'How much do you say?' (Simon had set a limit of £60.)

'40,000 CFA.' (£40)

His turn to shrug and scoff. We batted on, but I knew instinctively there was no mileage in this: he'd started far too high. After a few more exchanges round the circle, like mules stubbornly turning a pump at a well, I said thanks but no thanks and walked off.

The cousins took a while to catch up with me, and when they did, my exasperation spilt out. 'Excuse me, but the price that man was demanding was an insult, plain greed. All we've had in this country is "Give me a present . . . give me a Bic". It leaves us no room for generosity. If all we hear is "Gimme", before anything else is said, it leaves us nothing that we can give because we *want* to give. Nothing. You call Mali the land of welcome. "Gimme gimme gimme" is no welcome. Forget actually saying *thank you*. And to be asked such an exorbitant sum of money for that trip: you lose out on the money, we don't get a ride, no one's satisfied. You're disappointed, and we feel angry and pissed off. The only ride we have got is the one you're trying to take us for. You've tried to help, and I thank you. Forgive my candour, but that's it.'

They listened, shrugged their shoulders, seemed not unduly put out. Perhaps they sympathised. It felt so. My animosity was not directed at them, only at this culture of endless milking. Where else would cyclists in distress have to pay nearly a week's subsistence *each* to ride 20 miles in the back of a quarry lorry to escape a potentially dangerous – life-threatening – plight? And who implanted this greed? Our predecessors.

We trekked back to the camp. Ben sat on his own in the gloom: Simon had ridden off to find me half an hour ago.

I grabbed my bike and set off to track him down. It was, by this time, completely dark, and, at the far end of the beach, in the greying light, I discerned the shadowy bulk of a man. I called out. It was Simon, and suddenly, behind him, some 200 yards distant, a pair of headlamps, tracing a zigzag path along the beach, coming our way. Whether good news or bad, this *must* be for us, I thought, that's for sure. Police? It seemed unlikely. They were almost certainly too idle to be bothered. If they'd had any intention of hauling us in, they'd have done it long since. But if not police, *who*? The pickup pulled to a halt alongside me. I peered at the word painted on the cab door: not POLICE but CARE, the American aid agency. A guy riding the running board, arm looped through the window, said: 'I overheard you back there: you need a ride to Timbuktu.'

'We do. How much?'

'35,000 CFA.'

'Us and the bikes?'

'Yes.'

'Done.'

Simon arrived, wheeling his bike. He'd copped his second puncture of the day. I told him we were on our way.

'Right,' I said to our ride, 'follow me, give me the light of your headlamps.' I rode off, they drove behind. At the camp: 'Come on, Ben, get packed. We're off.' It was nearing 8 p.m. I had been toing and froing for nigh on four hours, but we would – wouldn't we? – be in Timbuktu that night after all.

Eleven

Everyman's Nowhere

Gilbert Scott, architect of St Pancras station and the
Glasgow museum, arrived in Glasgow by train once and
his mind went blank. He went to the telegraph office
and sent a four-word wire to his office in London. It
read: 'Why am I here?'

We broke camp, bundled everything into the panniers. The
driver and his mate whisked the bikes into the open back of the
truck onto a load of fibrous stalks matted in a heap. Shoulder
leaning against the cab, legs hooked over the side of the truck,
sat a young soldier in khaki uniform, an automatic rifle across
his knees. Simon and Ben were convinced that I'd fixed up
a carte-blanche ride with an armed police escort. The driver
secured the bikes in a heap with a long length of cord. I gave
the two cousins 1,000 CFA and thanked them for their help
and support. We shook hands, and so into the back of the
truck, Simon propped against the back of the cab, Ben next to
him, me next to the soldier, legs dangling over the side. All at
once, we were roaring along that beachhead we thought we'd
be stuck on. Destination . . . the end of the earth.

Through the back streets of this blighted town's eastern
quarter and out into the desert on Lanky's packed-earth road

sped the truck, its headlamps sweeping the alluvial plain. We saw briefly lit swathes of it dotted with scrub and stunted bushes, an eerie arc of white light from the vehicle illuminating no detectable roadway scored across the packed earth, only the vacancy of night and wilderness. Hence the ink-drawn line on Lanky's map, of course: there *is* no roadway, only the desiccated floor of the Niger's floodplain, soon, as every summer, to be inundated and become riverbed once more.

It was, we agreed, the worst journey any of us had ever undergone. I thought of adjectives to describe it – intolerable, unendurable, insufferable – but it was none of them. We had to tolerate, endure, suffer, we had no choice. It was, though, utterly frightful and frightening. The first 20 minutes or so were bumpy, fast, erratic, but that was nothing, a mere jaunt before the rough-ride proper. The driver flung the vehicle at everything, obstacle, ditch, rut and furrow, switchback, ricochet, off mudbank chicanes, over hummocks and ridges, twisting and skidding to lurch back onto the line of his imaginary compass pointing straight ahead through that trackless wasteland. He drove as if the entire Moroccan light cavalry were in hot pursuit on their fleet Arab thoroughbreds, firing from the hip.

We see-sawed through ditches, bounced over sudden bumps invisible in the full glare of the lights. We racketed and writhed through branches lashing out with their bony fingers at us, the bikes, the sides of the truck. All at crazy speed, gears thrashing, on yet another set of bald treadless tyres. When the rubber has no purchase, the only resource is to floor the accelerator. The bikes leapt and strained at their lashings, working the knots loose, like frantic horses yanking at the tethers.

Suddenly, the brakes screamed. We skidded to a halt, the front wheels clipped onto the lower rise of a 5ft embankment. Beyond it lay a wide irrigation ditch filled with water. To either side of the path we were on lay marshy ground. The engine still throbbing, the driver got out and walked ahead with a torch, probing the soggy earth for depth, left and right, scanning the ground on the far side of the ditch, wandering around in the headlights. He came back, said something in Bambara to our shotgun and climbed back into the cab. I asked the soldier to translate. 'He said: "Pray to God."'

We reversed a short way and then we were off. Hectic whine of high revs, clutch lifted, the truck's nose lurched round and we bucked forward up the ramp to the cut, one shimmy to steady the line and we went, full out. Fingers crossed. God does not sleep. The truck was flying, front wheels leaping, hungry for dry ground. The back wheels slipped and then kicked at the rim of the cut, and we were over, landing deadweight like an unsprung buckboard on the solid crust beyond.

And then, the *real* horror began. We jumped and dived like a dodgem car going full blast across a mogul field, veering and humping madly, the accelerator pressed flat, steering wheel spinning, yanked fiercely left and right as the driver split-second assessed the ground no more than a few yards ahead of the truck and jinked and slid across it.

He must have been doing a constant 60mph – the engine screeching like an amplified dentist's drill. Suddenly, the cord snapped. The bikes shook loose and plunged up and down with a harsh clang of metal. I grabbed for them, yelling: 'Stop the bus, stop the bus.' The soldier shouted the message on into the cab. Simon and Ben pummelled on the panels of the cab, the truck swerved and pulled over. Merciful release, a few moments' respite. Out sprang driver and mate as if this was the Paris–Dakar rally and precious seconds were being needlessly squandered on fripperies. Whilst they were at this, Ben and Simon stood up and clung to the cowling of the cab's roof, legs braced to absorb the shock and sway of the switchback. Driver and mate climbed in, motor roared, back to the frantic speed.

I was still sprawled in the back, hanging onto the bikes.

The driver and his mate knew as much about rope-lashing as I did about the private life of the slug. In next to no time, the bikes were bucking free again and I gripped the frame of the bike on top as firmly as I could and hung on desperately to keep them anchored. The weight of the metal hammering down was bruising and painful; it might easily have broken my arm. The crazy junketing of the vehicle might well have tipped the whole bangshoot over on its side. A second time, we stopped, and I tried to do the tying down, but the driver and his mate weren't bothered with tight binding, comfort or security. These bikes were our problem; getting this awful journey done as quickly as possible was theirs. No one said getting to Timbuktu would be easy, and the driver seemed to be manically determined to prove just how unpleasant it could be.

There have been times on the bike when I have roundly cursed the very invention of the machine and my passion for it . . . mostly when I'm cold, wet, tired out, far from home, on one occasion pedalling through East Sussex country lanes in the vicinity of Burwash and Bateman's, where Rudyard Kipling lived, late at night, far from destination and lover's bed, in the pitch dark, feeling myself damnably lost, my dynamo malfunctioning, the hills coming one after the other, steep and unseen. Such times I find a sore trial of patience, and I failed that one miserably in a torrent of invective directed at all things conspiring against me, it seemed. It's as if my adult mind reviews the situation, the No-Reason Negative zone, does not like it, gathers up its common sense and grimly takes off, leaving me to muddle through on wilful perseverance and childish petulance.

All through the length of that dreadful journey across the desert I cursed God, Life and Nature with a peculiar savagery. And came into my head unbidden the lines of a song I had written almost exactly 20 years earlier. It might have been a premonition of this very ride. It had come out of emotional blank, lost love, random anger:

> I took a broken bus to hell, full of demons,
> A nightmare ride through deserts of ice and sand.
> The ringing of the bell in sudden silence
> Brought terrors, nothing I could understand.
> The emptiness behind me now is vanishing,
> The chaos of a solitude too wide,
> Yet as the amber sunlight falls across my eyes
> I recognise no dark in which to hide.

> I saw laughing ghosts in tableau on a giant screen,
> The junketing of clowns upon my grave,
> A signpost reading: *Paradise – Infinity*,
> The sightless dreams of afterlife we crave . . .
> The tediums of suicidal visions are
> A deeper scar than anything unkind.

I was fast running out of resistance and strength, being shot from side to side, scarce able to hold onto the bikes pogoing up and down like saccharine-high kids on a trampoline. Frazzled, exhausted, terrified, bruised, on the edge of losing it completely, I cried out: 'I can't take much more of this.' The soldier next to me may have heard me. I neither knew nor registered – only that he seemed to be treating all this as normal.

I'd told the others that the last 22km of this road were on tarmac. At one point, Simon, hanging onto the lip of the cab roof, hollered to me: 'I'm not banking on this tarmac road.'

'It'll be there,' I hollered back, and even that reassurance, baseless as it might yet prove, gave me some extra will to keep going. Another pit stop to tether the loose bikes and suddenly, glory be, we were driving straight, the desert road carving past what looked like a sizeable concrete sty or stable-block, and there was a gate and the earth road merged with a curving strip of dark metalled road which appeared out of the night to our left and continued ahead into another dark mansion of the same black night. It was blessed relief.

There were only 17km of tarmac, in fact, but, after the jolting and jarring of that infernal pillar-to-post through the desert bagatelle, they rolled out smoothly beneath us like the track of a velodrome. Suddenly, I saw, way over to the north, a large eerie umbrella of light in the sky, hovering above a craggy silhouetted skyline, black crenellations picked out in the spectral glow. The soldier nudged me with the barrel of his weapon and said, in the French pronunciation: 'Tombouctou.'

It was a magical moment, gazing long at that blue-white electric glow staining the night sky, as it were the halo above a power station. We drove in a long smooth arc towards it, like a ship worn off direct course by contrary wind and current. It was as if we were being tugged away from Timbuktu by the black force field of the desert, a dark inhospitable emptiness, making a final effort to stop us getting there. Yet closer we came, drawn on magnetically by the far more powerful lode of the legendary city. At last, we drove into the outskirts, no other vehicle on the road, a sleepy calm, the tyres rumbling, hot rubber on a drag strip of dust and sand, lines of houses, square and rectangular sand-block, windows mostly unlit, bathed in the spillage of streetlights, an oasis of sodium glare in Mali. This was Timbuktu new town, tacked onto the old, the roundabout of the Place de l'Indépendance like a ball joint between them. We swung left down a wide street of boulevard proportions, but like a beach road cloaked in sand-drifts from hidden dunes. The truck drew up and, without a word to us, the soldier vaulted down, grabbed his haversack, gestured a wave with his rifle to the driver and his mate and was gone.

The driver's mate asked me where we were staying. I told him the Hotel Relais Azalai. We drove another half-mile or so and pulled up again. The journey, thank goodness, was over, and against the odds of this quite extraordinary day, we had arrived in Timbuktu.

We untied the bikes, offloaded them, our panniers and various items that had sprung astray in the ruckus, and suddenly two shadowy figures shimmered out of a side street. They couldn't have been forewarned of our coming, surely? But now I wondered if perhaps they did know, that the network which had conjured this ride out of nowhere had signalled our arrival ahead. At the time, it seemed that they just knew, or heard the truck and guessed, or were plugged into some divinatory wavelength as old as the caravans homing in on Timbuktu, the ever-alert desert telegraph.

'We can show you to the Hôtel Bouctou,' they said and started to load up with our panniers.

'We're staying at Le Relais,' I tell them.

'Have you booked?'

We hadn't booked. I fudged. 'We've fixed to go there.'

They shrugged, shook their heads. 'It's closed. Hôtel Bouctou,' with a nod of finality.

I counted out the agreed money in the light of the headlamps, handed it over to the driver, said thank you and that was that. As with the soldier, they did not say a word. They simply climbed back into the truck and drove off. Our self-appointed porters-cum-guides set off down the sandy side street from which they had appeared and we tramped in a straggle after them, clutching bikes, bags, loose bits and pieces, water bottles and tool pouches, etc. into pitch dark.

'Where is Le Relais?' I asked, stubbornly.

'Over there.' He nodded left. There were no lights. 'But there's no electricity. They only have electricity when there are enough guests. There aren't enough guests at the moment.' It seems that we had come off-season. At the time, this didn't augur well. In fact, it was a blessing.

Somewhere across an expanse of desert – how wide we could not judge because we could see nothing – stood the recommended hotel, Le Relais Azalaï, unlit, unpowered, shut. However, looming fully lit out of the darkness was the Hôtel Bouctou, known colloquially as Le Campement. We were tired, thirsty, hungry, in need of a bed: here was the Campement offering hospitality. We sloped in. The hotel/bar had two bits: the two-storey annexe across the way and the main building, a long bungalow with a verandah and wing of rooms attached. We asked for three air-conditioned rooms and were led out to see them. They were squalid and poky, furnished with flimsy bunk beds draped over with yellowing, stained mosquito nets, no bedding. Had there been one for me, I think I would not have used it. I decided I would unroll the lightweight sleeping bag. One early explorer ate the bugs and worms which supplemented the local staple diet. Perish the thought. A plastic curtain screened a basic shower cubicle. The third room was home to a very large cockroach – possibly an *amuse-bouche* for hardier individuals. I poked it with my toe. It was so lethargic it couldn't even raise a scuttle. The hotel man said offhandedly: 'No problem, no problem,' leant down, picked it up and dropped it in the waste-paper basket. (The best way to dispose of a cockroach is to place it on its back. Since they are reckoned to be the only creatures that will survive a thermo-nuclear explosion, this is homely.) Ben and Simon decided to double up: we didn't need the cockroach room. We dumped our gear and headed straight for refreshments.

The bar of the Bouctou was seedy, tattered, unforgettable. Strip lights flickered on the ceiling, the albatross-wing ventilator fans whirred like the hmm-hmm-hmm of men on holiday not knowing what to do, the jumbo-sized television on the bar droned like a disappointed woman desperate for flattery and the assembled company, the Bouctou clientele, watched the glittering screen hypnotically or, numb with indifference, ignored it completely, content to keep watch on the space into which people, known or unknown, came and went. (Ben, who lived in Casablanca at the time, recognised the programme being broadcast: Moroccan soap, dubbed by actors trained to deliver in shaved-down vocal tones, lots of orgasmic panting and tumescent huskiness, off.)

The assembled company was gathered on two ample moth-eaten settees set at right angles in one corner of the room: occupying one of them, two couples, white women, black men, all mid-20s, jeans, T-shirts, jackets; on the other, five black guys, indeterminate age, varied garb, native and European. One was brushing his teeth with the frayed end of a twig – a practice noted by the early explorers. The staff came and went through the door leading into the kitchen behind the bar itself. The bar was a high, cocktail-lounge-style counter, stools in front. Sellotaped to the wall, at the side of the shelves carrying bottles of spirits, was an Air Mali calendar, also the tariff board showing prices of Coca-Cola, mineral water, beer, gin, rum, whisky. The ambiance was decidedly *not* cocktail, but this was, most decidedly, the place where you stayed in Timbuktu, the meeting point where the serious Timbuktu watchers hung out. You could feel it. The atmosphere, the mood, the continuing style was languid, laid-back, cool, intuitively 'no problem'. Here we had a bare minimum of regulars convened on the regular patch. Our arrival caused no great stir. This was a living museum of so many exotics of one sort or another, a constant influx, that exotics from anywhere else unidentified had become the norm here. It was the place where people like us who'd come to see Timbuktu pitched up, and where the people who were already here came to see the people who'd come to see Timbuktu. I guessed that the other hotel, secluded within its own electricity-wanting curfew, was the starchy place that never hooked in to the local pulse. Indeed, it was built as a luxury holiday hotel but never attracted enough custom to justify its pretensions and now clung on in dwindling hope that, one day, the mirage of flocks of well-heeled tourists would fly in to deliver the bonanza to rescue it.

We ordered beers and sat on rickety chairs at a wobbly table whose plastic covering was encrusted with the dried slops of several days' worth of meals and infested with a thick swathe of insects. I stress infested: a close-packed layer of small, cochineal-coloured flying beetles over the whole area. We swept them off in brusque handfuls. They didn't even have the pep to fly. They simply plopped to the floor and stayed there. Sporadically, one would summon up the vigour to revisit, but another swat and it gave up.

That first beer was delicious, unsurpassable. We were in Timbuktu, after all, and we drank to the mad luck of our getting there. Simon had hoped that we would ride in 'like the cavalry coming to the rescue'. Somehow it didn't matter. We'd made it to the town they called 'the place of sweet words', from the days when it was one of the largest centres of culture and learning in the Muslim world. It is very far from that now. Timbuktu is drowning in sand.

Simon and Ben had had a swim in the river; I was filthy. My hair matted like kapok, every inch of me sticky with dry sweat, dust and sand, I went off for a shower – hot water, bath soap (provided) and shampoo. Refreshed, clean, revived, I rejoined the others for the evening's entertainment. It was by now around 11 p.m., and we babbled incredulously, exultantly, about the events of this day that had begun an epoch ago at 5.30 a.m. on the banks of the Niger. A week since we'd ridden from the airport into Bamako, a week, only. So much packed into those seven days, uncountable time. We had travelled into and across one tiny corner of another world, and here we were at the very end of that world, *au bout du monde*, at the ends of the earth, in the fabled city.

We ordered more beers and dinner – there wasn't much left on offer, but we tucked into plain omelette, followed by inedible meat and peas, followed by a sweet pancake. More beer, and Ben and Simon slid off to bed. I stayed: I wanted more time to savour the triumph and picked up conversation with a young man (20 years old, it turned out) who'd come in while we were eating. He was articulate, intelligent, amicable. Soon, we were talking, in French, about Tombouctou, and I very soon realised that here was someone who was not only knowledgeable, he was interesting, charming, friendly. We got on well. He was, I know now, making a pitch to be our guide the next day, but nothing so meretricious was evident. We had, indeed, lit on a friendship, an unlikely friendship, maybe, but for the first time I reached deep into the real *accueil* that Mali prides itself on. I do not excuse myself from not seeing it before. I had been embattled, suspicious, insufficiently composed to relax and be more welcoming myself. Yet, Sankoum *was* different. We clicked. The fact that he was speaking in French was useful, too: whatever story he told me I'd be able to translate and edit as I chose. And, his French was more cultured than most of the French I'd heard, the accent clearer. It was, above all, a treat to be talking about more complex matters than basic tourist necessities.

I very often found it quite difficult to decode the local Mali version of the language, as they did my Parisian. We were of course both speaking a foreign language, learnt from different sources and in different contexts for differing needs. Most of the time it got us by, no more than that. Sankoum had been educated, however – he was still at university – and I asked him if he would be willing to repeat much of what he had told me into the microphone the following morning. He said that he'd be delighted. He didn't ask me how much I'd give him.

He simply said: of course. And then, it must have been about 12.30 by this time, he looked at me and said: '*T'es fatigué*.'

It was, after all I had so far experienced in this crushingly impoverished country, remarkable: a gesture of unfeigned kindness, the kindness of strangers, without a price tag.

I confessed that I was very tired. We said goodnight and *à demain* (see you tomorrow).

I retired, despatched what I took to be a rather sinister-looking creepy-crawlie poised, in mid-lurch, on the lower of the other set of bunks in my room, and got ready for bed. I have never had any conscience about insects and had voided no shit since Monday. I had no timepiece, either, to tell me the hour. I had left at home the gold watch bequeathed to me by Grandad, given him by the community in Canada where he was living at the outbreak of the First World War.

Twelve

Timbuktu, Drowning in Sand

When I woke, the sun had already washed its face in the morning mist and was drying off on threadbare towels of cloud. I had another shower, even that a prodigal indulgence, gathered pen and notebook and headed for the bar along the verandah, past the terrace. A view out across the desert: startlingly bright radiance, a hard, lustrous, dazzling neon glare as if reflected off polished fine-drawn brass, a few trees, buildings, a uniformity of colour tone, metallic, the essence of harsh brilliance, a glassy quality in the sky, an opaque shimmer below, both signs of heat, extreme heat. As I walked along, I noticed several Tuareg men loitering about the outer wall of the hotel, several pairs of eyes regarding me through the narrow slits in the cheche – a light cotton scarf, white or indigo (pale and dark), wound about the head as a turban. Henri de Montherlant, whose *Les Jeunes Filles* I was still struggling with, said that the 'cheche is the turban the Arabs wear, and you can do anything you like with it'. He also tells the story of the young Bedouin alone and lost, dying of thirst, in the desert, who finds, in the sand, a pearl of inestimable value – spelling out the true nature of worth. Those gems apart, I found the book extremely heavy going and gave up on it.

The indigo dye favoured by the Tuareg is apt to run in the

coiling sweat and give the wearer a mask of woad, hence the sobriquet 'blue men'.

The tables on the terrace were thick with the local insect life. It was too hot and sultry to sit outside, in any case. I went into the saloon. The clock read 7 a.m., the television was on and the room was empty apart from a young black guy behind the bar. He looked up. I asked for some coffee and spotted the title of the book he was reading: *Half Asleep in Frog Pajamas*, by the peerless Tom Robbins. We conversed, in French, the Timbuktu Robbins fan and I. He must have been a fan. You don't read Tom Robbins without becoming either an ardent fan or – I know one – an ardent foe.

'You're reading Tom Robbins. Wow.'

'Yes, yes. He's a marvellous writer.'

'Don't you find him quite difficult? Not so much that the language is so difficult but the expressions are so eccentric, he has such an idiosyncratic style?'

I may have been doing his command of English an injustice, but Robbins flexes prose into wild comic invention studded with metaphors of poetic flight and ingenuity, with idea-spinning that makes the brain leap and race.

'Yes, yes, he's hard, very hard. I have to use the dictionary all the time.' (A scholar he must be. Perhaps the Islamic tradition at work: the virtue in long poring over texts brought to its zenith here at the old university in Timbuktu.)

'Is he translated?'

'No.' He shrugged his shoulders, paused, then said, casually: 'He stayed here a few years ago, with his wife. Five days.'

And, of course, I remembered (from chapter one of *Frog Pajamas*):

> Timbuktu. The end of everybody's road. The capital
> of Nowhere . . . The last pure place. Isolation being
> the mother of purity. All men are jealous of Timbuktu

because Timbuktu is removed from men, it's the wholeness men have fractured, the sacred extreme they've traded away. Like Hell, like Heaven, Timbuktu is a place in the brain, a place whose existence may be often doubted but never dismissed. Timbuktu. A constellation by which the imagination can navigate, the joker that haunts the map-maker's deck.

(In a letter, Tom Robbins told me that some of his books had been done into French, but the translations were awful.)

'Is he a good man?'

'*Gentil. Sympa. Génial.*' (Kind. Sympathetic. Good company.)

I could not have thought otherwise. So: Tom Robbins was here. Who else?

The sachet of Nescafé powder arrived with the cup of tepid water.

'Is there any orange juice?'

'There is Fanta.'

'No, thanks.'

I swept the cloth clear of bugs and sat to write. The TV brought up the European news. Bizarre. An item caught my eye: report of the Tour de France – a scant ten minutes. The doping scandal which nearly stopped that year's race was continuing to unravel – the Italian leader of the mountains competition, Rodolfo Massi, had been kicked out, a suitcase full of banned substances in his room. Said he'd been feeling poorly. But then the real sensation: the diminutive climber Marco Pantani, *Il Pirata*, was in yellow, holding a comfortable margin over the previous year's winner Jan Ullrich. The Pirate must have slain him in the Alps – a lone attack, no doubt, killer punch. Three stages only left to ride. One of the bar staff came in and I asked if he knew the story: Pantani let fly on the stage to Les Deux Alpes. Must have battered the rest of them by seven or eight minutes.

Simon came in at about 8 a.m. and we had breakfast: coffee, jam and the famous wheaten Timbuktu bread, a sort of double-layer, unleavened oval, not dissimilar from a pitta. One bite and we were into gritty sand: crunch crunch crunch. Pretty tasteless dough, and the jam was only one notch up from insipid, but the bread clung to the ribs and took your mind off the foul coffee. Simon's bed had half-collapsed in the middle of the night, posing him one of those intriguing conundrums that occupy the long reaches of darkness. The debate runs thus: *fact* – I'm passably comfortable as I am, even in the wreckage of the balsawood and the tangle of nylon shroud. *Thesis* – would I be so much *more* comfortable, *appreciably* more comfortable, if I got up and reconstructed what I could of the matchstick frame and the cardboard mattress? *Interim analysis* – perhaps. He'd got up, spent half an hour trying to re-sling the mosquito net and, thoroughly fed up, eventually climbed into the bunk above Ben. *Conclusion* – when will we ever learn?

Ben came in, needlessly cheery.

After breakfast, we donned our 'Simon Jersey On Location' T-shirts, printed with a map of Mali, and proceeded into the desert, with our bikes, for a photocall; two Tuareg obliged as local colour. The one standing next to me whispered out of the corner of his mouth as we stood there, not wanting to turn away from the camera, inviting me to come and have a cup of tea in his tent after the Intrepid Cyclist Explorers in Sahara commemorative shoot. Oh, I say, ta nicely. Then he says: 'You can see what we have for sale: knives, leatherwork, nice things . . . no obligation . . . if you don't want to buy, no problem.'

Hang on, matey: time for a picture. Everybody say 'Nes-ca-féééé!'

The Tuareg, once a proud nomadic military caste, had become loitering, not even travelling, salesmen, hawking their ancestral treasures, the heirlooms, in all probability (we were told) either stolen or many times already bartered.

There was the usual dawdling attendance of kids. Round Timbuktu, the approach was slightly more sophisticated – in the end, no less bothersome. The routine was for them to ask, in French: 'Are you English?' followed almost without pause to listen to whatever reply was forthcoming: 'My name is . . . What's your name?' to which, after the tenth, the fifteenth time of asking, I replied: *'Je suis le roi d'Angleterre,'* which, given my feelings about imperialist interventions, was a telling Freudian slip.

Waiting back on the verandah in a marginally cooler shade was a young guy with a familiar face. I recognised him at once, but couldn't instantly place him – but then, of course, it was Djal from the boat, in smart clothes, come into Timbuktu to see his pals. Affable greetings, a bit of the story, our epic ride, and 'See you later'. Waiting, too, was Sankoum, and we went into my room. I switched off the air conditioner, we sat face to face on the ramshackle chairs and he talked for about 45 minutes in fascinating detail – the history of the city, the legends of the famous holy men, the substance of Timbuktu's legendary standing. Enthusiastic, learned, with a light touch, he was a superb informant. He was pouring sweat in the airless room, heat squirming in from outside through every cranny, and there were plenty, and my arm ached with holding the microphone. When we'd done, I thanked him and he said: 'A pleasure.' He didn't ask for money, instead, he earned his wage as our guide, he and his friend Oumar, the young man with the Tom Robbins book.

A Frenchman, René Caillé, who came here in 1828, at considerable risk – it was a forbidden city to infidels – said of Timbuktu: 'There is something indefinably imposing about the sight of such a large town built in the middle of the sand dunes; one cannot help but admire those who founded it.'

Through the door of the mosque, we entered a strange cave of shadows. Transverse lines of slender wooden pillars, like parallel palisades, reached from the packed earth floor to the mud-brick roof and divided the whole building into narrow open rows, along which the worshippers crowded in to kneel for prayers. To the side of the main door was a recess, large enough for the imam – the religious leader – to sit in and lead the devotions, telling the story of the prophet's life, each imam in his own version. It was a place of great tranquillity, spare of ornament, as empty as the human heart which opens itself to the worship of God. The solitary prayers in the desert would find combined voice here when the faithful came each Friday, holiest day of the week. They come in, stroke the purifying wood three times and take its virtue into their body. We saw a niche in which one of Timbuktu's saints was buried. There are some 333 altogether, interred in the foundations of what were the boundary walls, a sacred pomerium about the city, protecting it against evil. We climbed onto the roof and gazed out across the other roofs of Timbuktu, jostling for breathing space in the dry choked air. And all around, the caloried haze, the blurring desert sand, the startling impact of the monotone colour. The same hue everywhere in everything: of bleached sand, of sand-coloured mud bricks, of a sky gritted over with sand, of a light which reflects only the ubiquitous, same same same dun hue of the sand.

Even 25 years ago, the River Niger flowed past the walls of the city, water ran between the two hotels, and the old mosque occupied what was, effectively, a peninsula, so that worshippers could reach it only by boat. The river is some 10km away now, and the desert continues to encroach.

From the mosque, we walked through the back streets of the old city. Many of the houses had distinctive lancet-arched, double-leaf doors, their wooden panels patterned with broad-headed iron nails or filigree ironwork – a Tuareg style of ornamentation: elaborate grille shapes, multi-pointed crosses, crystal forms, ornate lozenge designs and a big iron ring threaded through a central boss for a knocker. The windows, too: oriole-shaped with a close-mesh lattice across the lower half, an open fanlight at the top. Through these, the women could stare out at the world as it passed without the world being able to stare back, *oeillets* for the beautiful prisoners, locked away like rare gems in caskets with fretwork lids.

And so to the Grand Marché, which occupies a covered building open at either end, tin roof, sand floor, housing a cornucopia of produce. The place sizzled with lively chatter and blaring music. Faces all round lit with eagerness for business.

Here, Oumar explained that the oleaginous *beurre de karitay* is made from the sap of the karitay tree and used as a condiment for food and a cream for the skin. And he pointed out a thin white drink, made of fine millet flour and goat's milk, which keeps the workers in the fields going. We saw pots and pots of ochrous fabric dyes, earthen and vegetable, smoky reds and blues, oranges, browns and yellows that might have been squeezed out of mineral clays. What looked like narrow slabs of rough marble, a metre or so in length, a half-metre wide, 5cm thick, were actually slabs of salt, 50 kilos apiece, which are strapped to the flanks of the camels and ferried back on the Azalai. There were the usual dishes of herbs, but one oddity: dried lemons, the size of a squash ball. Because the citizens of Timbuktu can get nothing out of season, the lemons are dried and used as flavourings in stews when fresh citrus is not to be had. We bought some of these tiny near-weightless dried items.

I asked Oumar about the ubiquitous sand – doesn't it wear down their teeth? He smiled, showing a full set of white pearlies, and said: 'In Timbuktu, sand is an extra space.'

'Spice?'

'Yes, spice.'

He also said: 'You must see that Timbuktu is not only our

past, but it is our present, too. Of course we are proud of tradition, but it is not a dead city. It lives.'

Simon and I each bought a Tuareg passport. These ornamental tokens made of silver, frapped to a leather lace with wire and coloured thread, are fashioned in cabbalistic shapes – stars, triangles, squares and circles – and worn as distinctive badges to identify the wearer as the member of a particular tribe, necessary when drawing water at an oasis.

Sankoum and Oumar, close friends who try to speak English to each other every day for practice, *made* our visit to the city. Their happiness in the place went beyond the deference of guide to paymaster. They were a treat to be with, not in the least pushy, and well informed, clear-spoken, happy. Conscious of the legend, they also introduced us to the new reality, the abiding heritage. As a result, that melancholy of which so many travellers speak did not afflict us. We saw, beneath the surface layer of sand, that other spice, the peculiar genius of Timbuktu.

Oumar and Sankoum walked us back to the hotel, and we said goodbye. 'Send me a tape of Oasis,' said Sankoum, 'and a Manchester United shirt.' I did, of course.

Given that it *is* pretty strange to encounter the new globalism even in this tiny outpost of the ancient world, still the ancient world of guardian spirits and salt caravans, Oasis are, appropriately, his favourite band. And the football World Cup is beamed into Timbuktu as everywhere else.

In the bar, we drank a toast of cold beer, dew of condensation beading the glasses, to my mother, the news of whose death came to me this day a year before. Appropriate, I'm happy to say, to her quirky sense of humour that we should be at the fabled end of the earth remembering her in her resting place way beyond the earth.

Simon had bought a curved knife in a camel-leather sheath from Hamed, one of the Tuareg loitering around the hotel.

It had belonged, he said, to his grandfather, and he regaled Simon with its history. He didn't want to sell it but had no choice, and tears welled in his eyes as, for the last time, he fingered the pommel, a shiny nut of ebony in which was set the silver roundel clasping the tang of the blade. Sixty pounds and the knife changed hands. Simon said he felt sad taking it from him, but Hamed needed the money and the knife would always be a treasured possession. Next, a young lad sidled up touting a musical instrument. 'No thanks,' said Simon. 'I've already got three.'

Ben actually did buy a curious object, too crude really to be called an instrument: a thumb piano or *kalimba* – a box with a sound hole across which extended four thin strips of springy metal, each like the twanging tongue of a Jew's harp. On this dubious item, he was soon pinging out the first seven notes of 'Twinkle, Twinkle, Little Star' . . . again and again and a-bloody-gain.

Getting ready for our departure, I attempted to realign my back brake, a touch dislodged during the truck ride. Ben, expedition mechanic, watched me fumbling and said, in that faintly pitying tone of the expert disparaging the bungler's ham fists: 'Let me do that. You do what you're good at – go and pay the bill.'

If we hadn't ridden into Timbuktu like the 7th Cavalry, we did, at least, ride out in some style. First, we did the tourist thing and got our notebooks stamped with the official Tombouctou seal at the Post Office. There, too, we bought stamps for our cards – stamps incongruously emblazoned with *Star Wars* characters. So much of abroad has been shrunk by marketing. In the tourist season, the Post Office does brisk trade with the German tourists who fly in, grab a cab, dash round the town, video the sand, bat off the camp Tuareg cadging cigarettes or custom, eat a meal and queue up for their Tombouctou stamp . . . they and the inevitable Japanese tourists, togged up like moonwalkers in face veils, hats and gloves against the sand. Timbuktu has become just another destination for photocall, notch on the foreign travel tally and scoot back to safety when the plane has refuelled. Whether it be cycling to a col or the end of the earth, there is a vanity in reaching somewhere remote on two wheels. Being overtaken by sleek motorbike or saloon adds to the satisfaction of getting there by pedal power.

Riding away from the Post Office to rejoin the *African Queen* at Korioumé, my water-bottle cage came loose, and I stopped to fix it while the others rode on. I set off after them, flat out. It took an age to reel them in, and then I realised: they'd given it all they'd got to give me a race. I caught them, flew past mouthing ebullient imprecation and belted it all the way to the river, and there was the boat, the captain and crew, beaming faces, pleased to see us, probably amazed to see us.

Simon arrived ten minutes later, shattered, poached and gasping, and plunged into the Niger, fully clad. He peeled off his T-shirt to wash it but lost it in the swirl, even as the captain called out in the local lingo, Bambara, to 'cast off aft'. Cruising away, we watched a young boy diving for the shirt. On the third attempt, he popped up, gleeful, T-shirt in hand. We waved: may he have joy of it.

3 August: my birthday
I woke to Ben and Simon warbling 'Happy Birthday' greetings at first light. In my bag, I had a card from Lindy. Before opening it, the boat had to be shipshape: despite Ben telling me I shouldn't be doing jobs on my birthday, I tidied away, cleaned and reorganised, clearing the decks, and then sat amid the new order and opened the envelope and slid from it the card. It seemed so loving, that message, but only seemed, alas. She was somewhere else; I was somewhere else. Then arrived,

by Pinasse Mail, the small brown envelope made of a strip of cardboard peeled off a box, addressed to:

FIFE
AFRICAN QUEEN RIVER NIGER MALI
W. AFRICA
URGENT DELIVERY
From the passengers and crew of *African Queen:*
Simon. Ben. Captain. Chief Cook. Petty Officer.

The captain had signed with three parallel horizontal lines, Djal with a circle struck through with two horizontal lines, Lal with a cross. The picture was of the pinasse, Ben roasting nicely on the roof, Simon by the bikes in the prow, me inside, captain and cook in the stern and the petty officer peeing off the back. They sang 'Happy Birthday', and I felt as if I'd won a prize. The captain beckoned me over so that he could stamp the envelope with his blue rubber seal, like a franking mark.

That afternoon, we beached back in Mopti.

Next morning, I strip-rolled the birthday-celebration hangover out of me into the tarmac, a ten-mile gut-buster. Dreadful. Simon stuck to my wheel like conscience. We got to the airport by 8.30 a.m. to be told that the flight due to arrive some time that morning would be going to Timbuktu, or else the pilot would decide where it was going, but back to Bamako at some point, oh yes. Probably.

'When is the plane due?' I asked. I was told 10 a.m. There was no conviction in any of this. The airport terminal was a shabby, run-down, hollow shack that must have been a hangar once. A collection of chairs and settees that looked as if they were on display for a fourth-hand furniture auction adorned the lounge, along with a tiny bar and an unattended table which served as the check-in desk.

I staked our claim for seats with an official in a suit who was wandering about the place meditating on vagaries of inaction, lack of information and the strictures of his job, which was to cope with the irritating infestation – growing steadily – of passengers. He answered my questions without enthusiasm, concern or confidence. I concluded that he had to be kept an eye on. If anything did happen, he'd be the man on the ground providing whatever liaison Mopti airport ran to.

We whiled the time away; time we had, and we spent it on nothing.

At about 10.30, the twin-engined Fokker 28 landed, the captain strode into the terminal with a sheaf of paper – flight details, presumably – and I introduced myself. We shook hands, he introduced himself: Jean-Claude, friendly, relaxed and pleased to talk. 'Make sure they put your bikes in the cabin,' he told me. He was half-Mauritanian, half-Malian, spoke good French, excellent English, the man who knew the skies of Mali.

They did indeed insist on our putting the bikes in the cabin, in passenger seats at the rear: such reverence for the beautiful machine was wholly touching. We took a photo, of course. As soon as the bikes were installed, I was summoned back into the terminal building. Our man wanted to see me. He scowled. 'Do you think this is the right way to behave?'

I wasn't aware of any indiscretion or high-handed behaviour. I'd confirmed our telephone reservation, paid cash for three tickets at the price he'd demanded, told him we had bikes. So what now? What now was the bikes.

'You didn't say anything about bikes.'

'I *did* say anything about bikes.'

I walked out and boarded. The plane took off, and, as it flew across the landlocked desert, 'no smoking' signs ranged round the cabin and the stewardess went through the emergency precautions: 'In the unlikely event of our having to ditch in the sea, please extinguish all cigarettes.'

Cabin service was a plastic mug of water from a bottle, in-flight entertainment a free Malian newspaper, *L'Essor*, which means flight, a soaring (of a bird). On the horoscope page, I read this, for me: '*La tendance est propice aux investissements dans l'immobilier.*' (A good time to buy a house.) I needed somewhere to live, I had a certain amount of money, I had not the first clue where I would begin my search for a house, but here were the spirit voices of the dazzling Malian star circuits urging me to buy my house. Two months later, to the day, I bought the house where I write this.

When the stewardess announced that we would be landing in Tombouctou in a few minutes, I tingled with pleasure. Four days earlier, we had ridden out of Timbuktu, but here was further sign of the mystery: Timbuktu would not let us go. She added that the temperature outside was 35°C. We would be on the ground for only 30 minutes, to let passengers off and take on more. This is the usual way of visiting the place: flying visit to the sandcastle.

I was determined to get off the plane; the stewardess said it wasn't allowed. I stood in the doorway and gazed across at the terminal building. Under a canopy was gathered a large crowd, among them Sankoum and Oumar. Regulations be buggered. 'I need to go and say hello to our friends,' I said and was off down the steps, followed by Ben and Simon. Our Timbuktu buddies greeted us like old friends, and, in the way that time seems to expand in this place, old friends we were, friends of improbably long date.

We said goodbye again and went back to loiter by the plane. Standing on the tarmac, we chatted to the captain. It was all very laid-back. He'd probably have let us fly the plane if we'd asked.

'This is a beautiful flying machine you've got,' said Ben.

Jean-Claude shook his head. 'No, it's not. It's old, it's decrepit and it's not good in heat. Above 30° . . . very risky.'

(The temperature, remember, was 35°.) He hadn't a good thing to say about the poor old Fokker.

'Did you pay extra for the bikes, by the way?' he asked.

'No,' I said.

'Ah . . . I'm so glad.'

That second visit to Timbuktu was perfect, because so unexpected and so much a seal on the astonishment of the first one. The night before, in Mopti, the owner of the pinasse, Mohammed, had arranged a performance by local singers and musicians, part of my birthday celebrations, which I'd recorded. It had been exuberant, huge fun, and its intense excitement had delivered a pure full-proof shot of *joie de vivre*. When I'd first set out for Africa, I'd been aching for a renewal of joy, on the brink of accidie, that deplorable state of near-suicidal collapse condemned by theologians as mortally sinful despair. The visit to Mali had precipitated me into the spiritual vacuum, a dreadful null and void. The experience of Timbuktu had begun the cleansing of mind and spirit: in that brief time there, I'd reconnected the slender armature which links energy to need. Now I had something, a small something, on which to rebuild – the reality of the place that is, to many people, a symbol for Nowhere.

It was, I told Simon, an experience I would not have missed and one that I was in no haste at all to repeat. My feeling is that such experiences are an absolute privilege. The ride to Timbuktu had tested us all in different ways. For my part, I salute the uncomplicated friendship and support of my two cycling companions in helping me through. This fraternity of the two wheels is, indeed, unique.

I sold the hybrid bike I had bought for the expedition to a local man for the same that I had paid for it, and we flew home.

***

Going back to the Pond in the lull between the return from Mali and the move to the new house in Kent, I was greeted by an American friend: 'Hey, haven't seen you for ages. Where you been?'

'Timbuktu.'

'Timbuktu? Doesn't exist. Where is it? Wisconsin?'

Apparently the thing about Wisconsin is that it's east of Pittsburgh and west of Seattle.

Postscript

The BBC did buy the radio programme. I had presented the editor with a rough cut of my recordings and interpolated commentary put together in the downstairs loo at Simon's house in Oxfordshire . . . thus giving an entirely new definition to the epithet 'bog-standard'.

Thirteen

Atlantic to Mediterranean

The long open balcony of the Boulevard des Pyrénées in Pau affords one of the best long-distance panoramas of the central ranges anywhere, all the monsters, capped in snow, brimful of altitude. Pau itself is a gracious town, and the Saturday market is a very boom of good things to eat, drink and, in the growing season, plant. The Duke of Wellington's army took some overdue leave in Pau on the march north to Paris at the end of the Peninsular War. Their compatriots followed, and there was soon a sizeable English colony in residence, with, one presumes, a tidy complement of retired generals, clergy and remittance men. They imported fox hunting, built a golf course – the oldest in Europe outside Scotland – and Pau came to be known as 'Englishville'. A good place, therefore, to have an eccentric idea, Pau. And, one day in 1951, an old French *cyclo-touriste* was polishing his rims in his garage in Pau, or fettling his rear mech on the kitchen table of his house in Pau, or maybe sitting in a favourite bar in Pau, flicking through a picture album of what the French call 'the epoch', the good old days, and had an eccentric idea.

The Tour de France, he decided, had gone soft since the epoch, when men were men, the race was to a hardy few and bikes were a no-nonsense diamond, two wheels, saddle, bars, bean-pod front brake and not much else. In the good old days (1919–29), they did the Pyrenees – the whole range – in two stages: Bayonne to Luchon; Luchon to Perpignan, back to back. That's what you call a decent test of a rider. In a fit of nostalgia laced with the kind of sadomasochism which is the norm in such individuals who routinely attach 'good' to 'old days', he persuaded the local Cyclo Club Béarnais to institute the Raid Pyrénéen. Thus, a cross-Pyrenees ride, from Hendaye on the Atlantic coast (a few miles from Bayonne, traditional rendezvous for the early Tours) across the river from Spain to the border town of Cerbère on the Mediterranean, down the coast from the Tour port of call, Perpignan: 710km, 18 cols.

The Tour riders completed their first leg, 326km, including Aubisque, Tourmalet, Aspin and Peyresourde, in as little as 14½ or up to 17+ hours, depending on the weather, which can be foul. In the 1926 Tour, the longest ever, 5,745km in 17 stages, Stage 10, Bayonne to Luchon, served up a horror. The rain started near the foot of the Aubisque, then a dense yellow fog settled over the mountains: visibility, nil. The roads were awash with glacial rain and layered with gluey mud; the wind howled at gale force; bursts of lightning exploded behind the mist like incendiary shells. Engulfed in this Dantesque scenario, some riders slogged on as best they could; others had not the stomach for such madness and abandoned their bikes in doorways. The Belgian, Lucien Buysse, pressed on doggedly and eventually shook off a small group of equally spirited obdurate types to cross the Aspin alone. He rode into Luchon, unrecognisable beneath his carapace of mud, with 25 minutes on the Italian Bartolomeo Aymo and over an hour on the surprise of the day, the Frenchman Tailleu (his first name is lost) riding his first Tour. The Italian Ottavio Bottechia, winner in 1924 and '25, frozen stiff, wearing a coal sack as a make-do impermeable, rode straight off the mountains to the station at Bagnères and caught the train home. At midnight, 47 of the 76 riders still in the race – 126 had left Paris – reached the long tree-lined Allées d'Etigny into Luchon. Cars and vans set off to sweep up the other survivors stranded in the mountains. One of the rescuers later complained bitterly to the Tour officials: 'It's scandalous, a disgrace. I brought back 12 riders in my bus and they haven't paid me. Thieves, every one of them.' Only 41 made it back to Paris. Buysse (who took both Pyrenean stages and consolidated in the Alps) won overall; Frantz, the winner in '27 and '28, was second, Aymo third and the plucky Tailleu eleventh.

The second leg, 323km, took the pedalling mudlarks laden with all the clothing, food, drink and spares they might need, on their heavy, under-geared machines, between 13 and 14 hours.

The Raid rules, pandering to modern sensitivities, fixed the time limit for the whole chain at 100 hours. The French word *raid* was borrowed from our English word in 1864. This was for many years synonymous with *rád*, the Anglo-Saxon for road, and described a military expedition on horseback, a hostile and predatory incursion, pre-eminently the looting raids carried out by the lawless Steel Bonnets of the Anglo-Scottish Border Marches. Those bellicose folk, the reivers, were, by cynical reputation, 'Scottish at will, and English when they choose,' and gave the language *blackmail* – literally 'forced tribute or rent', protection money squeezed out of local farmers – long before the Mafia hoods set up the rackets in Chicago and New York. The French adopted 'raid' for an endurance test – of men and the materials that made up whatever vehicle they rode or drove.

There are some ingrained purists – Paris–Brest–Paris (PBP), End-to-End, Coast-to-Coast types, etc. – who will say that because having to get up each morning after a particularly brutal beasting the day before and then motivate yourself for yet another 150km over the mountains is so outlandishly wretched, far better to make it easy on yourself and do it all in one go, without stopping. Some of them do ride the Raid non-stop. One of my acquaintance, the otherwise friendly and inoffensive Australian Steve Wessel, assures me that the dead-and-alive feeling I had once at the end of a 150km ride through the Pyrenees, with outsized saddlebag, over three big mountains, was quite as bad and debilitating as what happens through the PBP. It just lasts less time, he said. As reassurances go, this, it has to be said, is no great reassurance, nor am I in any haste to test the analogy, for I am no purist of that extreme-endurance stripe. No stranger to brutal beastings, I also crave an ample slice of social after a day's worth of serious bodily and mental abuse on the bike. Thus, when Nick and Jan Flanagan, convinced social animals themselves, invited me to join their inaugural Pyrenean Pursuits Raid, I said 'yes' cheerily, nay blithely, and thought no more about it. Until I got the itinerary.

You always think you've done enough training, but lack of training, like the width of the waistband, has a very brisk way of acquainting you with the solid bulk of truth.

Four and a half days, eighteen cols, 710km. That's it. As soon as you leave the hotel in Hendaye where you get the first official Raid control stamp in the carnet, the clock starts running down. There are eight fixed controls along the route, and always the possibility of the organisers staging what was a regular feature of early Tours, a random spot check. One of Desgrange's officials – each of them, one imagines, hand-picked for utter indifference to mortal suffering and a deranged fanaticism honed to rabid inflexibility by a diet of iron filings – might leap out of a canvas booth in the swirling mist on a col waving a rubber stamp. The riders had to hold out their wrist, like a disco clubber, to get the ink tattoo. This didn't happen to us, fortunately. Given the effects of the thin air, the heat and tight nerves, there might well have ensued an altercation or profane comment at the very least.

The four of us who were booked to do the ride – Phil, Simon, Tim and I – met at the Flanagans' Guest House for Cyclists in the Massat valley, along which the 1997 and '98 Tours had passed. We did a couple of warm-up rides, and, as the others discussed the route animatedly, I listened and kept my counsel. Talking a route is a bit like talking about sex: fanciful, prone to exaggeration or misconstruction, a very long way off the real thing. I had what may have seemed to the others to be an advantage in that I had ridden most of the cols in prospect. I saw that differently, of course. I'd crossed them at rather more sedate intervals of time and intervening distance and was in a pretty alarmed state. There was nothing to be done about my training now – I was 54 years old to their mid-30s and further deterred by a 10-day lay-off (a touring holiday in Andalusia with Lucy) which restricted me to psychological stiffening – i.e. pretending I was tough – in lieu of putting real miles into my legs. Lucy and I had flown back from Madrid on a Saturday, I'd ridden 100 miles across Kent the next day and flown out to the mountains on Tuesday, my mood oppressed, my tongue stilled, my spirit unleavened. Even Aussie Steve's recommendation of liquid yoghourt as sustenance for the sapping long ride felt like short commons as a backup for what might be terminal ill-preparedness.

Hendaye: Sunday evening
Tim and I swam off the Hendaye beach in the Atlantic rollers, the others looked on and, when we came out, we were joined by a sinister creature – arguably female – who slunk up in a queer pink tartan outfit, loitered about somewhat unnervingly as we got changed and seemed more than passingly interested in my lower musculature. I avoided eye contact.

Monday morning

The Campanile chain of hotels cannot boast anything like personality, and the laminated menus tell the dull story: same choice every meal in every Campanile hotel across France, but they do lay out a terrific buffet breakfast. We packed in as much cereal, yoghourt, fruit, cakes, croissants, bread as we could. Eat before you're hungry, drink before you're thirsty and when offered easy pickings by a hotel, grab them. I pocketed a week's supply of sachets of the best hot chocolate outside Salamanca and Madrid.

At 9.30, cleated and clotted, we trooped into the foyer to get our carnets stamped by the guy at reception. All along the route, proprietors of cafés, bars, newsagents, restaurants, hotels, who've seen a thousand Raiders, reach for the stamp and do the business without a second glance.

Once the ride was on, I felt instantly better, for, like the Sundance Kid, I'm better when I move, and I had found the wait foully unnerving. Get the wheels rolling, breeze in your face, sun in your eyes and the spirits soar, as if at last the bike has its chance to take some of the brooding pressure off your mind. Also, I did have that secret booster in my locker: the liquid yoghourt. Magic stuff. Like Popeye's spinach. Driving like a team-car *soigneur*, Nick, ex-racer from Liverpool, followed – or preceded – us with limitless stocks of water, energy bars, juice, bananas, lunch makings, hot coffee and tea.

Into the Basque cols, a couple of humpbacks, the Col Saint Ignace 169m out of Ascain and a quick flip across the border near Ainhoa into Spain – Simon had never been to Spain: there was the frontier post, we made the detour (20m), had a pee and rode on over another titchy col, the Pinodeita, 176m, and down into the first control at Espelette, where the locals have a red-pepper festival every summer. They adorn all the houses with fresh scarlet capsicums, and not a few houses have frills of dried (or artificial) red peppers hanging from their eaves and sills all year round. It's a Basque thing, red being their traditional colour – a tradition which ETA assassins have for too long perverted into a sanguinary fixation.

We were rather preening ourselves on the hot sun and the fine form we were showing, when a dissenting voice – mine – interposed, like that of the celestial timekeeper, pointing out that it was almost noon and we'd done only 46km of that day's allotted 140km. Phil, who not only hadn't ridden this distance before and never a single col and thereby showed extraordinary courage (or foolhardiness) in taking on both at a swoop, nodded pensively and reached for another banana. We remounted, and, in no time, Simon and I were caning towards the Pas du Roland with delicious abandon. Along this defile, said to have been cut in the mountains by the paladin's sword, we did an evens 25, at one point passing under a great flock of buzzards – 200 by all estimates, every buzzard in the mountains wheeling overhead. A bit early in the ride, I mused, for the vultures to be eyeing the potential carrion, but they obviously knew that if it were cyclists involved in the raw buffet they'd have a hell of a fight on their talons.

From the Col d'Osquich, 500m, a known gathering point for big birds of prey, stretched wonderful views north over a broad plain. From its summit, with 29km to go, Phil and Simon took off in close pursuit of a couple of motorbikes and overtook even as Tim swished after them. I love the buzz of that kind of mad devilry but, fretting about punctures, rolled down way behind. I think I have probably never been a descender of any more than moderate skill except in the sudden rush of the moment when a rasher competitive streak takes over – memory still pricked of hurtling down precipitous Salt Box Hill into the trough below Biggin Hill when my front tyre blew. It was a touchy experience, trying to hold on to a bike going from a straight plummet at around 60kph to slithering about on loose rubber in front of a line of cars. When I asked

Sean Yates, a noted reckless downhiller, if he had always been a good descender, he answered with that pragmatism which is the hallmark of the true pro, in any sphere: 'I don't know.' Not being a very fast climber, he simply had to get fast – bloody fast – on the descents to limit his losses.

A few kilometres from the finish, we topped a little sod of a climb that the organisers don't tell you about because it isn't a named col. We passed a small knot of what looked like a patrol of German Alpenkorps on mountain bikes, backs bowed under rucksacks. Had they not heard of pannier bags? We swept over the hill onto a valley road that made some of the dodgier strips in south London feel like fresh-laid tarmac – the sort of surface that could easily turn the contents of your testes into a milkshake.

First night stop (swimming pool adjacent) in a converted coaching house, run by a flamboyant hostess who greeted us with warm smile and manner. She sashayed into the galleried hall at supper in a flame-coloured full-length gown, matching her lip gloss. Her startling presence in such *fin de siècle* operatic finery had an incongruous slightly melancholy aspect. She was, in this backwater of rural France, like the village belle dreaming of the Paris boulevards, the cabaret singer booked by the manager of a works canteen who turns up to find that the café-concert has been cancelled. Had she come to impress the clientele? The clientele were concentrating ravenously on the food: lashings of garbure (country-vegetable soup); salmon steak in hollandaise sauce; salad; potato omelette; large bowl of pasta; cheese; and either ice cream or Gâteau Basque. The five of us shared the dining room, a large inner courtyard roofed over in glass, with a chapter of elderly leather-clad Dutch bikies who'd roared in on Harleys like a lost patrol of unfrocked Hell's Angels.

Second day

What had looked like an easy enough 30km towards the foot of the Aubisque turned out to be the kind of warm-up ride the late Eddie Soens might have devised. Nasty little hills through a sunscreen of woodland that go on at you like a scold, gradients that seem like nothing but worm their way relentlessly up between your lungs and your sense of humour. It didn't help, either, that this supposedly easy stretch was knocking the stuffing out of us before we even broached the main challenge: Aubisque, 1,709m, followed by Tourmalet, 2,115m, 132km in all. Jan, who is the mildest-tempered, most helpful of women, had, for some reason – of subliminal mischief or sheer oversight – originally included the Col de Marie Blanque in the Flanagan Raid. It was I, like W.C. Fields hunting through the Bible for loopholes, who spotted that the official Raid route did *not* include the Marie Blanque and its 10km worth of sheer misery. I've ridden it. I know about the Marie Blanque. Even the pros hate that one. In the opinion of Fernando Escartin: 'As far as these Pyrenean climbs go, I think the Marie Blanque is one of the hardest there is. It's only 10km long, but there are four or five kilometres that really make you suffer. You will need a 19 to 23 to get up this one. A 21 is no good.'

I broke the happy news at supper. We rode past it along the valley, glanced complacently up at the high wooded slopes where my friend Bernard Thévenet's defence of his Tour ended in 1976 and gloated on our good fortune. In an e-mail to me, Bernard recalled that dreadful day when, having come to the race as the reigning champion, he knew he was finished this time. As the road wound up through the trees onto the long curves of the higher plane in thinning air, the mist closed in, cold and damp, soaking into his enfeebled legs and tortured lungs. His season had not been going well:

At the start [in Leyden, Holland], I was in fair shape – I thought I would ride into form after a few stages. It didn't happen. I feared this col because I didn't know it, although friends had told me how hard it was. From the first slopes, I felt bad. I had no strength. I was incapable of rising to this hellish gradient. At the summit, in that rain which I hated, I must already have lost ten minutes. I couldn't believe I was so shattered. On that climb, I went through one of the worst experiences in my life.

He abandoned on the lower slopes of the Tourmalet next day.

The Aubisque is probably not, in the scale of things, exceptionally hard. That is not to say it's easy: even if a climb isn't cripplingly hideous, it is best not to judge too closely. Mountains command respect. Take mountains, all mountains, seriously. If you don't, *they* will take *you*. *That* is serious.

I waved the rest goodbye as we rounded the first hairpin off the main road heading for Spain and watched them forge slowly ahead. Phil, who knew I had done it and come back for more, had asked me what riding the Aubisque would be like. I recognised the symptoms. Of course, you can't ride the climb for anyone, nor can you reduce the trial of it, but friendly encouragement, just talking through the nerves, will help to quell the latent anxiety a bit. Statistics are only ever virtual, but from the valley out of Laruns to the summit is 18km. The real climbing starts around Eaux-Bonnes, with about 10km to go. At some point on any major climb, you will probably feel gruesome, dogged by a chilling sense that you are not going to make it, can't make it, never had the inherent power to make it. For such moments, be forearmed, forewarned that they will arrive. Remember, too, that many great climbers say they ride the mountains quickly because the sooner they get to the top, the sooner the agony abates.

The thing about mountains, the main thing, is that they seem to take for ever and, when you reach the col at last, all time slips away into the airy vastness of the valley you survey from the top: it is a transcendent experience, a link between physical and mental triumph and a wondrous exaltation of the spirits.

The old station of Eaux-Bonnes' hot springs has a faded grandeur, but just beyond it the real attack of the Aubisque launches on a ramp of surpassing steepness and into the switchback of hairpins which measure out the kilometres like a dwarf in lead boots paying out an iron cable. The ski resort at Gourette is as charmless in summer as any ski resort, like a faded movie star caught slumped in front of the dressing-room mirror in torn peignoir, her tired face caked with cleansing cream instead of make-up.

From Gourette, 6km to go, through wooded twists of road. When the treeline runs out, you know you're getting close. Think of them in the 1920s. As the founder of the Tour, Henri Desgrange, wrote of those early days:

> There is nothing in the world more hypocritical than the 1,709m of the Aubisque. Because one rolls out of Pau on deliciously flat country. Because, from the beginning of the climb, all the way to Eaux-Bonnes, there are 5km of a very beautiful road, mounting 'prettily'. It isn't till after Eaux-Bonnes that the treachery of this Aubisque declares itself. It is cruel, tortuous, frequently thick with shit when it isn't choked with dust and littered with stones.

At last, there's the summit and that feeling – familiar, now – of a unique relief. It's rarely what you'd identify as pain, although my back always suffers badly, or even fatigue; there is certainly not the rasp of lungs which comes from racing. More it is the gratitude, the shadow of incredulity, that you have made it, when so many kilometres took so long to disappear under your wheels, the stupendous sense that you're *there*, when you'd begun hardly to trust that there was such a place as a top, a line where the up becomes a down.

On the road, just below the summit, to the illustrious names of the Tour men painted there, some saddo had appended a lonely hearts (in French): 'Young man looking for a young woman for the night' plus telephone number. Perhaps he subscribed to the cliché that surmounting Pyrenean cols is on a par with mounting . . . but the analogy is tawdry.

As we stood in the car pull-off, bikes leaning against Nick's van, and stoked up on food and drink, the mood was bright. The views up there, in both directions, were sensational. We'd done 50km *and* the first monster col. It was but midday, and we faced another 82km, but most of them were downhill or undulating, albeit rounded off by the biggest, nastiest climb in what Tour mythology calls the Circle of Death, all the cols between us and the Peyresourde. Phil turned to me and said: 'Graeme, tell me that the Tourmalet isn't as bad as the Aubisque.' I reckoned instantly that if I told him the truth, he might well feel like packing it in there and then. I replied, blandly, that all mountains are different, they each pose their own difficulties, you can't really compare them. Luckily, he didn't press me on the point. He must have known I was ducking the issue, but nor did I want to bullshit. I asked him for some more Vaseline (his tip, to smear on the eyebrows to reroute the sweat away from the eyes round down the nose and cheeks), and we were off onto the spectacular Cirque du Litor, the corniche road cut into the great curved sweep of rock which drops 4km or so to the level and races round at speed to the 3km climb back up to the Col du Soulor, 1,464m.

A picnic party of Basques had set up a portable stove by the side of the col, making their conical cakes, built of spirals.

We rode past onto the long descent into Argelès-Gazost. On the final run-in, Nick clocked us at around 56+kph: what Boardman did for an hour round the Manchester track in 1996, which puts *that* particular achievement into some perspective.

The approach to the Tourmalet is always taxing, a long, long valley road, that day in extreme heat, into the gorge whose gradients are just enough off the level to feel increasingly harder. And then the mountain itself, which I had first ridden three years earlier.

The Gascons, not a people known for their timidity – think d'Artagnan – named the Tourmalet, in their tongue, 'a bad detour'. The 2,114m mountain forms part of the mighty Massif de Néouville between the Aure valley to the east and the Gorge de Luz to the west. The more obvious detour, the roundabout way linking the lower-lying towns and villages on either side, is a 60km loop via Lourdes. The direct route lies over the col. For the Gascons to curse the short cut is instructive. They knew as well as any *commerçant* that time is money and first and freshest to market is quickest to sell. Their wariness of the Tourmalet is a salutary warning that no great mountain is reducible to arithmetic of distance, gradients, averages, and the giant of the Pyrenees, more than most, defies such calculations. This is partly why the French call it *L'Incontournable*, 'The Unavoidable'. To any cyclist clapping eyes on it for the first time, its power of intimidation is staggering.

For the record, the statistics read: from the west, via Barèges, starting at Luz-Saint-Sauveur, 18.3km, height gained 1,450m, at gradients which, most of the way, oscillate between 7 to 9%. Some of the gradients smite you like rank injustice. Yet, how can abstractions of number frame the onset of reality – accumulating fatigue and the extreme mental stress, the need, somewhere between god and guesswork, to keep going?

It begins with that mere sight of the mountain. Not just the first time, which registers a sort of bewildered disbelief, but every time. Most starkly from the west. As the road approaches the Pont de la Gaubie over the Escoublous torrent, the view of the mountain ahead is stupendous, shocking, formidable. Confronting you across the big curve in the road stands a huge buttress jutting out with a road carved into its flank at a giddying angle. Beyond it, reaching into the haze of distance, more and more rock. The first time I saw that long scar cut into the cliff, I thought: 'Can't be a road,' . . . then saw a car driving up it.

From this point, and you know it because of course you have done the calculations, there remain nearly 7km to the col. When Brian Robinson rode the Tourmalet in the Route du Sud, at the start of a brilliant and, for the Britons who followed, an inspiring career in the Continental *peloton*, he looked up at the vastness of the mountain so far off, so far overhead and, seeing winks of light, couldn't think what they were. Then, with a lurch in his stomach at the implication, he realised: they were flashes of the sun reflecting off car wing mirrors.

The Tourmalet is not only the highest col in the Pyrenees, it is the mountain most visited by the Tour de France. For that reason alone, riding it at least once is obligatory for any serious student of the alchemy of suffering on two wheels.

I had gone ahead onto the climb itself. My compadres were inclined to stop too often for my liking. One of them dismounted every hour for a complete rejig – shoes off, shakedown, check contents of rear pockets, rearrange disposition of balls, scratch fugitive itches . . . I plugged on and was, inevitably, overtaken and on my own again, behind the ride. As the heat began to drill into me on the bare road skirting the basin below the first of the many long stone ramps flying up into the thin air, I hit that mental blockage that always lies ahead somewhere: mind starts to ramble . . . not going to make this one . . . running out of strength . . . no way, no way, no way. This is the moment when your willpower's central control has to go out in determined search of the off-duty units absent on tea break, training course, or compassionate leave (shell-shocked from the Aubisque?) and dragoon them back – emergency, all hands to the pumps. The wavering mood will pass, and when it does, you will be perhaps a kilometre on.

Nick had parked near the café below that long steep ramp, and as I rode up, clearly wobbling, he called out: 'Graeme, do you want to stop?' I shook my head and whispered 'No', because I knew that if I did, it would be ten levels of torture to get back on the bike and recommence. Better to stay in the hard place and ride out the other side. Every pedal turned takes metres off the ride: the final quotient is all that matters, not the intervening arithmetic.

There is always a glorious jubilation as you ride up the final slab of the ascent – it is, of course, extremely unpleasant – and, this day, not to have succumbed to the Tourmalet. Nick levelled his camera and took a more mundane sort of photo finish, and there was the famous summit café for a celebratory drink. They keep a box full of newspaper ('Cyclists, help yourselves') – what Tour riders in the past took from spectators to stuff up the front of their jerseys to keep out the chill wind on the fast descent. All that was left was the long fast roll past the hideosity of La Mongie, which would look ugly even round the Elephant and Castle, to the night stop at the gîte on the site of the forge where Christophe welded up a new set of forks in 1913.

The local folklore tradition – originally for putting a hex on interlopers – is to park *mounaques*, large stuffed dummies, male and female, outside houses, seated at tables, leaning out of doorways, clagged onto window sills, seated by gates . . . unfortunately, a couple of them had been stuck inside the gîte to run it. There were regulation slippers to wear along the regulation corridors, regulation chapel pegs on which to hang regulation door keys, a complex regulation number of things not to do, an equally complex regulation number of things to do and a regulation alignment in the garage for the regulated parking of bikes. The regulation proprietors served, if that is the word for graceless delivery to cheerless table, a supper that wouldn't have filled a dormouse on a diet and crept about in open-toed sandals, their faces clenched in Creeping Jesus expressions of nauseating ingratiation. In fact, for my money, they couldn't have ingratiated themselves on vouchsafe of a free service for the bike and a buckshee bottle of Bollinger apiece.

When we asked for another carafe of wine to supplement the single (regulation) carafe they had grudgingly provided, the woman said they hadn't got any more wine. I detected in her eyes – so lifeless they might have been made of glass – a flicker, just, of embarrassment. There ensued a muffled argument in the kitchen – her berating her other half, who had sent her out to call halt on our Trappist festivities. She eventually emerged with some more wine and a smile she kept on a hook by the door.

The place ought to have been rich in atmosphere – walls lined with old photographs and the spirit of Christophe, and there was still a faint aura about the place, but Mr and Mrs Gumboil had done their best to stifle it, reducing it to the level of a '50s youth hostel. As for a '50s youth hostel, believe me, you don't need to know that badly. There are some who like heartiness and woollen bobble hats, jovial types claiming, with an idiot grin and a guffaw, to be mad, scoutmasters and the whole string-vest ilk. They make me shrivel, much as skin on custard used to make me shrivel.

Fourteen

Of Coffins and Bicycles

I wrote a story, 'Of Coffins and Bicycles', for Radio 3 about the composers Franz Suppé, a brooding, paranoid cove who, for much of his life, slept in a tailor-made coffin, and Ernest Chausson, who went for a bike ride with his daughter in the summer of 1899 in the country west of Paris. He crashed and was killed. Front tyre puncture.

When Phil rolled out his bike from the Sainte-Marie-de-Campan lodge next morning, the front tyre was flat – a sudden scary vision of a puncture on the descent of the Tourmalet . . . unless the pasty-faced loon running the doghouse had stealthily sneaked out and wreaked a condign nocturnal revenge on our extravagant unregulated consumption of his neck oil.

We braced ourselves for 164km and five cols: Aspin, 1,489m first, up to where the wild horses and cattle roamed, jostling car-bound tourists for snacks. Much amused when one woman, posing for a snapshot with a young steer, suddenly found herself playing at matadors. Silly cow.

I remembered the Peyresourde, 1,569m, from an earlier visit but could claim no special favours from it on such cursory acquaintance. That first time had been in light rain, with a saddlebag, and I had ridden it on the big ring. It seemed much harder this time. The others were dawdling about at the col, applying fresh layers of sunblock, tweaking shoe-clasps, munching sandwiches. Given that we had three more climbs to do and I am almost as crap on the downs as on the ups (sarcoidosis, age and dissipation have seen to that), I pushed on without stopping. Earlier on the climb, Nick had driven up alongside me and we'd chatted. I'd suggested that this stopping every hour was bloody nonsense: there was work to be done and I was not going to join the tea and embrocation break any more. I waited at the bottom in Bagnères-de-Luchon, and, once out of town, put the hammer down. About 24km on, I found Nick parked at the turn-off to the small road over the next two cols. I reined in, looked round: nobody there. Nick hadn't packed the small blackboard slate which shows riders in a break what time advantage they have, so he had to tell me the advance – about 20 minutes, apparently. There were climbs ahead: I decided to press on, and so began a weird experience. I know it wasn't a race, but we were all grown-ups: what was to stop me giving it a go on my own if I felt like it? So, I did and, romancing it or not, imagined my way into what the rider on the long lone break may feel. Certainly, I was reaching as deep into my physical and mental reserves as I had ever done, with the added frisson of being ahead, in the lead, one against three, a long way to ride and the growing thrill of being away, riding on the limit, because that's what you have to do, win or bust.

The Col des Ares seemed to go on interminably, even if it tops no great height (797m), but I was digging out all sorts of effort, exhilarated and full of riding. The country was an inspiration, too – one of the lush green pockets of these most beautiful mountains where the descending road swings its hips like a classy skier, all grace and speed, and, on the rise, constantly draws you on with hints of surprise round the next wooded corner, the seduction of secret views to glimpse between the tree cordons. Over the pass it went and plunged away in a sinuous run, dipping into the reaches of a lost valley, it seemed. The Col de Buret was a real treat: I really thought I had got my climbing legs at last, and there on the tarmac, in red daub, the countdown to Grand Prix de Montagnes. Through the village and I was heading for the Portet d'Aspet and the memorial to Casartelli, where we had agreed to stop for a group photo.

The first ramp of the climb is around one in six. Climbing legs? I might have been padlocked to a wheelchair. 'How much of this was there?' I thought, as I toiled exhaustedly up the precipice. And suddenly, there stood the white marble monument, which I had first seen two years before, on a visit with Lucy and Jan. It's a beautiful sculpture, and, for half an hour, I waited, lying in the shade next to it, soaking in the ambiguous tranquillity of that tragic spot. Sunshine and the dead racer's shade, the spirit of all who come this way. Nick drove up, reported the others far behind. I drank a pot of liquid yoghourt and decided to press on, after all. Tim later said that he had hardly felt the pedals as they rode up the rest of that hard climb. The gradient does even out, but the bracket seemed to be turning under its own power. There were other forces abroad. They certainly drove me the last 58km at exuberant speed to Saint-Girons and up the valley to Massat, where the day ended at Nick and Jan's guest house: a royal welcome, gargantuan feast, unregulated red wine and a tumble dryer for the freshly washed clothes, and Jan saying she was going to analyse the contents of my bidon.

Fourth day
The first 14km wind east from 650m up to the Col de Port, 1,249m, which I had ridden many times. Charlie Holland got stranded without spare tubes on his way down the Port in the 1937 Tour. The descent on the other side took us into Tarascon, past the prehistoric grottoes of Bedeilhac, refuge for

Cathars on the run. A Liverpudlian racer who was staying at the guest house joined us for the long fast haul up the valley to Ax-les-Thermes, and I made the grave error of matching his speed. I overextended myself badly on that ride and, leaving Ax after a lunch stop, entered the mild existential divagations of that peculiar phenomenon familiar to most cyclists: the *What possessed me to do this*? syndrome. The sun was hot, the road ought to have been untroublesome, but either my brake blocks were binding or I was hallucinating. I watched the others draw ahead and gradually began to cave in. I knew this climb from the other way round, and I had stared happily out of the train window once on the fabulous journey from Barcelona over the Pyrenees into France. But now I felt as if every particle of me, flesh, bone and spirit, was being stretched and pounded flat along the rising bed of those 18 dreadful kilometres. I was being overtaken by snails. At Hospitalet, a brief junction with Tim and Phil, who were doing some intermediate fiddling. I glanced at the carnet. It seemed to indicate that the col lay 15km ahead. This appalled me. At the rate I was going, I'd still be on this foul pass at nightfall. Nick said there were only 10km to go and joshed me. I snarled and said the carnet couldn't be wrong, could it? But there was no excuse for such surly back-biting.

I remounted and set off. The first gradients did nothing to encourage me, but, about 3km into the real climb, for no obvious reason other than the purging power of simply sticking at it, my brain cleared and I began to roll – not fast, but with something like fluency. And, even then, I saw the blessed sign: col at 6km. My heart lifted, I ignored the dizzying sight of another road shooting way off beam over the ridges into Andorra, which seemed, at first glance, to be where we were headed, and, at last, rode onto the Puymorens, a fairly shapeless col, no views from it and an abandoned warehouse like a drunk slumped forlornly by the roadside.

Downhill all the way to Bourg-Madame, a hard-riding 21km of gleeful vengeance on one bit of road for what another bit of the same road had put me through. *Now* I know what possessed me to do this, I thought, until we turned east and the gale blew up in our face. The next 20km were sheer misery – a combination of headwind and straight featureless roads which kept kicking away into a mean torment of hills. Fatigue bit into legs, willpower, elation. It became a cruel struggle to combat the darkening mood, and there was little to do but fight every inch of the way. Bourg-Madame stands at a bit under 1,200m, so the climbs from here up the ensuing Col de Lious, 1,345m, Col de Rigat, 1,488m, and Col de la Perche, 1,570m, spaced at around 6km, were nothing compared with the monsters we had surmounted, but they were punishing, horrible. Whatever else these rides do to you, they can introduce you to some interesting mental landscapes.

At Mont Louis, the calvary was over. The road smiled at last and cried out: 'Reward time, boys,' before hurtling off downhill Mediterranean-seawards all the way to Prades, cutting through ravines, roller-coastering over sharp rises into and out of villages, 36km of wild tarmac laughing uproariously with the breeze in its hair.

Fifth day
We had 82km to go. Nothing could stop us. Slowly, the pace gathered, and, an hour into the stage, we were flying: upwards of 48kph, bit and bit, exhilarated by the adventure of it, the whole four days behind us, letting rip in a fantastic salvo of strength and buoyant energy. On the ups and downs of the Mediterranean coast road, glorious views of the aquamarine sea far below us, we hit the niminy-piminy climbs with savage abandon: *We've* been up the Tourmalet, why're you midgets in *our* way? And, just after noon, we sprinted past the sign reading Cerbère, sat up and whooped as we swept down on

the momentum and pulled up outside the bar on the seafront, outpost of the Cyclo-club Béarnais. A couple of beers and into the sea and out again and lunch. A great feeling.

By way of the Pyrenees to Kent
I first rode the Col de Port, from the eastern approach, one early evening in May 1998. That was the long day I mention above. Working for a Dutch production company, I had flown from Barcelona to Moenchengladbach for a meeting, flown back, collected my bike, taken the train north to Ripoll, cycled on to Ribes de Freser and, next morning, set off for Massat. Collada de Toses, Col du Puymorens and Col de Port. Lindy had sold the flat and did not want us to live together. All my gear was in storage, I had very little money and I was going to lodge at the Flanagans' Guest House for May and June and write and write and write. As I rode up the early slopes of the Port, tired but, maybe perversely, liberated, the sun was hot, birds sang and my heart was full. A new departure.

I rolled up outside the house even as Nick emerged from the front door – almost a double-take on that first time of my arrival.

'We didn't expect to see you till tomorrow,' he said.

'Did you really think that, once I was on the road, I wouldn't get here?'

So began two months of gnawing discontent, a new friendship with Aussie Steve who came to stay, the rewriting of the Tour de France manuscript and the letter to Bill Campbell.

A week or so into my sojourn in France, I heard other guests arriving as I sat at my table in my first-storey room: the man speaking in a monotonous south London whine. This couple would be my companions at table for the next week, and I thought I was going to be hard put to it to socialise with them. We sat to supper; Nick brought in the food; we drank wine and essayed conversation. Within a few minutes, nasal drawl and prickly (temporary) expatriate were in animated discussion about books, he deliberating on Sebastian Faulks's *Birdsong*, which I had just finished and found unconvincing – an opinion which we shared – and, once more, a slovenly prejudice which made me blush innerly had been trashed. The prickliness came from being adrift, displaced once more. Geoff's twang came from Coulsdon.

On the Saturday, before going home, he and Gill brought a box of cakes from Saint-Girons for a farewell treat. I quipped from Pope's *Rape of the Lock* the line about 'great Anna! Whom three realms obey/Dost sometimes counsel take – and sometimes tea,'* and Gill said, casually: 'Do you know, I haven't read that since I was at school.'

They were my first allies in what became a new phase of my life, in Kent, and they continue to be fast friends, wonderfully supportive. Geoff will phone from time to time 'just to see how you are'. A latecomer to the bike, he is a member of the Old Portlians (Ports for short) Cycling Club, and through him, one summer down in Biert, I met another member of the club who has also become a great friend, Dave Hickman. Dave invited me to speak at the Old Ports annual dinner that autumn, and though the club practice of cross-toasting can be a bore, one of the Old Ports who had slept in the dormitory at the Lodge when I was there, stood and, with a fine sally of wit, said: 'I'd like to take wine with anyone who has seen our guest speaker naked.' This required my then girlfriend to rise, blushing, in company with a scatter of grinning voyeurs. She told me later, having been asked to give out the prizes, that she'd felt like the head boy's mother. 'More like the mature woman the head boy is looking forward immensely to going to bed with after supper,' I assured her. At another dinner where I had been invited to speak, one cross-toaster so hogged the

---

* Anna is Queen Anne (1665–1714) and she takes tea – note pronunciation 'tay' – in Hampton Court, then the principal royal palace.

early part of the show that one of the club men had to remind him that he wasn't that evening's guest speaker.

Those two months at the lodge in Biert in 1998 were a muddled time of unsated lust, mild depression, loneliness and creeping funk. Nick and Jan went off for a week with their two children to map out the route for a big charity ride that September (of which more later). I looked after the lodge and cooked and catered for any guests who happened to come, among them Aussie Steve. He was the first to read the revised text of the Tour de France book. I came downstairs to find him sitting at the dining table reading the last page. He looked up and said: 'Unlike any bike book I've ever read.'

'Oh,' I said. 'Is that good or bad?'

He beamed. 'Oh, *good.*'

Steve and I rode together in the short time he was there. Then I was back to riding alone, all the local cols, once over the Col de la Core, where a small string of riders from the Française des Jeux team passed me. The last man gave me a friendly wave – there truly is a fraternity of cycling which links us all. The ridge high above the Vallée de Massat gives a fine view north towards Carcassonne and south towards the beginnings of the main Pyrenean ranges. The two cols which give access – Crouzette to the west and Péguère to the east – dish out some of the most vicious gradients in the region. I've done the former twice, the latter three times, and I am happy in the knowledge that I am never going to ride them again. It's not always easy to renounce, but there are cases where it is. Nor will complaining always serve a useful purpose, while sometimes, as a release of mental toxins, it does. The stiff upper lip and 'play up, play the game' are relics of a race of men to whom emotional response was the unwelcome demon best kept firmly locked up in a closet. There is nothing to admire in that. Stiff upper lips in company with lots of stiff other things had their place on the battlefield and sundry associated theatres of action. To hell, I say, with all that.

I lived with two changes of clothes and an electric typewriter on loan. My library I supplemented with second-hand books, mostly French, from a shop in Saint-Girons to which I often rode, a fast thrash down the valley on shallow gradients and a return thrash back up. Saturday was market day. Any day made a welcome break from work. I love that road: I know it as well as any in the world. Riding back one day, the tar melting in broiling heat, I mused on the origin of the '*oui*' which was the northern French for 'yes' and the '*oc*' which the southern French, the people of the Languedoc, used. From the genitive and ablative forms of the Latin word '*hic*', I decided, '*huius*' and '*hoc*', crude vernacular as used by the household slave ('*verna*') with the masters. Suddenly, I found myself toppling over into the ditch – I'd lapsed into a grammatical reverie and veered off the road.

Three years later, I was riding that same road in company with the Old Ports to see a stage of the Tour de France go over the Portet d'Aspet. Breakfast: 6.30 a.m. The things we do to watch the Tour de France go through. At that time of the day, my digestive juices more closely resemble brake fluid. Eating at sparrow fart is a grisly business: chewing heated-up stale French loaf, toying with cold muesli, inhaling yoghourt . . . Outside, it was freezing, damp, misty, miserable, and we weren't even in England. We launched off into the fog. Halfway down the valley, only one bloke and I were left. He said not to worry, he'd blame me, and we flew on.

Of course, I did have that precious advantage over everyone else in any Old Ports bike ride: I knew the way. When the others caught up, the sun came out and we did the speed version of an Old Ports whip: 25kph, everybody in.

About 12km from the col, money started to change hands, the usual thing, and most of the party stopped off at the bar, figuring that they'd see the Tour glass in hand, whisk off back to Saint-Girons early for another beer to boost them back to the bar up the valley. There were the routine run-of-the-mill excuses: the freshly laundered Lycra getting sweaty, tyres picking up dust, metal fatigue . . .

When the club decided to ride the Raid in 2005, I seized the chance to do it again, with two of my dear friends.

I wrote up the ride afterwards as a diary, with a nod at the peerless Jerome K. Jerome, whose *Three Men on the Bummel*, following the glorious *Three Men in a Boat*, is a comic gem. Needing a change, the three men discuss possibilities:

"'I have it," said Harris, "a bicycle tour."

'George looked doubtful. "There's a lot of uphill about a bicycle tour," said he, "and the wind is against you."'

Me and Mountains

My first recollections of mountains, albeit the English and Welsh sub-Alpine variety, are of being wet, cold, tired and shouted at, whether as a Boy Scout (rain-sodden camping in the Lake District), an army cadet (military exercises on the rainswept Brecon Beacons) or a bumptious 16-year-old grammar-school boy at the Outward Bound Sea School in Aberdovey one February. We slept in bunks in unheated huts. At 6.30 a.m., the watch officer arrived, switched on the lights and counted one-two-three. If we weren't out of bed by three, the whole watch got extra duties. We pulled on shorts, vests, plimsolls, ran down to the parade ground, where we did 20 minutes' exercises, and from there to the bathhouse for a cold shower.

Thrown in with apprentices, police cadets, factory hands, young men not much older than me but already far more compact psychologically, streetwise and brisk with intellectual horseshit, I had a rough time. I brought it on myself, for sure: too angular, muddled, glib, cocky. Too different. I suffered miserably at the hands of one particular police cadet who ribbed, goaded and taunted me without cease. I took gloating satisfaction when, as he stood on the lip of a cliff, about to abseil down – we also did the climbing back up, which I was good at – his nerve went, his knees buckled, he gripped and ungripped the rope, and the gutless, blubbery bastard blubbed, chickened out and walked away. I didn't even need to catch his eye: he knew I'd seen. And, when I skipped over the side and danced off the rock slab away down to the bottom, he knew his brief tyranny was ended, crushed by what Shakespeare's despotic King John calls 'that idiot, laughter, . . . A passion hateful to my purposes'.

Our week-long expedition ought to have been a voyage on the school's clipper, but Greenpeace (I think) had borrowed it, and the boat had been impounded somewhere by disgruntled targets of their protest action. Instead, we went to the western Cambrian mountains and stayed in a refuge – bunks, stove and galley inside, loo and washing facilities outside. Also rain. We came back at the end of one day's trekking soaked through, got up next morning at 3 a.m. to pull on our wet clothes (disgusting) and set out for Cader Idris.

I'll never forget the magical sight of the mist swirling up from the valley bottom and spilling over the rim of the ridge like the quickening steam from Cerridwen's cauldron of regeneration. Ghostly vapour shrouding a part-obscured landscape of high summits silhouetted against a pale starlit night sky, the sinister dark abysms of the valleys below, their rivers and llyns haunted by kelpies. It seemed a Celtic faery realm. And, as a silver-bright sun brought up the dawn, we saw the great bulk of Cader itself, a prow of russet rock jutting out against the bright-blue morning sky. That must have begun it, the bewitchment of mountains. At the time, I was too much caught up in other things to register it, but the wonder and shock of mountains that has caught me again and again since surely stems from the enchantment of those early experiences in Wales.

I skied in the French Alps with Lucy three times in the '90s, and, staring out across the majestic snowbound perspective of spines and pinnacles, sun glinting off their ice coating, or shooting down the turns of the runs into the valley drops, I found myself being steadily lured to the momentous decision to ride them. I just knew it was something I had to do.

Shortly after my Alpine baptism on a bike, I wrote a piece for narrator and wind quintet based on my ride, into the full blast of the mistral, up and over Mont Ventoux. It contains the line: 'Mountains are rarely, if ever, finished with you.' Everything I have had to do with the geologies of altitude since has confirmed that truth. So when, in the early days of 2005, I was asked to write a big book about the Pyrenees (*The Rapha Guide to the Great Road Climbs of the Pyrenees*), I felt as if I had been preparing for such a job – privilege, rather – for a long, long time.

I drove the whole range end to end and north and south on my own to get a broad view, then individual sectors with my friend Nick for closer inspection and a growing familiarity with the variants in terrain and spirit of place. I took voluminous notes on cols, plateaus, towns, approach roads, topology, landmarks, buildings of interest, on anything that caught my eye. I wrote up detailed descriptions of climbs, gradients, distances, hairpins, road surface, tree cover, rock formations, views and panoramas, scenery, vegetation, rivers, lakes, gorges and gulches . . . memorably, on one narrow and very steep out-of-the-way col, the Spandelles, which branches off the foot of the Col du Soulor at its northern end, I drove up into snow on a remote high nowhere, pressing on as far as I dared, my hands clammy with fear, at one point along a ledge so constricted that I hugged the mountain wall as closely as I could, dreading the nauseous giddy pull of the sheer ice-encrusted precipice along which the offside tyres were crunching, inchmeal. I eventually nosed away from the exposed rock face into woodland on a flatter stretch of road, some 12km up the climb. Here I had enough space to turn the car round gingerly and brace myself for the edgy, terrifying descent back into the deep far off of the ravine.

In summer visits, I rode as many of the climbs I hadn't already ridden as I could. On my second Raid, with the Old Portlians, I rode most of the route by myself, taking detours to scout additional climbs, riding them one-handed as I talked into the recording machine. This so twisted and strained my entire frame that on the penultimate day, the marathon leg from Massat to Prades, I was in agony: running sore on my buttocks; right side, arm and leg in constant, throbbing pain; and, on what ought to have been the exuberant 30+km downhill off Mont Louis, my right foot joined the pain party as I squirmed and shuffled in the saddle in a futile attempt to find some relief.

In October 2005, Pete Drinkell, the photographer for the book, and I set off for the photo shoot. We began with a boisterous swim in the rollers off the Biarritz beach and a cheery reunion with my friends André and Françoise Darrigade in their bookshop at the top of the steps near the casino. Our itinerary was scheduled to take 11 days. I had planned every stage of the route precisely, factoring in the time Pete told me he would need for photo stops, hoping that we would encounter no snow. Thus when, on the first crossing of the Aubisque, a col we absolutely had to illustrate, the whole massif was obscured in mist, we had a problem: do we stick to the itinerary or delay overnight in hope of clear weather? I had pretty well decided but put the question to Pete. We agreed that we must go ahead as planned and gamble on securing the Aubisque on the last but one day of our return loop.

On the Route des Corniches, far to the east in the Ariège, we drove into a tiny hamlet called Appy. I had an idea. As you leave any French town or village, the sign shows the name crossed out with a red diagonal line. So, we had APPY and, with the deletion, *not* APPY. There followed SEIX . . . MONT . . . LES, and, as we headed back up the Arrens valley on the home run towards Pau, the Aubisque ahead, the skies loaded with sunshine, I spotted another sign for the collection. I stopped the car, and, so spontaneous had our complicity become in the work, I simply said: 'How far is it?' It was nearly noon, when the weather hereabouts tends to turn nasty over the tops if weather is going to turn nasty. Any detour was a risky frittering of time. Pete scanned the map: 'Half a k,' he said. Without a word, I swung off the road into a sleepy, flower-girt hamlet, and we got BUN *no* BUN.

The fogs fell on the Aubisque as Pete wound up the shoot on the Cirque du Litor, and he got one final, riveting, atmospheric shot of the restaurant on the neck of the col, far off, lit by a nimbus of magnesium-white sunlight with a horror-movie torn shawl of mist drifting across, before the horizon was blotted out and we headed for lunch in that very restaurant.

The Franco-Spanish frontier follows the main crests of the Pyrenees, from the low verdant hills of Basque territory in the west, where Lammergeier vultures fly, the pleated and interfolded spurs cloaked in trees, over the mighty bare-rock passes of the 3,000m-high central massif and the stupendous snow-tipped amphitheatre cliffs of the cirques de Lescun and Gavarnie. The range gradually dips through the gorgeous rustic wilds, forests and ravines of the Couserans in a long seawards descent to the vineyards of the Roussillon and the Vermilion Coast.

From 1910 to the mid-1920s, Tour riders crossed the entire Pyrenean chain in two massive stages: 326km and 323km. They called the daunting cols of the middle section, prowled by bears, the Circle of Death. Even the fearless Gascons called one col road – the shortcut to market in the next valley – Tourmalet, 'a bad detour'. This col, at 2,114m, marks a distinct cultural shift: from the proud Basques with their *pelote*, tugs-o'-war, fandango, dried red peppers and unfathomable language of the westerly half, to the gentler dances, songs and *demà* (in French '*demain*' – 'tomorrow', '*mañana*') attitudes of south-western France, the Languedoc or Occitanie.

The Occitans said '*oc*' for 'yes', their language closely related to the lyric tongue of the Provençal troubadours, also to Catalan, which Franco banned because it was threateningly nonconformist. Similarly, the sunkissed southern French – ever despised and mistrusted by the frosty northerners, the powerbrokers in Paris, who said '*oy*' ('*oui*') – lost out. But, along the eastern Pyrenees, you'll hear the '*oc*' on market days, in bars, town squares, at village fetes when they sing.

On one trip, I made recordings for a projected radio programme about the transhumance, when the cattle, sheep and goats are moved up from the winter byres to the high mountain pastures, an occasion for much jollity and *festa*. Talking to one old man who spoke Massatois, a local dialect of the Languedoc, I spoke to him in French and he replied in the old tongue, which I followed like the Catalan I knew from Mallorca.

As one of the big herds ambled into the village, the night before, I chatted to the little guy leading them in, a short, wiry, mustachioed individual wearing a blue pancake beret, shirt sleeves, braces and baggy-kneed corduroy trousers, stout boots. He paced his steady gait with a shoulder-high stave, absorbed in his day's work, no more than that, bringing the cattle in. I asked him about their day, where they had started from and when, had they stopped halfway – yes, to shelter from the worst of the heat – and was he glad to be nearly done for the day? He answered, nodded, smiled . . . no big deal. Then I said: 'Even so, you must be tired.' He looked at me briefly, smiled again and said: '*Toujours fatigué, jamais fatigué.*' Always tired, never tired.

The agriculture is as ancient as the songs. Herdsmen and shepherds still tend sheep and cattle on the high pasturage all summer, wary of bears (recently reintroduced), wolves, harsh weather. In the Second World War, such men acted as *passeurs*, guiding Allied airmen and young Frenchmen evading forced labour across the mountains into neutral Spain. Whereas smugglers dodged *aduanero* bullets and incarceration in the notorious Bayonne gaol, the passeurs, pursuing 'the road of freedom' dear to their hearts, risked German patrols and the hated French Milice. There are memorials to them, on one mountainside a tiny chapel. As the plaques record, 'They chose the chancy perils of crossing the Pyrenees for the honour of serving.' Many of them were caught, delivered to the Gestapo, and died during deportation for 'infraction': that is, infringing *French* law. Not surprising, their cussed independence. What had Paris – and now Vichy – ever given them? Taxes and gendarmes.

One hazardous route the passeurs took runs up the steep slopes from Aulus-les-Bains, one of several thermal spas snuggling in the Pyrenean valleys close to the frontier. Pete and I concluded our work on that memorable trip with a visit to the thermal baths at les Eaux-Chaudes on the lower slopes of the road that crosses from France into Spain over the Col du Pourtalet. Mineral bath, hose down with a power jet and sauna, followed by a relaxing half-hour in a beach chair inhaling the faintly sulphurous fumes (like bad egg) that are reckoned to be so good for the lungs and a general propensity to avoidance of stress.

The journey across the Pyrenees has many charms, not least in observing the glorious changing folds of landscape, the patterns of life – the faded grandeur of the spas, the bucolic rhythm of the remote villages. And, like the people who inhabit them, the mountains refuse to conform. They are by turns rumpled, jagged, long, petrified spines, huge cones, mighty shield bosses, and their valleys sumptuous cascades of variables of green leaf and moss and lea. Any adventure in these most beautiful and forbidding mountains is tough and exhilarating. Riding them, we marvel at their power to deter and to inspire, and laugh like kids on the last downhill away from them to the sea.

Lipstick and marshmallow

So, I'm cycling down the Otford Road, preparing myself for another session of retail dysfunction, when a red saloon screams up alongside, does an offside wheelie, shoots straight across my front tyre down a side road and screeches into McDonald's – presumably for a mad-cow burger and chips cholesterol shoot-up. Any closer and I'd have been a stain on the paintwork. There are some car drivers, it's quite apparent, who can't have their motor running at the same time as their brain – one or the other but not both simultaneously.

Now, I do try to avoid confrontation, but having narrowly escaped being chopped in half by a Ford Sierra, I thought something needed to be said. I collected myself and rode round onto the Big Mac tarmac as the car pulled up and the occupants got out. A man and a woman. Possibly. It wasn't easy to tell: they were wearing his and hers shell suits and face hair. I gave them a friendly wave to catch their attention and greeted them chirpily: 'Hello,' I said, 'you rather carved me up back there, nearly sliced me off my bike, ho ho.' I didn't catch the exact detail of the immediate response, but it was in the vicinity of negative. I said, 'Sorry, I missed that,' at which the driver – the nearer of the two to identifiably female – said: 'It was your fault, you were going too fast. You should look where you're going.'

What? I thought. Too fast? Does this imply that they glanced out and said: 'Ooh, look, cyclist. That'll be walking pace. Hang on, though: where's the bloke in front with the red flag? Ah, never mind, 'eave a left at 'im.'

My fault? I returned the unblinking gaze. I began to speak, hinting that the mitigating explanation for vehicular GBH

I had just been offered was straining logic just a weeny bit, didn't she think? Maybe we could discuss the matter, you know – in the interests of harmonious road sharing, live and let live, no hard feelings? At this point, the bloke, a double for one of those Bulgarian weightlifters who has melded with his bar-bells, clumped over and stuck his nose right in my face. Not the whole of his nose, there wasn't quite enough room in my face for all of it. He delivered a short speech. I translate: he put it to me that if I did not see my way clear to maintaining a judicious silence he would forthwith feel obliged and compelled to obstruct my organ of speech by forcibly introducing his clenched hand into the aperture much as a Dutch boy's finger into a leaky dyke, OK?

I paused. On brief but, I hope, mature reflection, I decided there probably wasn't much future in the conversation. We definitely stood either side of a language barrier here: I was talking joined-up English, he was paraphrasing the SAS manual on unarmed combat. So I smiled, remounted and set off to Sainsbury's after some cheap lipstick. You don't know about cheap lipstick? It's a real pig to get off, particularly after a too liberal proffer of neck linen at office parties. Also off glass. See, I thought I'd just slip back and scrawl a message on their windscreen in lurid pink gloss: *Have a nice day*. It'd be on there for months. Unfortunately, Sainsbury's don't sell cheap lipstick, not that I could find, anyway, though I did walk unwittingly straight past the marshmallows. I discovered later, from someone who is an expert in the like skills pertaining to urban survival – my daughter, actually – that if you open up a marshmallow and use the squishy inside bit, those mothers stick really well on glass. I could have left them a nice pink heart effect to look at.

Fifteen

Blazing Saddles

I'm on a flight to Pau packed with pilgrims heading for Lourdes, and it's a faintly indigestible experience. Their faces, young and old, wear a revivalist glaze. Happy-clappiness out of a bottle of holy face cream. Post-confessional serenity. The odour of sanctity smothers the pong of the airline air-freshener. I feel hemmed in by unremitting goodness and recall those Mormons who knocked at the door of the flat in Camden Town, starched smiles, teeth like wall-to-wall tiling, Sanforised suits. The leader asked me: 'Good morning, sir, and how are you?' and, before I had time to unburden even a scruple of the baggage of my angst, *Weldschmerz* and profound disquiet about the impossibility of infinite regress, he continued: 'We just called today to ask how you feel about world peace.'

'I'm for it,' I said and closed the door on their unctuous tendentious concern.

The atmosphere in this Bible-meeting cabin is as close as bad BO. We're flying through cloud nine of 'Closer my God to Thee' on a wing and a prayer, lots of prayer. I mumble garlicky obscenities to myself to keep the vampirish piety at bay and, after shuffling through passport control and retrieving my bag from the carousel, sit outside in pagan sunshine, glittering gold as Agamemnon's death mask, and meditate on fornication – rude, energetic, satiating sexual intercourse – to dispel the sanitised chatter of the pure at heart, the rustle of scripture, the prudish odiums of chastity, until Nick arrives to take me back to Massat for that summer's visitation of Americans.

Thing is, I know about Lourdes. I went there first in 1998.

While I was living with Nick and Jan in the Pyrenees, they were asked to plan the details of the route for a charity bike ride under the auspices of the Blazing Saddles, a freewheeling association founded in 1991 by Eamon Duffy, director of the National Council of the Blind of Ireland. Duffy had the idea of inveigling a motley bunch of cyclists to foregather in parts foreign and exotic, and there to pedal their socks off for the NCBI's war chest. The Blazing Saddles (hereafter Saddles) were born. The terrain would be varied, the itinerary always testing, the fund-raising bunch made up of all levels of bike-rider, but first and foremost good humour and a full heart were enjoined. For what discomfort in the saddle, blazing or not, can ever compare to the permanent trial of being blind? Moreover, the stars of the team would be the tandems, with a sighted pilot and a VIP (visually impaired person) in the engine room to force the pace. The Saddles rode their first tour in California in 1992, and since then, motivated by velocipedimania and a piratical way with sponsors, the outfit has raised around £200,000 a year.

On 4 September 1998, the Saddles wheeled out from Lourdes on the Expo '98 Challenge to ride some 930km through France and Spain into Portugal. Together with a young club cyclist, Chris Southworth, another friend of the Flanagans, I'd been jobbed in to ride as a safety marshall.

We met at Carcassonne airport, where Chris was hauled off to the local nick on suspicion of falsifying his passport photograph. He took the hour-long interrogation in good part, soothed in his comic bewilderment at such flagrant and unwarranted mistrust of his open nature by the attentive presence throughout of an extremely attractive female gendarme.

The Saddles, around 150 riders plus support team, gathered in Lourdes. The Tour leader, Sean Kelly – who hadn't bothered to shave his legs, even – has ridden for the NCBI since 1993, out of devotion to the Saddles' freewheeling cause and sheer love of the bike. Having won the Paris–Roubaix twice, the man is an adept at rut-jumping, cobble-dodging and all manner of rough-riding agility . . . bike-handling skills of preternatural balance. He has a trick of biffing empty cardboard boxes into the verge with a sideways flick of his back wheel and a grin at the tomfoolery of it. First morning in the hotel, Kelly sat down at Chris's table for breakfast. Chris looked across, flashed him a smile and said: 'Hi, I'm Chris, who are you?' Kelly's reply had that flavour of 'Are you kidding?' with ripe overtones of a rather pungent Attic sauce laced with brusque profanity.

The Saddles' chairman, Fergus O'Hagan, SC, of the Irish Bar, rode with us. (The SC stands for something abstruse in legal circles, although it might more pertinently refer to the Silk Cut of the weed to which he is addicted.) Fergus's robust commitment to long-distance cycling is famous, and he pursues, to use the word at its very loosest, an idiosyncratic fitness regime that leaves most so-called amateur gutbusters gasping. What precise ascription he would give to the word 'fitness' in the context remains debatable. Even so, and notwithstanding the man's desire to punish himself without mercy *in* the saddle *for* the Saddles, selfish puncture victims, heartlessly presuming on their chairman's sanguine temper, would quite offhandedly importune temporary loan of his front wheel, thus consigning him, all a-fret, to the padded smoking lounge of the broom wagon. He was ever, it goes without saying, bitterly reluctant to cede the loss of a few hours of athletic action in a baking sun on unforgiving roads, jostled by a *peloton* of certifiable lunatics. Yet, wedded as he is to philanthropic principle and selfless care for the less fortunate, his own native magnanimity won through. I passed his trim and trig figure (that is, from certain angles and with eyes narrowed, trim) at the foot of one climb, 2km of vicious 7% hairpins up a bare hillside into conifer groves balmy with resin and sun-roasted pine cones. He stood at the side of the road fuming – Silk Cut – as chief mechanic Fintan McGill loaded his now unrideable monocycle once more into the trailer.

I hailed him. 'You'll have been sorry to miss this climb, Fergus.'

'I was looking forward to it,' he replied, wistfully, 'but, as you know, I'm here on a scholarship from the Samaritans.'

(Incidentally, Fintan's adept wielding of toolbox, tyre-lever and monkey-wrench helped many a stranded Saddle out of a hole, and the man's grace under pressure never yielded to impatience or ill temper. 'Fling the bloody crate in the trailer, won't you, and let's get on,' he'd say, amiably.)

The chairman's Olympian reserve cracked but once. 'What's the Portugese for "thick as a plank"?' he asked me one day at the lunch stop. 'I'm going to snarl at one of these policemen and get myself arrested . . . I could do with a ride in a motorised vehicle.'

In the interests of keeping him at full racing peak, I bit my tongue and callously withheld the information.

On the first afternoon, Duffy and Alfie Acheson of the Garda, who joined the Saddles as motorbike outrider, levered Chris and me into a corner. Duffy narrowed his eyes and said: 'Listen.' We listened. Alfie looked on with that quiet authority that comes with an all-over shiny leather motorbike suit and a certain experience and forcible way with people who don't listen. 'We want you to take the hard men, as think themselves the hard men, that is, and give them a bit of a battering. They'll be reckoning they're hot, so it's your job to put a bit of cold reality between their ears. Do you see what we mean?' It was hardly worth our while to gainsay the proposal, so off we set in the direction of the Col du Soulor, west from Lourdes.

It was a pleasure to get out of the place.

Unless you have a perverse taste for the grotesque, the maudlin, the lurid, for pietistic excess and the kind of canonical trinketry and consecrated kitsch for which the Roman Catholic Church has a particular fondness; unless you exhibit an irrational craving for holy water dispensed promiscuously from rows of taps in standpipes into opaque plastic demijohns (on sale everywhere) the colour of glaucoma; if you suffer, even intermittently, from pangs of a dark, sanctimonious, brooding introspection or morbid intimations of mortality ('Being immortal is to be half-dead,' said Antoine Blondin, that peerless chronicler of the Tour de France), then, for your own sake and peace of mind, avoid Lourdes. Alabaster-visaged identical nuns scurry like scary troops of cloned triplets. Soutaned priests loiter like traffic wardens with quotas to maintain. Creeping Jesuses shuffle more holily than thou along every pavement, and there are vastly more churches, chapels, shrines, seminaries, pilgrim hotels (and pilgrims) than good bars and restaurants. Not an attractive imbalance. The 3-D eyes of numberless crucified Christs blink open and stare with the blank intensity of zombies from holograms impaled on card racks as you hurry by looking for a way out. The forecourt of the basilica is miraculously smooth and perfect for cycling, but beware: the odour of sanctity can be quite as noxious as the sulphurs of Old Nick, and the forecourt of the basilica is perilously close to the *source* and the grotto of St Bernadette. She was, like most of the saints, a remote stranger to personal hygiene and *mens sana in corpore sano*.

We scorched the tarmac out of town in fine style, and whenever one of the Saddles presumed to get to the front in a blatant attempt to suppress the pace, Chris or I, correspondent to command, snuck in and upped the tempo. By the time we got to the turn off for the Soulor, complaint and protest burred down the line like whooping cough.

Kelly, the soul of discretion, didn't say a thing, but he is famously taciturn, of course – one of the few men to respond to a question in a radio interview by nodding.

Some way up the valley, at the start of the climb, Chris went to the front of the bunch, and I, being at best a sloppy climber (OK, rubbish), took the rearguard. I hadn't gone but 20m when one of the guys got off to walk, blathering under his breath about a late night. I was soon to learn what *late night* meant in Saddle-speak. How many degrees of legless pissed are there? I lost count.

I rode on, supposing that the gradient had unnerved him and that he would soon remount. Then I looked back, took in the glaze of his fish-like eye, the bilious green hue of his complexion, the waxed sheen of his brow, and heard the rattle in his chest as he blurted: 'Ah, it's me hairt.'

Fuck. First day out and we've got an imminent cardiac arrest in the bunch. Nothing for it, I thought, better summon help pronto, and I proceeded to fly up the climb. I tell you, I devoured that mountain. Urgency pumped oxygen by the gallon into my decayed and bursting lungs, red corpuscle-rich blood into my arteries, visions of unsullied youth into the wishful thinking of my brain. In the café at the top, not having my glasses with me, I waited while the patron searched out the telephone number of our hotel and then dialled it. I delivered the Mayday call and went back outside to dally. Or should I go back down? I went back down and met the man with the hairt riding up, oblivious to emergency. He rode by, without a blink of recognition, if he could see anything at all. Alertness to immediate surrounding or circumstance wasn't always apparent on that ride, even in the sighted brethren. I rode back up and waited for whatever next might transpire. What did I know?

As I sat by the side of the road, a car parked on the grassy knoll opposite started to roll down the slope towards the road, its hapless owner half in, half out of the front door, trying, presumably, to reach the handbrake. He spilled out, the car kept going straight across the road at speed and snubbed its nose with force in the parapet wall below where I sat.

The man with the hairt was already riding on towards somewhere or other in the vague direction of the Bay of Biscay. Another Saddle appeared. 'Are you the last?' I enquired.

'The last what?' he replied. I resisted any play on 'Mohican', 'sober man in Christendom' or 'clown on earth', and we set off back to Lourdes.

Jan Flanagan and Anne Carey, responsible for daily signposting of the route, skulked out of the hotels unbreakfasted every morning at 6 a.m. like a pair of double-room moonlighters, to paste, pin and post arrows, notices and fingerposts from start to finish of the daily rides – crucial roundabouts, tricky side turnings and all. Often to no avail. Many of the Saddles are blind; quite a few of the other Saddles habitually act blind, and, as the sweeper, I spent many a lazy half-hour dozing on the grass verges in the afternoon sun waiting for stray breakaway groups who'd shot left past signs pointing right, or right past signs pointing straight on, to be hauled back onto the strait and narrow in the shimmering slipstream of Dublin copper Alfie's powerful Garda motorbike. Indeed, one balmy morning, from a high bridge on the designated minor road, with the sort of affectionate amusement normally reserved to a mother coot gazing at her fledgling brood as they head for the reeds, I watched a party of the Saddles forging purposefully up the inner lane of the motorway in a southerly direction, towards Gibraltar.

Taking my sweeper duties seriously, I found myself, much of the time, riding at a speed that was barely faster than a track stand. Early on, at the back of the ride, I waited for the man Kelly himself – he'd elected to make a bit of a clothing change – and, once he was re-garbed, I conscientiously tucked in behind him as we headed back up to the bunch. Since I had seen countless pictures of his rivals in the professional *peloton* glued to his back wheel with a look of drenching horror on their faces, this put me in something of a quandary. Clearly, the man needed no help from the likes of me. As I observed the mesmeric twirl of that famous 11 rear sprocket, it assumed the menace of a naked saw blade. On the other hand, there is a sort of democratic equalising inherent in the cycling fraternity, is there not? I decided I should take my turn and, with some trepidation, I went through, and was, in theory, towing a man whose more usual sight of a back wheel was in flashing past it. But that was just the nerves in me.

One of my Classics tutors at Durham was partially sighted – he read Cicero from a Braille copy and knew the whole of Euripides' *Medea*, for instance, by heart, but he could still read the dial of his watch, by holding it to his dim eyes and feeling for the hands with his fingers. However, I realised that, before this trip, I'd never talked to a blind person. When I confessed this sudden awkwardness to one of the blind riders, Geraldine, she said to me: 'We're the same as you.' Kind words, if inexact. The cheerful resource of those without sight over their affliction is humbling. How many of us expend so much effort on the easy labours of their day as it takes a blind person merely to get about, to fumble around in a strange bathroom, to eat a plate of food, to make a cup of coffee? And, at the same time, spice it with humour. In Oporto, we visited the HQ of Sandeman's. Our guide, togged out in replica of the famous logo – black Spanish sombrero, Coimbra University student's cape – switched on the slide show and asked if everyone could see. Stefan Grace, who's blind, said he couldn't see a thing. The guide feverishly tweaked the knobs and twiddled the focus and asked if that was better. 'I still can't see a thing,' said Stefan.

Stefan went blind late in life but seemed quite unfazed. Indeed, he said that he'd seen far more of the world since he lost his sight than ever before. Like Gloucester, perhaps, who 'stumbled when [he] saw'.

After the guided tour, the Saddles were parked at refectory tables to sample the drink known as 'bottled sunshine', ruby and white. Plainly considering this beverage to be a teetotal drink, resembling the true Guinness only remotely, by its deep red colour, one of the company, when informed that he was drinking a vintage over 20 years old, peered dolefully into his minuscule glass, the fourth he'd swallowed, and replied 'It's very small for its age.'

Ah, the drinking. Many of the Saddles resemble Flann O'Brien's *Third Policeman* not a little, in that they must surely be well over 50% bicycle in constitution, for, like the bike, they generally find themselves unable to stand up without something to lean against. To be fair to the philosophical notion of bicycle qua bicycle, this is because, come the evening, many of the Saddles are often more dished than ever are their back wheels. One of them, standing in the doorway of a bar whose exact location he could not quite put a memory to, nor the way back to the hotel if indeed he could remember its name or even his own, was overheard to say: 'If I was as wet inside as I am outside, wouldn't I be as dry as a bone?' As to water, this is a substance deemed by most Saddles to be fit only for the locating of punctures.

One debutante to the ride, when asked what she thought of the whole shebang, replied, with a distant look in her almond eyes: 'There are no words in life to describe these people.'

Chris piloted Geraldine towards the end of the ride, and, first morning out, giving the tandem an airing, they went over in the hotel forecourt where we had assembled. He came over to me, spluttering with laughter: 'Eighty miles to go and we deck it in the car park.'

Chris and I got on wonderfully well, despite the age difference between us. First evening, I strung a long strand of string across the room we were sharing.

'What's that?' he said.

'A washing line.'

'What for?'

'The washing.'

'What washing?'

Towards the end of the ride, I skirted his bag as it lay on the floor of the room like the rotting corpse of a beached porpoise and reeled from the violent emission of a rank odour through its open flap. It was the sort of noisome stink that used to come in tiny glass phials, evil little schoolboys for the mischievous hurling and planting of. When he emerged from the shower, smelling all over of perfumed soap and Brut, I said: 'Chris, there is something dead in that bag. You need to investigate.'

He investigated. The defunct item had once been a sock.

The last port of call was Fatima, and on the ride into that other shrine to Our Lady, Stefan Grace was partnered by Sean Kelly. This necessitated a change of footwear – the tandem pedals didn't take cleats. Even Kelly, who seems to be capable of divesting himself of most items of apparel whilst in the saddle on the move and, sporadically, losing them by the side of the road, had to admit defeat here and dismount. Stefan, ever alert for a dose of tar, puffed away the delay cheerily. When at last they were off, Stefan, sensing that Kelly was going particularly well that day, leaned over his man's shoulder to spur him on, adding that, since he seemed to be surplus to requirements just then, he was going to serenade the company. He leaned back, pulled a mouth organ from his pocket and launched into the Saddles' anthem. Someone chimed in with the words:

If you follow the Blazing Saddles, clap your hands
[*bis*]
If you follow the Blazing Saddles
You must really push the pedals
It's the greatest cycling team in all the land
etc., etc., blah blah blah.

(Authorship of this stirring farrago of twaddle is, for patriotic reasons and in the interests of the perpetrator's personal safety, kept a closely guarded secret.)

Before lunch that day, Eamon Duffy reminded the Saddles that if anyone wanted to ride into town they should be sure and take their bicycle with them. Given the prevailing record of forgetfulness among the party, this advice was timely. (One of the more committed hangover and lie-in men left his guitar behind in the hotel room on the first morning and himself behind in various other hotel rooms on most other mornings. His accumulated taxi bill at the end of the trip brought tears to the eyes. Of laughter, mostly.)

It was only when we reached the perimeter of the sanctuary that we discovered that cycling is not permitted therein, nor are dogs, beggars, bag-snatchers, mobile phones, radios, brass instruments, ball games, decolleté off-the-shoulder beachwear, brawling, etc. One of the Saddles, scrutinising the list of banned activities, murmured: 'Well, we're going to have a ball in here.'

We cycled through villages quaintly named Chaos, For Sale and Water All-Year-Round. The route took us along wild sea-coasts, dipping and soaring over cliff edges with the Atlantic surf coursing in onto smashed causeways of gleaming black rock and half-moon bays of smooth sand, over the ups and downs of the lower Pyrenees as they peter out westwards, by winding riverside paths, through the eucalyptus forests of northern Spain and Portugal. On a Sunday morning so tranquil and still, down green country lanes so rapt in peace you'd have known it for the Lord's Day even without the church bells, we rode out of Orthez, where, the night before, a Basque choir had charmed the fatigue and clamour out of us with songs in harmonies that dropped from a clear blue heaven and words of that queer impenetrable language. I turned to Chris at a break in the singing and whispered: 'Sure as hell beats Molly fucking Malone.'

For three days, echelons of Basque motorbike police escorted us through their province as if we were visiting bike-racing royalty. Out of Bilbao, I punctured. This was a godsend. Although I was occasionally relieved of sweeping duties, the opportunities for flat-out riding were few. (On one such occasion, I was flying down the line exuberantly and heard one of the riders I passed say, in startled manner: 'Fuck, it's the sweeper, we must be at the back.') The delay of changing a tube would give me a chance to cut loose for a free interlude. One of the motorbike cops sat on his purring machine watching. I took my time, then, all set, remounted and got stuck in. The motorbike glided up alongside, I felt an enormous leather-clad paw grasp my saddle and suddenly the engine roared and off we shot, 60mph, side by side. One jiggle of the front wheel and I'd pop up like a clay pigeon. A red light, the cop peeled off and I decelerated into a juddering pocket of wind resistance. Then, once again, I was on the end of the motorised Basque track-sling and we were accelerating to 60mph, me in an ecstasy of terror. At the border, my late riding companion lounged on the big motorbike, smiling from behind a drooping bush of a moustache and shades as black as diesel. Warily I went over, having survived what was, I suppose, some obscure Basque initiation ritual. We shook hands.

On the final rest and recreation day in Tomar, Kelly and five of us went for a ride. Feeling good all through, I lost contact on the last big descent onto the main road back. Neither of my brakes was functioning that well, and I watched Kelly flying off, wrong side of the road round corners, right foot trailing the tarmac to steady himself, and he and the others were gone. At the bottom, I gave chase hard and nearly caught them, but the turbulence of the small group, blasting along at some 60+kph, buffeted me away. It was a cruel disappointment – there were riders in there of whom I had the full measure. Back in town, I met Kelly and told him how bad it felt to be dropped. 'Ah, but I was dropped, too,' he said. By a puncture.

Changed and ready for the recreation, I walked out and met Nick. 'Come with me,' he said. 'A treat.' We strolled round to a local bar, where we drank fizzy *vinho verde* on tap and toasted the generosity and good companionship of this great brother and sisterhood of cycling.

Oh, *en passant*, and in the interests of group hygiene and one particularly fragile reputation, I wish to scotch unseemly reports that the following exchange did actually take place:

Male Saddle to group of female Saddles: 'Who's for an orgy? 2 a.m. till 5 a.m., room 312.'

'You're disgusting.'

'Oh, come on. It won't be a dirty orgy. There'll be no smoking and no coffee breaks. It'll be clean, totally clean.'

It's that *disgusting* that sticks in the craw.

Lacking the plastic

Assigned by editors to write articles or else despatching myself to garner material for submissions on spec, I have only ever three times possessed the plastic accreditation that grants access to riders and enclosures at a cycle race. First at the 2000 Giro d'Italia when I joined the McCartney team for a week. Famously, and eccentrically, they were riding on vegetables. When David Mackenzie won stage seven after an epic lone break of 164km, the Italian paper *Gazzetta dello Sport* heralded the victory with the incredulous exclamation: '*Li mangia in insalata*' (he eats salad). Bike-riders traditionally did not win races on greens and soya, though Sean Yates, *directeur sportif* of the team, had been a vegetarian when he went to the Olympics. He only became a meat eater because the French pro-am team he rode for put meat in front of him – manky steaks with frills of yellow fat before a race. Ever the pragmatist, he ate what he was told to and because that was what bike-riders had always eaten. The McCartneys, new to the Continental scene, were also making a splash with their aggression in races. When I got to the hotel by Lake Garda, I met Graham Watson, whom I knew a bit, and he said: 'No one's attacking except *these* boys'.

I'd arranged to write two articles about the team – for the *Daily Telegraph* and *The Times* – as well as a contribution to *The Food Programme* on Radio 4, paid for my own flight and was a guest of the team in the seven days I spent with them. I had huge fun riding in the team cars. Yates was a famously incurious descender on the bike, and, sitting in the team car next to him as we hit the hairpins down into Genoa at 80kph, I saw him calmly reaching for the phone when it rang and working the steering wheel one-handedly . . . well, it went beyond fear, for me. But the man has a calm that would make the Mona Lisa seem twitchy. Next day, we roared through Genoa in the team's minibus on a wide empty road past the assembled crowds and there was a giddy childish thrill to it. In the Giro . . . no jams. A few days later, I'm hanging out of the window in the second car, on the Col d'Izoard, behind a struggling Ciaran Power, yelling at the Italian *tifosi* '*Spingere! Spingere!*' (push him, push him). They cheerfully obliged. And as he neared the top, a couple of kilometres or so to go, having nearly missed the time cut the day before, I said to the driver, 'Topper' Taylor, 'Tell him if he gets to the top, he's made it to Milan . . . no, say *when* he gets to the top . . .' Power, to whom the fear of punctures and vertical plummets is no more intelligible than Mandarin Chinese, descended like an overflow down a drainpipe and was home, a time-trial and last stage only to ride.

The McCartneys had hired three chefs from Un Punto Macrobiotico, who produced a menu based around organically produced rice, millet, barley, wheat, pasta and unsalted bread. I interviewed and recorded them in the kitchen for the radio piece. I must say their earnestness had a very vegan, sourdough, starved intensity about it. Luckily, we on the management table had the pick of what the regular kitchen chefs offered.

The second official laminate I got was for the World Track Championships at the Manchester Velodrome in autumn 2000, and then only because I turned up at the desk with Phil Liggett, who vouched for me. It was my first experience of track-racing, and I was captivated: the thunder of high-inflated tyres on the wooden boards, the daring, the flashing speed, the roar of the crowd . . . Even the fact that I had left my house keys in the front-door lock could not dampen my spirits. (The Kent police bailed me out of that one – a patrol car called by in the early hours of the morning and posted the keys through the letter box.) Phil and I walked to and from the stadium each day along the Manchester ship canal and talked, Chris Boardman broke Merckx's hour record at the end of the week, the rain fell in torrents and I caught the train home with wet feet in saturated shoes.

As a result of the two articles I had written about the McCartneys, my friend Ron Webb, a former track rider whose wooden tracks – including the Manchester track – have produced more world records than any other's, got me a ride to Adelaide to follow the 2001 Tour Down Under. He was, at the time I met him, European coordinator of the race.

I arrived in Australia on the verge of complete exhaustion. In three months, I had spent only thirteen days at home, and those not consecutive. I had been travelling, on work, to France several times, plus two weeks in Mongolia on an assignment, to Tenerife to see my father, and to Manchester. In Christmas week, I went to the cinema. As the place went dark at the end of the film, I stood up and, for about two seconds, did not know where I was *in the world*.

For the week of the Down Under race, Phil and Pat Liggett and I started each day at 6 a.m. with a bunch of the local cyclists for a two-hour ride. I borrowed a red Colnago from a local bike shop, gratis. 'Did you mention me?' Phil asked.

'Of course I mentioned you. I didn't come down with the last snow.'

On the Sunday, last day of the race, we rode out to Cudlee Creek, in company with Phil Anderson, and saw wallabies in a small zoo and koalas up gum trees – they drink not at all, depending for liquid on the sap in their favourite eucalyptus leaves.

After each morning's ride, we breakfasted, set off to the start, where I conducted interviews for articles, begged a ride in a French team car so that I could talk to Thierry Bourgignon, the *directeur sportif*, joined other race followers in the official minibus . . . Back at the hotel, we worked in the press room till about 8 p.m., the ever-sociable Michael – i/c lubrication – slinking up to our desk, eyeing the progress through the Jacob's Creek and whispering in a sing-song jocular reproof over each scribe's shoulder: 'I can see that that glass is empty,' before topping it up. (I never, ever, ever, want to drink a glass of Australian red again, nor the Chardonnay, no. A French wine-grower was asked to sample a much-vaunted buttery Aussie urine-coloured plonk once, sipped, grimaced and said: '*Oui, c'est un Chardonnay Australien.*' (Yes, it's an Australian Chardonnay.)) One evening, as I sat morosely at the computer, my brain turgid with lack of sleep and dehydration, recalcitrant words refusing stubbornly to be levered into sentences, I heard Rupert Guiness behind me say: 'That's me done.'

I turned round and said: 'Can you come and do mine, then?' It really did feel like being in a homework class at prep school. When the slackers and speed typists had finished and lounged about and got rowdy, the remarkable Gennie Sheer would march in and bark: 'Anyone not working, go to the bar. This is not the bar.'

When the copy was filed, we'd go out to supper. More social. I never slept past 3 a.m.

Gennie, a woman of powerful intelligence and personality, invited me to join her and Rupert in the second press car. She had friends who ran a restaurant, 1918, in Tanunda, at the foot of the Mount Lofty range. We called in for a picnic: hors d'oeuvres, mini pizzas, oysters packed in ice, various salads, freshly baked rolls, strawberries and cream and a superior bottle of local white. Ah, the delight to cruise up to the first press vehicle, hand Liggett a single consolatory oyster from our cornucopia and cruise smugly past.

Gennie and I became friends, too, and I have learnt much from her involvement with the Australian pro cyclists – she is a no-nonsense journalist, adviser and consultant of wisdom and good humour.

In four days of the second week of my visit, staying with my cousin Terry in Tea Tree Gully, I wrote two chapters of *Inside the Peloton* to meet the deadline, eight days away. My work done, we toured the wineries of the Barossa Valley, including Jacob's Creek. Terry told the woman serving that I had been following the bike race, and she reached under the counter for a vintage that the firm doesn't export, because they don't make enough of it. I wish they did: it was superb, complex, big, long on taste . . . all that frilly wine-buff bombast. We also went up to Terry's shack on the Murray River and swam across the wide water. I know there are no crocodiles in the Murray, because of the barrier, but I was terrified. I knew that if there *was* a crocodile in those turbid waters, it was right underneath me, ready to grab me and haul me down to its decomposing pantry. On the way back to Adelaide, a kangaroo bounded out of the late afternoon sun right across the road in front of us, and I thought, 'Hurray, I can go home now,' and three days later did so. I was homesick, worn out, wrung dry.

Sixteen

Lance's Muffin

I got some accreditation for the 2000 Paris–Roubaix by a mixture of chutzpah, blagging and the flourish of a professional Sony Walkman with a BBC sticker affixed. That morning, I had interviewed Bernard Hinault in Paris. He'd asked me whether I was going to Compiègne and how was I getting there, then offered me a lift. Hinault never was what you'd call a shrinking violet, probably the last of the true *patrons* of the Continental *peloton*, but his courtesy and directness were, are, typical of all the racing cyclists I have met and talked to at any length. The commonplace 'we are all cyclists' is no platitude.

For the Tour de France that summer, I had an assignment to get a story about Jacky Durand, a story on Pascal Lino and anything else I could trawl in the process but no plastic.

I rode up Ventoux a couple of days beforehand from Malaucène and neared the top as riders of the Étape began to descend towards me. Ignoring police orders to dismount and walk, I got to the top just before the Étape organisers closed the race down – the mistral was in its frosty savage pomp, temperatures were falling, ice congealed on parts of the road, the field back down the route was scattered numb and shaking to the wide.

In Carpentras, I prowled the perimeter of the *village du départ* in mounting gloom. Phil Liggett and Paul Sherwen were already at the finish, no chance of an *entrée* through them. Guards patrolled, the gates were manned by the sort of expressionless gorillas paid to interpose themselves to stop bullets for bigwigs between 9 a.m. and 5 p.m., team buses lumbered in and I was in trouble. However, as I stood by the barriers, the Cofidis bus drew up alongside, leaving only a small gap, close enough to make a blind spot. I didn't hesitate: flipped the bike over and then scrambled after it. I was in. Waddling about in cleats, shades like a tiara on my head, goblin-silver alu frame without decals, no plastic, I chatted to a very pensive George Hincapie – sunken mood, mint-blue sunglasses – noted the pear-drop pungency of one Belgian team's massage oil, had a brief word with David Millar, our first encounter, got my interview with Pascal Lino and then Jacky Durand, laid-back, smiling, bandanna, no poaching on his time refused. Durand was a famous *baroudeur. Baroud* is the last fight in a lost battle, to save honour. He attacked, he told me, 'because you feel something, you do it. Consequences?' The question was rhetorical. 'The best moments are those you can't foresee, the fugitive moments. To win on l'Alpe d'Huez would be *the* win, but . . . you never know where else.'

The night before, I had dreamed I found Marco Pantani unconscious after a heavy fall, wrapped in two bits of torn cardboard. I eased off his shoes and put him to bed. It brought me up with a jolt when I saw him ride past me in the village, black bandanna, piratical silver earring. Given the wretched manner of his passing, that dream has a nasty premonitory chill about it now.

Ten minutes after the race rolled out into the streets of Carpentras, heading for Ventoux, I followed. The police waved me through, but, as I paused at the exit, one of the spectators cajoled me: 'Hey, you're late, the race has gone.' I laughed and rode off down the race route to a rolling volley of cheers and applause from behind the barriers, which was nice if faintly embarrassing – fake *lanterne rouge*.

Of course, no one needs plastic to see the Tour from the side of the road.

In 2003, I was down in Biert at Nick and Jan's request, to act as guide to a bunch of visitors, mostly American. I'd got my wings by showing some of the regulars around in previous years.

At Gaillac for the individual time-trial, when Ullrich beat Armstrong soundly, I felt a boyish compulsion to beat the plastic ring-fencing keeping the public out of the central warm-up area and drifted through a gap in the barriers, shadowing someone with the laminate flapping at his shirt front. It was ample enough to cover the two of us, anyway, so I escaped the scorching sun into the tree-shaded central compound and had a close-up view of Armstrong warming up.

Driving home, up and over the twists and turns of the Col de Port, I somehow put my back out. The pain was so sharp, the collapse of my lumbar region so complete, that I could barely walk. Since I had to be at the top of the Bonascre next day to join David Duffield in the Eurosport commentary box, this was bad news. I slumped out of bed next morning in extreme pain and discomfort, got dressed somehow – it was (as I imagine) like trying to pull a skin suit over a stick insect. My feet were almost beyond me even to reach and cover in sock. I hobbled downstairs in great pain and some trepidation, and David, from Boston, asked me if I wanted some vitamin I.

'Vitamin I?' I queried.

'Ibuprofen,' he said.

There was no way I could get to the Bonascre by car – the approach roads would be shut long before the first outriders of the race arrived anywhere near, and the cul-de-sac of the ski station would be closed to them already. Bike it had to be. I rolled out Shorter, leaning against it for support, and somehow managed to swing my leg over and find the saddle. It was frightening to be so incapacitated. Yet, once I'd mounted, the pain and discomfort in my lower back subsided – I guess the traction of the stretched riding position effected that – and, hope restored, I set off with the rest of the party for the Col de Port and the valley road to Ax-les-Thermes.

The 11km horribly steep ride up the Ax Trois Domaines to the *arrivée* in blistering airless heat was purgatory. Anxious about the 3 p.m. rendezvous time, I asked one passing car for a tow but was refused. I made it, at last, to the media village, to be confronted by a ring of about ten stony-faced gendarmes. I struggled off the bike and said I had an interview appointment. They looked back at me as if I were a bad smell. I may well have been a bad smell. Then I saw Sean Kelly walking up behind them, come to greet me. 'There's my man,' I announced to the constabulary, and Sean was leading me through the maze of trucks, caravans, media buses and Portaloos, over the interlooped sinews of cables, to the Eurosport commentary box.

Sitting along from David and Sean, Laurent Fignon looked up and nodded greeting. Earlier that year, I had asked him repeatedly for an interview and got no reply. Even when I was in Paris, I'd got no response to my messages, so I'd decided to turn up unannounced and try my luck. His office was down by the River Marne, near where it flows into the Seine. I rang the bell by the large blank portico door. A secretary called down from a first-storey window. No point in fudging. I told her I had come to see M. Fignon.

Two minutes later, I had been shown up and, after brief deliberation between Fignon and the secretary, was ushered into his office. He explained politely but firmly that he was too busy to see me, he had no time to see me or talk, and, yes, he had had my messages but had no time to reply, he was very sorry, but if he *had* had time, of course he would have been only too happy to talk. I interpolated various blandishments about being sorry he hadn't got time, and, in the event, I had ten minutes of the time he couldn't spare, a precious chance to get the feel of the man. I liked him, instinctively. He'd been famously rude to intrusive journalists and was outspoken about any rider's merits and demerits. He lambasted David Millar for a slack approach, and I think Millar would agree, now, that he had been just in his critique. What I liked best about Fignon was his straightforwardness. I admired him hugely as a rider, too. In my view, the 1989 Tour was rightly his: Lemond shared no work in the mountains, but he was unshakeably resentful of the French and, in particular, about Fignon's old boss, Bernard Hinault, who, in Lemond's view, had robbed him of a Tour victory in 1985.

Back on the Ax: in the television monitor I watched the riders hitting the lower slopes. One of them took off his helmet and hurled it away – a nice gift for someone. I talked to David Duffield about the race. He, generous as ever, plugged my books and then told me to make way for Christie Anderson. When the commentating was done, I sought out Phil and Paul, had a chat, somehow relocated shoes and feet and then set off.

The others had made it to the top in the cable car, and I caught them on the way down after all the riders had come in. Just off the top, though, police were holding everyone up, until a rowdy bumper-to-bumper procession of caravan vehicles had gone by. One French guy pedalled up and simply brushed past the gendarme and carried on. A salutary lesson learnt.

The following day, we were at Orgibet on the climb to the Portet d'Aspet just above the feed station and just short of the restaurant I always take visiting cyclists to. I'd already taken this class of 2003 there on a day's ride out to see the Casartelli monument. They hadn't grasped the importance of getting to restaurants in rural France well in advance of 1.30 p.m. at risk of missing lunch. I stressed we needed to reassemble at the col by 12.30 p.m. at the latest. As they straggled in, late, I told one member of the party that I was going to head down as fast as I could in search of an eatery and to follow with all haste. Nothing in the first village; the restaurant owner in the next village barked the dread curse '*Terminé*' at me so I stomped on to Orgibet. It was by now well past 2 p.m. I walked in, dripping sweat, lungs heaving, and gave the *patronne* what I hoped was a winning look, between foundling and favourite uncle, I guess. I didn't explain *why* I was there. She knew why. I said only: 'Is it possible?' There was a pause, into which I could have poured 'please' in all the languages I know. Then she said: 'How many are you?'

'Eight,' I said. 'They are on the way now.'

There was another pause, but I had run out of pleases. Then she said: 'Would cassoulet be all right?' I nodded with all the force of my gratitude, ordered a beer and sat to wait.

We sat down to crudités (which my mother called 'crudities'), charcuterie, soup, cassoulet, salad, ice cream . . . we left a splendid tip, and I had made friends whose gracious hospitality I try always to repay whenever I can take people there to eat.

So, a few days later, as the race came through, riders were rummaging through their food sacks and throwing out reject items, mostly energy bars. Then there was Armstrong, sitting up in the saddle. He flung a spherical object wrapped in silver foil across the road at the feet of Karen, from Rhode Island. When the fanfara of the Tour de France had whirled on and left that strange silence that its parting conjures, we walked up to the restaurant, sat outside and watched as Karen laid the unexpected booty on the table. Gingerly, she unpicked the shiny envelope to reveal what was inside. It was Lance's muffin.

'Are you going to try it?' I said.

She brought it circumspectly to her lips and nibbled a crumb.

'Well. What's it like?'

Her nose wrinkled. 'It's terrible,' she said.

Next day, we took a hire coach out to Bagnères-de-Bigorre and cycled out to the Tourmalet. Nearing the top, I passed Larry, Karen's husband, sitting with his bike by the side of the road amid the crowds of spectators. He looked tired and disconsolate.

'Are you going to the top?' he called out.

'Yeah.'

'I'll follow you.'

We got to the summit line just as the police walked across it and closed the road. I was so pleased that Larry had made it. He had had a small doubt, that's all, a sense that he couldn't go the distance. Instead, he went home with the Tourmalet.

Back in La Mongie for lunch, I watched the race go through and, at the back, a long way down, Axel Merckx in patent distress. His face etched with misery, he'd been suffering from a stomach bug but did not want to give up, although it was plain that he would miss the time cut this day. His very public suffering, his body finished, his mind, his will, refusing to give in, was a vignette of what elevates those who do honour to this beautiful sport to heroic stature.

My friendship with David was forged on a long ride we did together that summer. I took the party up the Col de Port. The morning was beset with a rheumy cold, dank and cheerless, and when we got to the col, everybody except David eyed the restaurant with piercing interest and the consensus was to scrub round the rest of the ride and settle in for lunch and an easy scoot back down to Massat. David, however, announced that he felt like pushing on. This entailed a loop of an extra 75km. I was not being paid to show them round, but my responsibility was clear: 'OK,' I heard myself saying, 'let's go.'

In the valley on the other side, the sun came out, I showed David the Devil's Bridge outside Foix, we had lunch in the market square. He was brought up in Alabama, and I asked him what it was like there. He paused, gave me a long look, smiled and said: 'It's terrible.'

On the long climb up the back (easier) approach to the Col de Péguère, we rode side by side and talked. Along the ridge towards the Col de Portet above Massat, a buzzard flew up from below the road and right across us, almost close enough to feel the beat of its wings – a fine brush with a magnificent bird.

On the last day of the 2003 visit, the ride split up in Saint-Girons – people needing Internet café, bike shop, last-minute souvenir hunting – and Karen, Larry and I rode up the valley together, very weary but wonderfully content. The riding, the companionship, the burgeoning of new friendship, this was the acme of the love of the bike. I was already showered and sitting on the terrace outside the Lodge, beer nicely in hand, feet up, when Larry, still in bike clothes, hauled the heavy bike boxes out.

'Always worth an hour's entertainment, watching someone trying to get a bike into a box,' I said. 'Cheers.'

'Watch it,' Larry said with a big grin. 'I get scratchy when I'm tired.'

16 July 2004

In company with what seems to be the entire cycling fraternity of the Pyrenees, I ride up towards La Mongie in blistering heat, well ahead of the race, trying not to remember how hard the climb is, thinking of last year when we had to go all the way to the col, 4km beyond the ugly ski station. At Sainte-Marie-de-Campan, the foot of the climb, the woman gendarme told me to dismount and continue on foot. I recalled the guy on the Bonascre. Thus, civic disobedience being a sort of tradition in France, I ignored her and carried on riding.

I'm wearing a yellow top. A man lounging at the side of the road with his family cheers and claps. 'It's the *maillot jaune*.' I nod, blink the stinging sweat out of my eyes, and say: 'Ah, last year's.' Remember the Campan *mounaques*? The harder the gradient gets, the more the acid sweat floods my eyes, the more I am overtaken by other cyclists, who, like me, glance fearfully at the line of cars cut across the wooded mountain slope way above us, the more I feel like a straw dummy propping up an old house. Even so, I don't envy the crowds lining the route. A foolish pride stirs. We're riding the route of the Tour de France; they're just looking at it. I see a picnicker lounging in the shade wearing a T-shirt with the legend 'Steep is good' and wonder what his problem is. A beaming woman sits next to a banner with the painted legend 'Richard, *ton bidon*' – will Virenque see and obligingly toss her his bottle?

On the lower slopes, the road winds through trees, but around 7km from the *arrivée* it breaks clear of the woods, and the ridges and craggy humps of the high range loom into view, stark against the clear blue sky. This is the moment when the awe of climbing way beyond the reach of sanctity and beanstalks swamps you, when you surrender to the sheer enormity of the mountain's power. The daunting prospect, the thrill of natural grandeur and, like a memento mori to you, the puny mortal on a frail bike, the wearing expense of the effort needed to keep the pedals turning. Every revolution of the cranks brings us nearer the top. Got to keep on, don't think too hard, stay loose.

A thought lights up in my soggy brain: a sudden boost to the confidence. I realise that the banners telling us '5km to go . . . 4km to go' relate, of course, to the race. We certainly won't be allowed beyond the red kite. Hurray. A surprise gift of one whole kilometre less to ride, one whole kilometre less of being ambushed by idiots straying into the road across my wheel.

The local paper, *La Dépêche*, has vans plying the Tour roads lobbing out batches of the latest edition to all and sundry. One of the bundles nearly decks me. Higher up the road, in one of the tunnels, my back wheel clogs up – a loose page of that wretched despatch caught in the rear mech. I straddle the bike as a friendly cove leans down and unpicks the rags from chain and cogs. '*Merci, merci.*' '*De rien.*' (Thanks, thanks. Think nothing of it.) Out of the tunnel and along the road daubed with the white scrawl of the Tour riders' visitor's book – Vinokourov . . . Jaja . . . Bobo . . .

Basque fans everywhere. The *L'Équipe* cartoonist has depicted La Mongie as 'The Orange Planet', a strange lunatic world overpopulated with a cloned tribe of corpulent, smoke-jawed, jet-eyed men in tangerine bolero tops, bikini bottoms and frizzy wigs, some distinguished (if that's the word) by red tie-on clowns' noses. The elders of the clan, possibly. They speak a strange tongue. It's said that when the Devil tried to learn Basque, he could master only seven words – perhaps the deadly sins, in which he has a vested interest. Luckily, the idiot Devil who haunts the Tour (a Dutch fan well known for turning up in red tights, black cape and horned cap, brandishing a trident) is nowhere to be seen . . . or caught diabolical whiff of. Peugh. Sulphurous fumes ain't in it. The year before, a bunch of the Basque corsairs had taken him prisoner and tied him to a chair, perhaps to coax him into indulging in a wash.

Dark clouds gather over the peaks as I rejoin my companions: four of the Americans I'm introducing to Tour and mountains. We peel off into a clearing with beer tents and televisions. Wait a minute, man, isn't that Sheryl Crow checking out the blond (Kronenbourg) and the small screen? Sure is – Sheryl Crow. She looks kinda nervous, don't she? But say, we come to the Tour, which is neat anyway, and now we're watching it with Sheryl Crow, too. Man, that's awesome. Cameras out.

Larry from Pennsylvania, his face glistening with drizzle and sheer delight, looks at me and sighs: 'Wow, man, every day something noo and I owe it all to you,' which was kind if not wholly accurate.

The rain comes, the cold, cold driving rain. The Basques sing and party on, al fresco. The rest of us huddle under the beer-tent canopies, watch coverage of the race through a blur of static interference and spray-shot lenses. At last, the storm passes over, sun comes out, and we're at the side of the road with the countless others, waiting, waiting. Gendarmes try to stem the encroaching tide of fans, but the Basques seem to have the situation under control. This is their stretch of tarmac, a bare 2.5m wide, claimed and occupied, and they mount guard across it jealously, joshing the police, guffawing at the very idea of meekly doing what they're told. Suddenly, the familiar klaxons hee-haw hee-haw from down the road, Jean-Marie Leblanc's red car speeds through, and motorbikes and press vehicles follow, like tailors' scissors ripping cloth, and . . . and . . . it's Armstrong and Basso, at terrible velocity, faces drawn, bodies hunched and taut. In the vivid snapshot of their flying past us, inches away, I say to myself: 'Armstrong just won the Tour.'

Seconds tick away, too many seconds, before the chasers squeeze through in a burst of speed. The dense crowd opens and closes to allow them narrow passage, like a boa constrictor digesting mice. Pallid masks of pain and shock stand out in this bunch of men who've been dropped: Hamilton, Ullrich, Mayo, the named contenders who may even now be seeing contention slip away. But here is the gutsy Voeckler, hanging onto yellow . . . and the sprint specialists O'Grady and McEwen, who might offer some ripe Aussie response to Monsieur 'Steep is good'. Finally, like the Grim Reaper, the broom wagon trundles by, and La Mongie begins to spill its vast flood of Tour pilgrims back down the mountain.

17 July

I've decided to ride the 13km up from our base in Massat, to just below the Port de Lers. The view is stupendous: I look across a deep basin to the ramparts of rock towering over the Col d'Agnès. Folds of mountain plummet down to the lake below the road along which the riders will first descend and then climb once more. I and a thousand other spectators, more, will see them coming, tiny figures far in the distance, plunging off their fifth col of the day, brief respite before they climb up the next one, past me, and onto the last descent and the day's grim finale: 16 withering kilometres to the Plateau de Beille. And from where I sit, a grand tableau of what makes this sporting event unique: 5km of serpentine road lined with people come to linger for hours so as to snatch a glimpse of a race that, from the very start, lit a fervour across the entire hexagon of France – the 'giants of the route' riding like mythic heroes into even the remotest regions, appearing on mountain tops and vanishing into the long perspective of the endless road. Epic stuff – always was, always will be.

People who've camped up here are well provided. I passed one family tucking contentedly into barbecued steak, green leaves, chilled rosé. Transient chancers like me liberate a banana from the back pocket and sip the last of the lukewarm water from the bidon. The *Vélo* car scorches through – a commentator tells us over the loudspeaker that the *maillot jaune* is in trouble on the vicious ascent of the Agnès. An Irish voice behind me tells a mate he's heard that Mayo climbed off on the fourth climb, got an earful from his manager and climbed back on.

A flurry of excitement ripples along the road: action in the distance – the publicity caravan approaches. The very different Tour de France surges by: motorised Aquarel bottles . . . a glum-looking bloke driving a giant Crédit Lyonnais winner's lion clamped to a pop-pop tricycle . . . a large cylindrical cheese with no visible means of locomotion . . . in quick succession, a rubber duck, a garden gnome and a horribly sunburnt pink pig, each mounted on what may be a stripped-down Robin Reliant. Girls with glassy smiles hurl out the free gifts, and an elderly couple next to me pitch in to amass the full collection, everything from sticks of liquorice to Mickey Mouse magazines. At one point, Madame scrambles off down the precipice to retrieve, at close risk of a long fall, what turns out to be a pair of mulberry-coloured flip-flops. Their battle for the bonbons is ferocious, though what they'll do with a pair of ill-fitting Champion polka-dot caps, who knows?

A lull. Five helicopters herald the arrival of the riders. At the foot of the climb, the little troop of Boy Scouts in cornflower-blue shirts take up the cheering again – they cheered me as I went by, but they cheered everything that moved – and two riders fly past us: Rasmussen, the bald ex-mountain biker, and Chavanel, whose break will take the pressure off his team trying to defend Voeckler's lead. The Postals go through a couple of minutes later, a compact ruthless hunting party, chasing down the escape. And here's Voeckler, riding with enormous courage, only a small gap, he's fought his way back. After him come the stragglers, heavy with fatigue – the drama at full pelt along the narrow road on whose verge we stand. It fills out what the television can never show, just as riding the mountains is the only way really to know what the effort of the Tour riders costs.

When the race has passed, I ride down to the junction and turn off on the descent – cars facing both ways parked either side, others trying to shimmy through. There's already a jam – cork in the bottle, the French say. I shoulder the bike, scamper down over mud and boulders across the hairpin and remount on clear road. I'd talked to Phil Liggett on the way to La Mongie. 'You're lucky,' he said, knowing he'd be stuck in the media village at the end of the stage, 'you'll be able to get off the mountain – you're on a bike,' and it's somehow reassuring that the best way to see the Great Bike Race is on a bicycle.

Back in Massat to watch the last hour on television, Larry and Peter, my American buddies, report from their pitch on the Col de la Core. 'We're next to this camper van, OK, folks from Colorado, they've stayed overnight. Suddenly, their cellphone rings and they're laughing and shouting into it like crazy. Turns out the girl, who's really an exceptionally hot-looking chick, dropped some stuff, and when she leant over and displayed her rear, the camera moto swooped and there she is all over the TV coverage Stateside, and the folks back home are phoning to tell her. Man, did she blush. It was wild.'

And this day, 18 July, the flat stage to Carcassonne, I sit to write the account of the past two days, glad that I can take a rest from 10 miles' worth of 10% gradients and look forward to some chilled rosé of my own at lunchtime followed by the continuing spectacular of the Tour de France, albeit crammed onto the small screen, from the comfort of a chair. *Santé*.

Saturday, 16 July 2005
Back on the Tour route one year on. We set out at 8.30 a.m. over the Col de Port. It's no killer of a climb, but hitting the gradients first thing always sorts you out. Note the euphemism: for the first 6km of the 12.5km I suffered (in the words of the great Sean Yates referring to his early-season racing) like a pig. There were compensations. The glorious early sun was burning off the mist, the views across the gorge opened wide and, from the summit, we gazed north across the Ariège valley, roofed over by the famous Pyrenean 'sea of clouds' – an archipelago of mountain peaks poking up out of the low cloud.

On the descent, we passed a bloke scooting round the hairpins on long rollers, whacking the tarmac with ski poles in manic rhythm. Didn't stop to ask what *his* game was. At the foot of the descent, I was hailed by two men in a car wanting to get to Spain. 'Forget it,' I said. 'The road's closed 12km up ahead. The Tour de France is going through.'

They looked at their map. 'What about Andorra?' they said. (Andorra is a shithole. Rejoice any day you *can't* get to Andorra.) I shook my head. 'Sorry, Andorra too,' and set off towards Ax-les-Thermes, noted for sulphur springs and a military hospital built in 1260 for Crusaders returning from the Holy Land with leprosy.

The invading cars dwindled to a trickle, and cyclists had the road.

At the foot of the Bonascre, I plumbed that self-delusion we all practise, imagining this brute of a hill might really not be as bad as when I did it two years ago before that other *arrivée*, of the Centenary Tour. Simpleton. At the first hairpin, I saw once more the white graffito on the rock: '100 years of history', and felt every pedal-stroke of that momentous century beginning to pour lead into my legs. No statistics can overrule the steepness, the ugliness, the lack of shade, the snarling tarmac of that merciless 11km climb. Within half an hour, you are in your own isolation zone, more or less oblivious of the crowds lining the route, deep in the strange quadratics of physical stress whose rationale no 'why' or 'how' can pierce. The only good to come out of it – aside from getting to the top without expiring – is reinforcement of one's awe at the speed at which the pros devour these slopes.

From behind the barriers in the media village, I watched the photographers with their bazooka lenses screaming at another bunch of happy snappers in front, crowding their zoom-shot. I saw that day's winner, Toschnig, come in, collapse and get pounced on, like a hot bargain at a Harrods sale, even as I berated a woman standing next to me for lighting up a cigarette. Coming off the mountain shortly after, as I changed a punctured tube, the motorised plastic pink pig of the caravan loitered briefly alongside me. Then a green watering can drew up, its driver flipped out a cigarette butt. 'Stand on that for me,' he said. I nearly picked it up, dropped it in the car and said: 'Stand on it yourself,' but, instead, remounted for the hurly-burly of the downhill through the slalom of Tour cars, caravan wheelie bins, Basque fans in orange bunny-girl outfits, the weird geezer in sheer black nylons with suspenders, gendarme hat and coat, and the tosser who strolled out towards my front wheel in a haze of Heineken. I delivered a short speech in Anglo-Saxon to deter him from advancing any further.

In the five hours I spent on the Bonascre, I cadged and stole water with the alacrity of the Ancient Mariner and didn't pee once. That dehydrated.

Sunday, 17 July
Off to the Portet d'Aspet at a leisurely 33kph along the valley to Saint-Girons. The gendarmerie had closed the barriers ahead of time. We were told they were making cyclists walk. As you will know by now, that cuts no ice with me: I rode through, and off we went, up the route of the Tour de France, cheered all the way by little knots of people gathered betimes to see the royal progress (not us) pass, families *en fête*, the party-time of locals that has lined the small roads of France since the race began, to marvel, to cheer, to clap. We, the cyclist guys and dolls, reap a strange benefit of that – their enthusiasm and encouragement heaped on us merely because we are riding the bike on the day the Tour comes through. It's humbling.

At the intermediate Hot Spot sprint in Argein, two of my compadres went too early. Being a McEwen aficionado, I bided my time. (Yesterday, on the descent of the Bonascre, a feckless youth lurched wildly into me and I shouldered him off with all the brisk bruising panache I've learnt from the Aussie scrapper.) I took the prime, indeed, and shot across the line to rapturous applause from a company of oversize Pari Mutuel Urbain (the

French tote) green hands, and a shiver went up my spine, a palpable thrill. The emotion spooling off the road as you go through is really that hot. I later traded in my notional six bonus points for a beer.

We had to stop to make way for the publicity caravan and were thankful there were no gimlet-eyed old ladies in the vicinity, toting sharp-pointed walking sticks. They are definitely *not* to be messed with in the matter of amassing caravan goodies. So, we had a clear run on the Crédit Lyonnais bags, the Gummy Bears, the Champion and Skoda hats, the key rings, the cyclist-shaped Haribo sweeties and the minuscule slabs of chocolate that came winging our way.

The Aquarel guy hosed us down.

Back down in the hamlet of Moulis, my friend Nick Flanagan and his 11-year-old son Dominic stood almost alone at the side of the road when the race went through. Dominic said: 'Dad, Dad, look, there's Lance,' and the big man, no rider between him and the kerb, heard, turned and smiled, an unforgettable glowing smile, at the lad.

Tuesday, 19 July

I'd agreed to help a friend's non-cycling father (73 years old) see the Tour if at all possible and, after reflexion, decided that the best way was to chance the Col des Spandelles, a backstairs bucolic route linking the main road from Argelès-Gazost to the Soulor descent. I've ridden some of it, couldn't imagine why it would be blocked: with luck, only cyclists would know about it. Worth the risk. The valley road west from Argelès affords one of the finest views in the Pyrenees, towards the range of massive peaks of which the Aubisque forms part; the panorama from the top of the remote Col de Couradouque stops the breath, and the dizzy perspective from the even remoter Col des Spandelles is a wonder.

So we drove, up and over the narrow, partly unpaved,

twinkly, rustic road to the junction with the D126 of the Soulor descent, and lo, we had the liberty of the Tour route with a straggle of other spectators. (It's not often you can outsmart the Tour route, and, the day after the Soulor, a blast from the past – riders ducking under the closing bar of a railway crossing not to be held up while following team cars backed up, waiting for the train to pass. That happened to the young Romain Maes in 1935, who raced into the lead on the first stage when the bunch got held up by the level-crossing barrier which had just closed behind him. He took the overall lead and never relinquished it.)

We strolled 300m down the road to the Le Moulin restaurant and sat by the cool of the mill race with a beer. Perfection. And suddenly, a shocking intrusion of noise – klaxons, blaring music, tannoys . . . bloody Tour de France. What? We're here for a nice quiet lunch (*salade verte, poulet Basquaise, pommes frites, fromage de brebis, vin rouge*) in a backwater of rural France and, startled, glance up from our table to see a motorised garden gnome fly past, followed hotly by the Champion lorry, albeit the man with the microphone saw us and generously called out: '*Bon appetit, messieurs, 'dames.*' The yellow-jersey pompom girls flounced past on the back of their lorry, and a blizzard of packets of pretzels and coffee sachets, baby sausages and Bouygues lanyards landed on the patio.

The Aquarel guy hosed us down.

Then, a lull, the curious bating of breath that tracks the caravan ahead of *Le Tour*.

All at once, the break hurtled down, heralded by two police *motards*, blue lights flashing – four riders, on the money, they'd make it. A bit later, a lone escapee, then another. Further pause and it was the yellow-jersey group, compact, intense. Then a whole rout of riders, weaving in and out of jostling team cars, like penguins slicing underwater; one guy rocketing towards the bend, hands off the bars, stuffing a drink down the back of his jersey; others, with bottles between their teeth, slipped into invisible gaps, and when they were past, it was rush hour choking the Col du Soulor – cars, motorbikes, vans in a jam, horns honking, impatient to get through. One rider, all but decked by the Assistance Médicale van (there was irony – nearly trashed by the guy who would scrape you off the road), battered on its side window in a fury.

Finally, another lull, foreboding this time, because it counted in minutes the pain and toil of what had happened on the mountains behind, the last summits of the Tour. And a melancholy moment: here came Beloki, solitary, bemused, way down on time, a leader *manqué*. Four years ago, when the Tour had last come this way, he'd arrived in Paris third on general classification. Now? Nowhere. But, that was the race, just another particle of the 100 years' history.

Seventeen

Rhode Island, Cape Cod and Massachusetts

The Amtrak train from Penn Station, New York, pulled into Kingston, Rhode Island, at 6.58 p.m. on Monday, 29 September 2003. Away from the sawtooth skyline of upper Manhattan, up along the east coast seaboard, past small-town outcrops, parking lots crammed with yellow school buses, nosing round inlets of ocean and river, through reedy marshes as the sun sank with all the sky's colour in its pocket and the copses of alder and willow put on the sombre greys of the dusk. Under a cone of sherbet pale light from the platform lamp stood Larry and Karen Purtill. As I walked towards them, I said: 'I don't believe this.' One evening on the terrace down at Massat two months earlier, after supper, warm night air, convivial mood, they'd said: 'Any time you think of coming to the States, you're very welcome to come visit,' and come visit I had, to Narragansett, an English settlers' corruption of the Indian name Nanhigganeuck, 'people of the small point'.

Next morning, I drove away in the jeep they loaned me, Larry's own bike in the back, heading for Cape Cod. Nearing JFK once, I'd gazed longingly from the air at the surf-trimmed white-sand beaches of the Cape and decided that I had to swim there some day.

I skirted Buttermilk Bay around 10 a.m. of a bright warm Tuesday morning and did the sensible thing: pulled in at a diner and ordered a plate of pancakes. The waitress, obviously thinking that the rest of the famished family were outside parking their bikes, staggered in with a loaded plate the size and volume of a ten-gallon hat plus bottle of syrup. Reminds me of Handel, en route to Ireland, ordering dinner for two in a hostelry in Fishguard. When the landlord asked where his companion was, Handel replied: 'I am der two.' I chomped through about half the heap and departed feeling mildly sick but dutifully carbo'd up and ready for the first ride, along the Cape Cod Canal Bikeway, a 12km smooth concrete route between the Sagamore and Bourne bridges. Partly maintained by the Army Corps of Engineers (there's a National Guard base nearby), it's fast, flat, two-way (yellow line down the middle) and designated for government vehicles, pedestrians and bicycles only. A perfect warm-up, there and back, 24km, ozone fresh air and the bracing sight of boats, large and small, plying the waterway linking Buzzards Bay south to Cape Cod Bay in the north, wearing big, white, foamy bow waves like walrus moustaches. I hit the gears hard, wound up to a high-tempo cruising speed and snipped away the frayed edges of travel-weariness. America may be the home of the big gas-guzzling automobiles, but there is a distinctly bike-friendly code in play, too. There is a real, not imagined, sense that riding a bike does not instantly mark you out as dangerous or eccentric. In fact, where the cloth-cap proletarian image still dogs cyclists in the UK, in the USA, most cyclists are moneyed professionals.

From the canal, I drove a short way south and rolled out of a woodland park near Sagamore heading south-east down a green route for my second ride, past town names reminiscent of the old country: Sandwich, Barnstable, Yarmouth Port. Clean, white, colonial clapperboard houses stand proud of trim green lawns in Sandwich, the open-box belfry on the church familiar from movies. The town approaches are leafy and wide. Out into country, rolling hills, wide, smooth-paved, tree-lined roads, very little traffic and signs to the place names of far older stock than those the early settlers imported: Hyannis, Cummaquid, Wequequet Lake. I called in at the Tourist Center near Barnstable – a smart, airy, brick-built facility – picked up a pamphlet about the Rail Trail and advice on somewhere to stay for the night, then looped back to the motor after a good four-hour ride and drove on to a hotel in Hyannis Port, a popular fishing harbour and ferry terminus on the southern shore. A swim off Craigville Beach – fine white sand and the cool waters of Nantucket Sound – was nearly as good as a massage for tired legs but even better for the thrill of being afloat in that sea, the tidal flood of New England. Just up the coast, north from the Cape, lies Plymouth, landfall of the *Mayflower* with its freight of Pilgrim Fathers in 1620 after a voyage of 66 days. There is history here, for sure. The writer Henry David Thoreau said that when he stood on Cape Cod, he felt all America at his back.

I turned in early, too pooped from riding, sea air and bathing to eat more than a delicious bowl of clam chowder, the famous creamy, butter-yellow, chunky clam and fish soup – from *chaudière* (pot), originating in the fishing villages of Brittany.

8 a.m.: I spurned the clammy chlorinated hotel indoor pool, headed for the beach once more, the perfect start to any day, and, two hours later, pulled into the car park near South Dennis at the start of the Rail Trail, 45km of gravel asphalt along the track of the Old Colony railroad which carried passengers and freight from the early 1800s until the mid-1960s. It cuts through wooded avenues, past furze heath, salt and freshwater marshland, broad lakes opening out to either side, sometimes winding with a relaxed swish through

hamlets of houses lurking in leafy glades – on a line in the garden of one home, a bunch of protest banners hanging out to dry, each with the legend 'No More Lies'. One house called 'SUITSUS'. I saw chipmunks skittering in the undergrowth, blue jays and orioles aloft. The Trail twice crosses a road: cars are required to give bikes priority, and they *do*. In our dreams. Early in the ride, I passed an impressive two-storey wooden building, formerly a cranberry factory, now housing a bike shop, repairs and rental. Crimson cranberries, attached to wiry creeping stems, cushioned on evergreen leaves, poking up out of the turf bogs which speckle the low-lying terrain of the Cape, have been a staple of Cape Cod diet since the first settlers arrived. In the factory, workers picked the berries off the stems ready for processing to feed the hungry clamour at Thanksgiving.

At the Wellfleet end of the Trail, there is a smaller building with a bigger culinary treat in store: The Blue Willow, quite the best café stop I have ever encountered on a bike ride and handily situated in a quiet turn-off beyond the rail end. Lisa Wheeler's cheery boast – 'Everything you need for a Great Meal' – is not idle. Oven-roasted herb chicken, crab cakes – 'We'll ship them anywhere' – Home Sweet Home meatloaf, stuffed cabbage, balsamic caramelised salmon, bagels, sticky *sticky* pastries, muffins and oh my, my, jen-you-eye-n American deep-dish apple pie.

Gourmet coffees and teas and a cool 45km to ride back to the motor. This lone wheeler without a silver bullet to his name bade the home-baking, comely, smiling Lisa Wheeler a rosemary for remembrance-flavoured goodbye and got on his way again. Rode up alongside a guy who seemed to be having trouble with his back wheel. 'Spoke,' he said in an accent hovering around the banter of a French country market. I offered '*rayon*', and it turned out he was from Quebec. Until he turned off, we bowled along at a sweet brisk kph, jabbering the *parlez-vous* – I got about half of what he said, French Canadian being a peculiar mishmash of the language, but enjoyed the *craìc*, nevertheless, and the company.

I swam in the Sound once more and set off back to RI past a billboard heralding 'Bug of the Month'. Beauty contests for vermin? Actually, the currently most prolific house-pest. Now a sign to Centerville intrigued me. I'd heard of two Canadian women driving around France who saw signs to *Centre Ville* everywhere but never could find the place. So here *was* Centerville, and it had a historical centre, so I stopped to visit – a wonderful local museum packed full of interesting exhibits, expertly displayed, the whole vista of Cape Cod life from early days – and I met the curator, Britt, and she was a cyclist, in training for the Last Gasp ride of the season. So began a friendship, and three years later she came to the Pyrenees to contribute to the book I wrote about those loveliest of mountains.

Next evening, Larry, Karen and I drove up to their condo in Lincoln, New Hampshire, via Manchester – Tyler Hamilton's home town, east of Mount Moosilauke and west of the White Mountains, among them Mount Washington.

First ride took us through town down the Kancamagus Highway ('the Kanc') which cuts north–south along the western flanks of the White Mountains, and up through Franconia Notch, part of the way on an off-road forest path dappled with sunlight. The leaves were blushing with the acids of fall, the hillsides overlaid with a soft-layered tapestry of burnt orange, mulberry red, plum purple highlighting the spread of dusty greens. We stopped to look at the Old Man of the Mountain, a series of five ledges in a towering cliff of Profile Mountain etching the giant craggy outline of a man's visage gazing eastwards. He's lost his jaw, sadly – wear, tear and weather led to a calamitous fall of rock. Local man Daniel Webster, the nineteenth-century statesman, said of the face: 'Doctors and lawyers hang out signs to announce their profession. In NH, God almighty has hung out a sign to say that is where He makes men.' I filled my bottle from a tap hoping for a miracle infusion of the local hero's ichor to waft me to the top of the Notch and down the sweeping 9% descent into Franconia – large perspectives opened out ahead of the big road, and the spirits surged, even if the damp silted lungs still resisted.

I know the names of the places we visited now, but at the time it was all a blank, and when the man behind the counter in the Franconia sandwich bar asked me where I had come from, I replied: 'I don't know.' Then, to 'Where are you going?' I said: 'I don't know.' So much for our gibes at the average American grasp of geography. Not the least charm of riding in these parts is the exotic colour of the place names: skirt the Ammonoosuc and Saco rivers, 15km to Kinsman Notch, short 4km climb to Lost River and Kinsman Pass and a photocall by Beaver Pond before the sweeping downs to home.

Next morning, the rain had set in, but we did a 45km there and back to a 10km climb on the turn – steep first section, gradual interim, steep to the top – which must surely be a glorious ride on a dry late fall day and was a pleasure even so, imparting that happy sense of defying the elements as you head back off the ride, shoes sloshing with water, spray stinging your eyes, brakes slipping on the wet rims, for an early hot bath, lunch and a lazy slump in front of the television to watch the Boston Red Sox taking a good win.

Sunday morning, sitting to a more manageable dish of pancakes with oak-cured streaky bacon and maple syrup on the side, the doorbell chimed and here came David, from Boston, to join us for a 100km cruise along the Pemigewasset River, past a house where the poet Robert Frost once lived. 'The woods are lovely, dark and deep,' Frost wrote: 'But I have promises to keep/And miles to go before I sleep.' I'd wanted those woods to be aflame with red and goldburst, the postcard moment, but David assured me that the postcard moment is always fleeting and anyway quite rare, so Frost's quieter painting of the foliage and our own miles to go had to do, through the verdant byways, the quiet roads, of this lovely state in the company of warm-hearted friends.

David rides occasionally with the Charles River Wheelmen, a Boston club dedicated to 'the enjoyment and advancement of cycling and other healthful sports'. They organise season-long rides, beginners to hotshots – Wednesday evening Ice-Cream, Fitness and Masters rides, a Thursday Fitness ride, a Friday Unwinder ('ice cream is optional') . . . 'experience the fun and camaraderie of riding with others in a friends atmosphere' – frequently up to 100 riders gather on Sundays to head out into Norfolk and Suffolk County, adjacent to Boston. One thing they don't do is socialise. A few of the more ardent members have tried to chivvy the wheelers out of their Lycra into party casuals, but the first essay at off-road clubbability, held in the basement of a church hall, apparently had all the conviviality of a convention of accountants, who, as we know, are actuaries with the sense of fun surgically removed.

I returned to Boston with David on Monday, had a happy day walking Harvard Square and Beantown, saw the Sox go through in the play-offs and caught the train back to New York next morning. I glanced idly at my plane ticket. It was for Monday. Got to the airport thinking I had just casually blown three hundred and fifty or so quid out of forgetfulness, told the be-turbanned Air India man at the check-in I was a bit late and he said: 'That will be forty dollars.' Keen price to prolong my stay. Home by 10 a.m. next day and, two hours later, to Paris to help Jane with an exhibition . . . another detail I had overlooked. But the visit had been a treat after finishing my big book on the French revolutionary Terror (published in 2004). That I had been so relaxed is entirely to be applauded.

21 September 2006, the autumn equinox

David and Lauren have just got married, so I'm back in the land of hand-cut doughnuts and fries, hand-crafted salads and crab-cakes, hand-fashioned oyster crackers to eat with clam chowder. This is the land where a rotary is a roundabout, an efficiency a bedsit and the *summum bonum* of contentment in any given situation is to be 'all set'. Here lived the Indians called Massachusett, an Algonquin word meaning 'at the range of small hills'.

Before heading out there, I exchanged e-mails with Pete, a Bostonian, Sox fan, whom I'd met down in Massat when he was there with his girlfriend Chaylee. He cyclist, she wine expert, they live in San Francisco. He wrote:

> Too bad you won't be there end of August, we are going to be there for my grandfather's 90th birthday and one of Chaylee's old friends is getting married on Cape Cod, both will be amazingly fun events.
>
> And I won the lottery to purchase tickets to sit atop the green monster at Fenway August 31st!! I have 2 extras, I would take you if you were in town, instead I am selling them for about $500 a piece – should provide some nice beer money for the evening. Regardless, I'll keep it in mind that you make trips out to Boston for the weddings of former Pyrenean visitors.

Ah, the generosity of my cycling friends.

David meets me at Logan and says: 'Baseball is over. The Sox were going great, then they fell off a cliff. It's all football now.' We call home in Cambridge for his wife Lauren and stroll up Massachusetts Avenue to the Central Kitchen for supper. They serve meat and seafood, but the names of the shellfish in New England have a particular briny poetry about them: bay and diver scallops, littleneck and softshell clams, Jonah or 'Peeky-Toe' and rock crabs, Maine, blue and Massachusetts lobsters, Wellfleet oysters and the chowder clams known as quahogs (pronounced 'co' hogs) from the Narragansett Native American name *poquauhock*. They used them to make beads for purple *wampum*, money, twice as valuable as white *wampum*. (Hence the Latin name *Mercenaria mercenaria*.)

I spent next day in Boston, walked through Charlestown up over Bunker Hill, scene of the first major engagement of the American Revolution. On 17 June 1775, General Howe's army seized the peninsula from the rebels but lost a third of its force and were soon cooped up by a tight cordon. Howe eventually extricated his beleaguered men by sea north to Nova Scotia in March of the following year, nothing much achieved.

I caught the bus over the water to Downtown, spotted a market just past the bridge and hopped my ride. I stepped, first, into what claims to be 'the oldest tavern in the USA': the Bell in Hand, established in 1695 by a local auctioneer. 'I'll have a Harpoon,' I say.

'Small or tall?' says the barmaid.

Thirst quenched with a 'small' of the nutty-flavoured Indian pale ale, the colour of clear toffee, I strolled along to the Haymarket – stalls laden with fruit and vegetables, a couple with fish and seafood. An underground dive purveying 'fresh meat' looked like a hastily converted urinal. The pavement of Haymarket is inlaid with curious intaglios of gleaming brass shaped like squelches of discarded fruit . . . which is exactly what they are intended to represent, the trade stamp of the market. I noted the punnets of raspberries, strawberries and blueberries to buy on my return and walked on into North End, home of Paul and Rachel Revere.

Revere, a Boston silversmith, joined the Boston Tea Party on 16 December 1773. Three companies of fifty men each, disguised as Mohawk Native Americans, boarded three British ships in Boston harbour and tipped their cargo of tea (on which, by orders of the Crown, the British paid no import duty) into the bay.

On the night of 18 April 1775, Revere made his famous ride west to Lexington. Longfellow romanticised the exploit in a florid poem, but the truth is more prosaic. Revere was already active in coordinating the armed resistance to the British in New England. Using his numerous contacts in eastern Massachusetts, he set up a relay network for the rapid call-up of the local militias. Several messengers rode longer distances and alerted more soldiers than did Revere that legendary night, but they did so at his initiative.

As night fell on 18 April, to the steeple-top on the Old North End church were hoisted two lanterns, signal that the British were crossing the Charles River en route to Concord to seize munitions stockpiled there by the local militia. Revere borrowed a horse and, in company with one William Dawes, set off from North End, Boston, at 10 p.m. To folks along the way, he probably did not cry Longfellow's 'The British are coming' but the brusquer 'The regulars are out'. He reached Lexington by midnight and, an hour later, set off for Concord, was captured and, *sans* horse, released. He continued on foot to Concord to deliver the warning. Meanwhile, 900 British infantry were marching west under General Gage, royal governor of Massachusetts and commander of the king's troops in North America. Barring their way across Lexington Common stood 75 men of the local militia, the so-called Minutemen, who were required to be ready for action in 60 seconds. Shots were exchanged; the British regulars marched on to Concord, where, on the far bank of the river at the North Bridge, another company of Minutemen confronted them. A yellow house on the east side of Monument Street across the way still proudly boasts a bullet hole from that day: as they withdrew, the British fired at the house-owner. A plaque by the bridge records:

They came three thousand miles, and died,
To keep the Past upon its throne;
Unheard, beyond the ocean tide,
Their English mother made her moan.
James Russell Lowell, 'Graves of Two English
Soldiers on Concord Battleground' (1849)

The first encounters were no more than scuffles, but handfuls of untrained militia facing a regiment of disciplined redcoats was no slight bravery, and those acts of defiance roused the 13 colonies to the American Revolution, birth of the Republic, *E pluribus unum*. Who pulled the first trigger is hotly disputed, of course, but that musket reined memory as changing history:

By the rude bridge that arched the flood,
Their flag to April's breeze unfurled;
Here once the embattled farmers stood;
And fired the shot heard round the world.
Opening stanza of the 'Concord Hymn' (1837),
by Ralph Waldo Emerson, native of Concord (his
grandfather had watched the engagement from his
house, The Old Manse, close by the bridge)

The patriot who organised the stockpiling of munitions in Concord was another man of Boston, Samuel Adams, who organised the Boston Tea Party and famously refused to wear a ruff or bend the knee to the king or his minions. 'If ye love wealth greater than liberty,' he told all waverers to the cause, 'the tranquillity of servitude greater than the animating contest for freedom, go home from us in peace. We seek not your counsel, nor your arms. Crouch down and lick the hand that feeds you. May your chains set lightly upon you, and may posterity forget that ye were our countrymen.' He is rightly and gratifyingly commemorated in a malty conkerbrown pale ale of New England, the relative scarcity of which in Old England I lament. Another example of local manu-(i.e. 'by hand') facture, its makers 'use only classic ingredients: hand-selected Hallertau Mittelfrueh and Tetnang Tettnanger hops, two-row summer barley and pure water'. Bottles of it come free of state tax. In Massachusetts, alcohol isn't a luxury, it's a necessity. Oddly, though, to dial the speaking clock in Massachusetts, the code is N-E-R-V-O-U-S. In California, you spell out the letters P-O-P-C-O-R-N on the keypad.

Across the street from Paul and Rachel Revere's khaki clapperboard house, kids played primary baseball in a school yard, with a plastic woofle ball that has the hanging flight of a shuttlecock. I stood and watched awhile, then hit my first burger (which came with enough fries to feed the entire playground) in a nearby grill across the street from an Italian barber shop. This planted the idea of a shave. Later.

I walked back across town over Mount Vernon and Beacon Hill, once pastureland, then claimed as a residential enclave by Boston's richest citizens in the nineteenth century. From the bus up Massachusetts Avenue, I saw a poster: 'Parents, talk to your kids about Not Drinking' and hear ornery, weather-polished, whiskey-sour pop berating pasty-faced junior: 'OK, son, guess we should talk. I'm getting rumours here, ugly damned rumours, that you're not drinking. Beats me. What's up? We didn't treat you right? You turning into a wuss? Or worse? Not on my watch, kiddo. Fix yerself a Dogfish, an Improper Hopper, a Rotating Dark, whatever, and let's have no more talk of tee-darn-total.'

David and I drove off to collect a hire Specialized from a shop in Watertown, and he asked me where I wanted to ride next morning, Saturday. I hadn't been on the bike for a while, didn't fancy a hard kicking from any of the local sadists and, besides, was keen to see a bit of historical Massachusetts. He suggested the Charles River Wheelmen's regular Thursday evening ride, from Hanscom airport, once a military base, out to Concord. 'Near Walden Pond?' I ask. Walden, a mile and a half from the town, is where Thoreau, one of Concord's several illustrious literary sons, was born, and where he lived in a rough lakeside cabin, built by him, for two years, two months and two days. Reputedly self-sufficient, he seems to have taken occasional clandestine delivery of essential provisions from the home-town stores, but his account of the experiment, *Walden*, published in 1854, was one of the inspirational books of my youth. He speaks of his desire to 'front only the essential facts of life'. How little of that mystery I had as yet plumbed, but I knew its direct inspiriting sense. 'How vain it is to sit down to write when you have not stood up to live,' he said, too. I'm OK with that apophthegm of his, less so with another caveat that 'writing is an excuse for not living' – mouthed, it's clear, by someone (and I can't recall his name) who struggled with both. I wanted to swim in Walden Pond and took my swimming trunks on the ride . . . except that even as we unloaded the bikes from the motor, rain hosing us, it was clear we were in for a certain ducking long before we got to any standing water.

'You sure you want to do this?' said David through the liquid gauze of the downpour.

'Sure. You?'

'Sure.'

We rode 30 miles, through woods and skittering wet, by way of Concord. Riding down Monument Street, the way the British had marched, we turned off to North Bridge. A monument to the Minutemen stands on the far side, where the rebels had lined up. From 1842–5, Nathaniel Hawthorne, he of *The Scarlet Letter*, etc., and his wife Sophia, newly married, lived in the Old Manse. (The book he wrote there named it.) Sophia miscarried and, with the diamond in her wedding ring, scratched on the window pane of a small upstairs room: 'Man's accidents are God's purposes.'

North Road took us across the Great Brook Farm State Park, colonised by transcendentalists in the nineteenth century. There was much seeking after backwood pioneer wisdom hereabouts in those days of railroads. Machines rampaged the land like vandals bringing the hostile intransigence of forged metal and belching steam and coal smoke in the name of progress. Taking to the forests for the simple life was in fashion among the liberal set. As Thoreau wrote:

> What after all does the practicalness of life amount to? The things immediate to be done are very trivial. I could postpone them all to hear this locust sing. The most glorious fact of our experience is not anything that we have done or may hope to do, but a transient thought, or vision, or dream which we have had. I would give all the wealth of the world, and all the deeds of all the heroes, for one true vision.

There is a sort of truth, or at least a path to it, in the daily culling of hand-planted vegetables, wild mushrooms and fresh-caught freshwater fish.

Lowell Road took us back on a loop through the dripping oaks over the glistening sopping tarmac, past Tophet Swamp, which seemed, this saturated day, to be encroaching, but it didn't matter, for we were riding through Massachusetts, back into Concord and out again past Sleepy Hollow Cemetery, where lie Thoreau, Emerson, Hawthorne and Louisa M. Alcott, she of *Little Women* and resident of Orchard House a little way along.

The tyres hissing on the meniscus of rain over the road out of Carlisle, I noted Blimey Drive (which is odd) to the right and also the seemingly eccentric numbering of the houses: as it might be 1135 then 1143 then 1160 . . . But I recognised this from parts of rural France. The numbers mark the distance in yards between mailboxes from a designated point outside the town line. Where two townships, such as Concord and Carlisle, converge on the same road, the numbers increase to the meeting point then decrease to the next town line. And 'blimey', I found, means 'sentimental', of a music-hall song. Well.

Round Concord lived the Nipnet peoples, an Algonquin word meaning 'small pond place', but of those ponds, Walden lay just too far away this sodden day: my swim would have to wait. When I took the towel and bathers out of my musette, they were soaking wet. So, too, my wallet. Buying some postcards in the Theatre Pharmacy in Lexington, I said to the old guy at the counter: 'I should tell you that these dollar bills are somewhat damp,' as I peeled them from the wad.

He looked at me through owlish glasses, took the greenbacks, liver spots on his hands, and said, in a hushed tone of old-world courtesy: 'Thank you, sir, for advising me of that. I'm going to set them here on the counter to dry out before I put them in the till. Your change, sir.'

All Lexington is dry – no bar, no booze outlet, no alcohol-fired bonhomie. Tee-darn-total.

Out of Lexington, we passed Wright's Tavern, HQ of the Minutemen that morning of 19 April, and Munroe Tavern, built in 1695, painted the dull maroon of many of these houses here, which is also the Harvard University colour. It served as the British HQ and hospital that day of the first clash of arms.

David and Lauren's wedding celebration party that night was at Fruitlands Farm Museum, on Prospect Hill near Harvard village in west Massachusetts. The start of another Wheelmen's ride, it stands near the Johnny Appleseed Trail. Long, long ago, Johnny went walking with apples in his knapsack, and everywhere he went he laid apple pips, and, lo, the orchards of New England came to be. (The real historical figure was John Chapman, born 26 September 1774 in Leominster, close by. Chapman roamed the wilderness with a bag of apple seeds on his back seeking likely spots for planting. There he would clear the land, tugging out weeds and brush by hand, plant his apple seeds in neat rows and build a brush fence around the area to keep out straying animals. His nurseries varied in size: from one acre or so to many.)

Prospect Hill, a small stone slab tells us, was the name given, in 1800, to what had been Makamachekamuk. The inscription adds, somewhat gratuitously, that this was 'an old Indian name'. Fancy that. The hill, 557m altitude, affords a fine prospect west across the Nashua River valley, the blue shapes of Wachusett, Watatic and far-away Monadnock, of distant forest, a quilted spread of variables of green, dark to pale, even now beginning to colour in the slow alchemical burn of fall. In a hollow to the right, a clutch of houses, a Shaker village.

On the way to the party, I spied a market garden in one corner of which stood a mighty pile of regular-sized traffic-light-orange pumpkins and a regular pile of mighty-sized pumpkins, imminent Halloween jack-o'-lanterns. Then we passed a man on a motorbike, to the luggage rack of which was tied a mini-sized pumpkin, no bigger than a melon, a sonny-jim-o'-lantern, perhaps.

Eighteen

'OK, You're Set'

Next morning, David and I strolled along the Charles River, me agog to see any racing shells skimming by. Just as well we were not joining the Charles River Wheelmen. I'd been introduced to a couple of them at the party: very intense, morbid, obsessive types. I did not wish to find myself in the thankless position of upholding the honour of the Kentish Men, if not the full roll call of my cycling brothers and sisters across the UK, in the high-octane company of any slick-geared morbid obsessives. Not at all sure I'd have been up to the task, and pleading excess of Cabernet Sauvignon would have been unseemly and lowering. Instead, David and I headed out at lunchtime into another sector of the 'burbs east of Framingham – Needham, Medfield, Sherborn – no history attached, but 'This is real McMansion country', he told me. Mac as in Big Mac: large and unimprovably *same*, applying to the mock-colonial houses being built by the nouveau riche, for whom Boston old money had a distinct contempt. Of two such families, it was said that one spoke only to the other, the other, only to God, and some of that quaint snobbery persists.

One very far from nouveau and never riche home I spotted in an overgrown patch more closely resembled a Bates (*Psycho*)

Motel, its eaves warped, paintwork flaking, lintels curled with desiccating age, windows smeared over with a cataract of grime and neglect. It almost certainly suffered from bad breath, psychotic delusions and vengeful malcontent, too.

The day was sunny and warm, the roads of this Wheelmen's regular Saturday ride, 45km with an optional extra 22km loop, quite as pleasant and bosky as the soaked roads of Nipnet. Oaks spat acorns at me along Hunting Lane, a sign by a bridge suggested that I 'Slow Down. Enjoy Dover', another alerted me to the fact that we were entering an area that was 'Thickly Settled'. Yet another warned cars to 'Yield' to pedestrians. I loved that soft 'Yield', more commonly associated here with mediaeval jousting and nick-of-time rescue of damsels in distress by straight-backed, strait-laced, young derring-do saviours with the emotional age of a pre-pubertal swot. The Yanks do have a bizarre way with language, it's true, jostling meticulous gentility against a hybrid of military and computer gobbledygook which brings obscurantism to new strata of impenetrability, that and the chancey sprouts of immigrant literal translation from the imported languages. Absolutely no chance of getting a decent subjunctive out of most Americans. 'If I would have done such and such, I would have . . .' Bollocks. Yet it was not always so. When Leo Rosten had his fictitious character Hyman Kaplan learning English in 'beginnis grate' ('beginner's grade' in Kaplan's rumbustious Central European pronunciation) for the citizenship exam, the 'schplitt infinitif' was anathema, *zakazany*, *verboten*, a stylistic ukase, a verbal 'do not walk', as the American pedestrian red lights warn jaywalkers. Now the Star Trekkian solecism demeans and pollutes English wherever she is spoke. Nevertheless, they do get some things routinely correct. In the USA, there is no such thing as 12 p.m., because 12 p.m. is an absurdity, a physical impossibility. I know time moves swiftly, but it cannot outstrip its own essential being or instance, even within the scope of nanoseconds. The 'm' in both p.m. and a.m. means '*meridiem*', which is noon, halfway through the day. Twelve cannot be after or before itself. Their contemporary novelists, too, many supreme in brilliance of language, thought and invention: Tom Robbins . . . Philip Roth . . . Donna Tartt . . . Michael Chabon . . . Jeffrey Eugenides . . . Stewart O'Nan . . . sublime craftsmen and women.

In Dover, on the way back, we did slow down, and though the town itself had no great bounty to offer – a church, a green, an intersection – the sandwich shop at the crossroads did. Of the Pantagruelish selection of bulging Dagwoods on offer, I chose an NJ Sloppy Joe's: pastrami, Swiss cheese, coleslaw and Russian salad in a white bloomer studded with sesame seeds. I would have done without the coleslaw, that universal, unasked for, inedible condiment of English pub food, but I am a nut for pastrami. Pastrami was also on offer in combination with corned beef, turkey and chicken for those carnivores who can't make up their minds. To my decided mind, pastrami is best with mustard and pickle (large gherkin) on rye. Boston and its satellites is not the best place for such archetypical, starchy-tip-pickle, Jewish fare. Go, rather, to Manhattan or Chicago. But, my sandwich was excellent and the coleslaw toothsome, of not even far-fetched relation to its bottled apology for an off-side order on these shores.

I was, I told my friend David, mightily glad to be there, so full of contentment, riding the Massachusetts roads, historic or obscure, yet familiar to him, as he had ridden mine, rain or shine, on a hired machine, albeit, but a machine which served me well, bearing me fast and away through placid woodland, wetland and farmland.

On Monday morning, I caught the bus out to the hire shop in Watertown to retrieve the pedals I'd inadvertently left *in situ* when we returned the bike. In and out of the shop and back to the same bus that brought me. I asked the driver if he had change of $10. Due to leave in a minute's time, he shook his head, reached for a transfer chit, handed it over and said: 'OK, you're set.'

Hurrying from the stop in Harvard Square, I passed the foreign bookshop in whose window sat a copy of *Essential Scots Dictionary* – not quite as slim as the Blue Guide to Albania but close – and so on to Central Square, where a Spanish barber gave me a shave with a straight-cut (cut-throat) razor. Apparently, J. Edgar Hoover, the cross-dressing head of the FBI, quizzed applicant agents as to whether they shaved with a straight-cut or a safety. If they admitted 'safety', he brushed them off as nancy boys. He could talk.

Male reader, if you have never had a shave in a barber's shop, you have missed one of life's treats. I told David and he frowned. But he has never had a massage, even, and does not want to be told about treats he has missed. I demurred.

Pulling out of Boston South Station, Amtrak #137 grazed the view of a skyline building surmounted with letters reading: GILLETTE. WORLD SHAVING HEADQUARTERS. I turned my smooth cheek complacently. This was a quiet car, too: 'This policy [no cellphones] will certainly be enforced.' If only in Britain. Someone has just composed a concertino for orchestra and mobile phones. Apparently, audience participation is enjoined. One to avoid.

The train arrived in Kingston at 2.42 p.m., and Larry walked along the platform to greet me with a big hug. An hour later, he, Karen and I were riding up Lee Ann Drive at the start of a 48km loop through the coastal town of Narragansett to the lighthouse at Judith Point and back via Galilee, Jerusalem and Bonnet Shores – a private beach. The route was a gentle roller, the sort of ups which have not the clout of identifiable hills, being no more than intermittent drags only marginally off the level. In all conscience, you can't take the punishment too seriously, but the lay-off was hurting me. I was on Larry's wheel, suffering, near that threshold of resistance where the outer edge of what's comfortable is getting friction burns from the coarse edge of what's uncomfortable. My mind was beginning to splinter into doubt, dislike and indecision. Could I stay here? Stupid question. I was staying here. Did I want to stay here? Irrelevant. Such questions, indicative of the advancing disintegration, do not help. Larry pulled ahead up a slight incline. I felt myself drifting, going slack, and I did not like it, nor did I think, for a few merciless seconds, that I could do anything about it, even if I also knew that I *had to* do something about it. Why did I have to do something about it? Nugatory. There is no reasonable, sensible or apposite answer to that. Knowing I had to do something about it had the logical consequence of being able to do something about it. Simple. In a process similar to that of breathing itself – natural compulsion – I inched back and, having caught the ruthless wheel upon which I had been forced miserably to sit, I rode alongside for a while, wondering how the hell this sequence was going to proceed. Then I went through, half-wheeling Larry, and instantly felt better: strong, less distressed, clear-headed. This is a strange chemistry but no more than a demonstration of how the psychological barometer operates, siphoning the juice up from the lower bilges, where physical and mental substance crumble and decompose into a useless slurry, to the higher plane, where they somehow transmute into pure spirit. The fact is that if I lead, I do not mind the unpleasantness so much. The sense of responsibility for those whom I am leading overrides the displeasure. I have felt this since I became drum major in the cadet corps band.

There are wild acres along the shores of the Pettaquamscutt River, which flows near the Purtills' house. Coyotes and fisher cats, as the North American marten is called in New England (also *pekan* in the Algonquin tongue), had moved in. I listened out for the eerie yowl of the wild dog that night but did not hear it. Nor did I see any woodchucks this time, though the inane ditty did float back to mind – American, it transpired, another bit of puerile surplus courtesy of the 5th Army in Italy: 'How much wood could a woodchuck chuck if a woodchuck could chuck wood?'

I got my swim in the ocean next morning, at the beach called Conachet, after a local Native chief. Wetsuited surfers idled in the feeble rollers like mutant seals, gulls wheeled, squinnying for small fry, and I walked with delight down the white-sand beach into the jade-green water to luxuriate, while Larry took in some rays on the beach.

The ride that followed started ill. I could find no pace no poise no push. I was in real trouble, so far *off* the pace it was embarrassing then tedious then an insult – the beautiful machine, in this case Karen's ultra-light Colnago, reduced to the role of a potato trolley, a rustic bier, a builder's wheelbarrow for sacks of rubble. 'Ride like there's no tomorrow,' said Merckx. I was riding as if there was no chance of my making it to the afternoon, let alone any tomorrow.

To North Kingstown, tranquil wooded lanes, along Snuff Mill Road to the home where the noted portrait painter Gilbert Stuart was born, in 1755. Another maroon-painted clapperboard house with Dutch gable ends, a large mill wheel with pond, race and sluice. No visitors this day, I chafed at not getting another card of George Washington, face only on an unfinished white canvas, seeming to ask Stuart dolefully: 'When am I going to get some trousers?'

After an hour plus of staring dully at Larry's wheel, I started to feel dizzy. Onset of the bonk. We spun through Wickford overlooking the water near Cocumscussoc State Park and I pleaded the wolf, badly needing to eat. Club sandwich in a café on the jetty, two inches thick of soft pink beef, tomatoes, bacon, salad, mayo, no cheese – most of the meat comes with cheese – on brown wheat, though I asked for rye. Coffee and a brownie. Was I set? Too soon to tell.

Out of Wickford, Larry said: 'We've got another 32km, mostly flattish, one hill – pretty steep but not very long. Are you OK with that?'

Me (thinking: 'Do I have a choice? Probably not.'): 'Fine.' (Also thinking: 'Shite.') The hill to which he alluded was very sharp, up to Rhode Island's only ski station. At the top, I rode alongside Larry and told him my legs were OK, my head was clear, only I had absolutely no power in my heart or lungs. 'Must be cold still from the swim,' he said. This was charitable.

We rode through a turf-farm neighbourhood, one establishment called SODCO – sod as in grass, not Sodom twinned with Gomorrah, the Soho and San Francisco of the Bronze Age. Open fields of golf course, baseball outfield, bowling green and chapel lawn, one where the turf of a new garden, perhaps, stood waiting in earth-caked rolls. There's a Hell of the Turf bike race round here in March. On these smooth roads, the only resemblance to Paris–Roubaix, surely, the abrupt right-angle turns into blustering headwinds.

Some of the maples and birches were lit with the fall fires, the foliage gashed with blazes of blood-red leaves, rarely the full bonnet. And, slowly, my own system took fire, a blessed heat in mind, stomach and legs, till I was pumping hard, back to normal. Another stretch of rail-trail helped, south from Kingston station through the woods – 'Pedestrians keep to the left facing bicyclists' – and Larry spurred me on with the promise of a coffee shop some way along which did great pastries, and, of course, me being the guest, how could I refuse? Since I had very little willpower to play with at this point, refusal was out of the question anyway.

By the time we reached the cake emporium, I was going a ton, and it was shut. The place was run by a mountain biker, and, when asked why he always closed at 2 p.m. on Saturdays, he replied: 'I need to go riding.' This was Tuesday;

he'd obviously sneaked off for some fresh air and fun, but I was back on song and happy and indifferent to cakes. We sat outside the café, drank water from the bidon and cared not a jot. We were at peace, on bikes, a good ride behind us, near home.

I'm often asked, by non-cyclists, how far I've been on a ride. I can't tell. I never take much account of how far I go, nor do I compare minutely how long the same route takes me on successive occasions. My Dutch friend, the writer Tim Krabbé, is a hog for records and split times, and I understand the mania. But it has never interested me. I do the ride, as strenuously as all the contributing factors permit, and that's that. George Bernard Shaw, informed that an athlete had improved his performance for the 100 yards by a fraction of a second over a summer's training, asked him: 'What do you plan to do with the time saved?'

The counter-claim of the White Horse Tavern in Newport (established 1673) to be the oldest in America beats the Bell in Hand by 22 years. The oak-planked floor, ceiling and walls of the dining room are handsome, the clam chowder is excellent, the burger succulent and the choice of ales ample and satisfying. Larry and I had spent the morning touring the peninsula and visiting the Vanderbilt mansion, Breakers – from the crash of the surf against the cliffs atop which it stands. One of a number of other magisterial summer homes, lesser in size, Breakers was designed and built in two years, 1893–5, an exorbitant confection of Italian renaissance palazzo, French Louis Quinze and architectural whimsy. There's absolutely nowhere in its cavernous rococo halls or rooms where you could hang a damp maillot or park a bike without feeling just a tiny bit out of order – one of those houses where the guests are permanently on call to be on show, every hour of the social day minuted. The beds in the vast rooms of single occupation looked uninviting and austere, and I wondered how often slipper-clad feet padded the marble-tiled floors to and fro between one sleeping chamber to the adjacent, via intervening bathroom – four faucets, two for seawater, hot and cold – for rumpy-pumpy on the lumpy conjugal – or visitor – mattress.

Karen arrived after high-school math teaching. We changed on the harbour front opposite Goat Island and set off on a 48km circuit by way of Fort Adams, the mansions and the opulently appointed Salve Regina Catholic University campus, then down to the shore and Ocean Avenue, Brenton Point and Ridge Road. Noting a sign for Gooseberry Beach and another for Purgatory Chasm, I reflected: apt indicators for two distinct phases of my state of collapse and misery on the Tuesday ride. Full of riding this day, I let rip, all cylinders, and over the last five miles or so broke clear. I rounded off my New England sallies with a swim among the moored yachts in Newport Harbour.

The Red Parrot in town was shut for a 'Staff Appreciation' end-of-season party; the Cheeky Monkey tempted me, but it was a nightclub bar, so we had our farewell supper in the Clarke Cooke Candy Store restaurant on the wharfside. Shops on the walkway offered T-shirts emblazoned with the legend: 'I support two teams – the Yankees and any team that beats the Red Sox', and 'Real women don't date Red Sox fans', in shameless pandering to the well-heeled New Yorkers who flocked to Newport to disport themselves.

Larry and Karen's hound dog Coee is named after the white-water River Ocoee in Tennessee, where they kayaked once, and the hoarse contralto bray of the Amtrak train calling ahead to the stations we whisked through north to Boston echoed Coee's lugubrious chin-up one-tone howl, whether greeting me or saying goodbye. As the train drew into Back Bay station, Boston, an old guy in the seat in front got up, glanced at me and, putting on his jacket, smiled and said: 'You look like one of those Boston sports writers.'

Why he said such a thing, a complete stranger, for the life of me I cannot tell.

[Note: the first evening I asked Karen if she still had the muffin. She still has the muffin . . . in the freezer.]

My last day, I said farewell to David and Lauren, breakfasted on pancakes with maple syrup and hickory-smoked streaky bacon at The Green House in Harvard Square, bought some presents, found the Central Kitchen closed, searched out a tavern and lunched on clam chowder and Maryland crab-cakes to the sappy accompaniment of Lefthand Sawtooth ale from Colorado.

Phil and Friends

In 2005, David, a law professor at Boston University, had come to London to run a summer course. Geoff, one of my taller friends, loaned him, a lanky six-plus footer, a Geoffrey Butler machine, and he came down for a weekend in Kent. We rode out into the Ashdown Forest, Yates country. (A club cyclist pointed out to his wife Arthur Conan Doyle's statue in Crowborough, now weathered black with age. 'I thought he was white,' she said.) Top Hill out of Groombridge looks worse than it is. The sun shone, and it was a pleasure to introduce a friend to the lanes of Kent which I so love. The following weekend, we took the train to Sheffield for the annual Phil [Liggett] and Friends ride, begun in 2001, in the High Peak district of Derbyshire. Phil was kind of stuck with me, having originally asked me along as 'a celebrity of the sport and the pastime'. This was kind, if unwieldy. (Someone I hadn't seen for ages, learning that I was a writer, asked if I was famous. I told her: 'No. I'm quite well known in the cycling world, but that's a bit like being president of the Fancy Rat Society.')

David had needed no persuasion to come to the ride, which was preceded on Saturday night by a dinner to celebrate the 50th anniversary of the first ride in the Tour de France by a

British team. Brian Robinson, the star of that show and great pioneer of Brits racing on the Continent, hosted a pre-dinner drinks party at his house. Among others of the team, Tony Hoar was there too, the only other finisher in the '55 race. I introduced David to a number of the cycling luminaries in attendance and had a long talk with another rider who has become a friend, David Millar. I would wish on none the hell he has been through, and I reserve any comment on the mistake that cast him there. David has come through it, that's all that counts, his spirit intact, ambition renewed.

Phil, as president of the Cyclists' Touring Club (CTC), inaugurated the ride as a fund-raiser. (Jon Snow succeeded him as president in January 2007.)

The background:

On 24 May 1997, Darren Coombes was riding his bike along the road near his home on the Isle of Wight when a car drove into him and left him with severe brain damage. A happy little boy of eight years at the time, he will live the rest of his life with the mental age of a child. His parents determined to sue the woman car driver's insurance company, for compensation to provide Darren with essential care; the insurers threatened to counter-sue on the grounds of 'contributory negligence' because he had not been wearing a helmet. The wrangling dragged on for years. Several different groups, outraged at the monstrous injustice of the case, were involved before the CTC joined the fray, but it was they who put the headlock on the insurers with a concerted boycott on their policies. The insurers finally backed down. The Coombes family's claim was upheld, and the CTC's Cyclist's Defence Fund was set up to subvent action in any similar cases. A number of annual money-raising events were inaugurated to support the fund, including the Phil and Friends.

Rudyard Kipling, who said of his Lanchester that it 'sang

like a six-inch shell across the Sussex Downs', applauded the advent of the motor car because it had, finally, introduced a major blood sport to England. It still goes on.

Someone suggested a route in Essex, but Phil wanted a more demanding circuit than the byroad past Theydon Bois golf course and Toot Hill, the promenade at Frinton-on-Sea and the Billericay ring road. Not that he has anything against Essex. In fact, he told me, he even drove through a bit of it once. However, he was more drawn to country he used frequently in his 22 years of directing the Milk Race. The High Peak offered climbs like Holme Moss, Snake Pass, Winnats and Monsal Head, which so resonate in the history of bike racing. Besides, it was ground Phil had never ridden himself. There are two courses available: 100km or 150km, and the longer route is a registered Audax (Latin for 'bold, daring') event, which speaks for its toughness. Putting themselves through misery in the saddle is central to the Audax riders' purpose in life, a core element in their idiosyncratic sense of fun.

The CTC may not be everyone's idea of a beefy organisation. From the window in my workroom, I often see a string of the local CTC wallahs go by on their weekly bracer at a speed that would seem to defy gyroscopic motion. Lycra? They're still using up stocks of alpaca, corduroy and four-ply handknits. But, join the CTC in High Peak and the other venues for its challenge rides and you find a very different animal. I invited Brian Robinson to come along the first year, and he's ridden ever since. So, too, his daughter Louise (silver medal in the Worlds' cyclo-cross, national champion) and Isla Rowntree, also national mountain bike and cyclo-cross champion. I'd met Brian a while back, and we hadn't by then had a chance to ride together. He lives not far away, and this is country he knows well from his beginnings in the sport.

That cold dismal morning in August 2001, a huge mob

of riders shot off down Bankfield Lane into the dip and up onto the long uphill bully of a road west, just the wrong sort of start to any day, in truth. Not properly warmed up, over-exuberant, imprudently tempted to give it more than you've got, and pop, lungs and legs go into minor seizure. I turned left onto the long slow drag towards Dungworth in a state that can only be described as pitiable and was immediately engaged by Carlton Reid, editor of *Bikebiz*, in penetrating colloquy about Dr Ferrari's views on orange juice and asthma medication. That is, he talked, I wheezed. Normal speech patterns gradually resumed. I told Brian I'd overstretched it. He just laughed.

First bit of the route, up past Wigtwizzle, bites into strines country. Strine is dialect for a stream or rivulet. It can also mean sink-hole, rough analogy of my insides as we sped down the winding incline to the muddy foot of Ewden Bank. There follows a murderous twist of 20% up from Ewden Beck onto a slightly gentler haul on towards Dungworth – further comparison unnecessary – and over the edge of Strines Moor. Brian recalls having to walk it on his first encounter when he was 14. Sixty years on and he padded along, in the saddle, making it look easy. In 2002, Yvonne McGregor joined the ride. Apparently, she shot up Ewden as if she'd left the milk on the stove and needed to get home. I'd interviewed her earlier that summer for a radio programme, and, talking about her training runs, she made some remark about 'toiling up hills'. I said: 'I'd be glad to know just what you call *toiling up hills*.'

The High Peak covers some of the grandest country in England: deep-set moorland, long, long vistas over forest and valley, big ridges far above the road, broad stretches of water in the reservoirs. And the punishment of the ride itself is mollified by the *craic*. Hurtling down at speed into Holmfirth, I was reminded by a fellow rider – in the politest terms, I might add – that didn't I know it is customary in the UK, even in Yorkshire, to use the left-hand side of the road? You don't get that in London. 'Woss your game?' more like.

We always forget the rotten steep climb from the breakfast stop in Holme to the start of Holme Moss. It may be the coffee or nature's jocular way with disremembered pain. Brian still holds the record for the Moss: from the shepherd's hut at the bottom to the opening of the radio mast, six minutes ten seconds, in a hill climb, 1951. As I saw him pulling away, Liggett tucked in, I thought: 'I could do that once, tuck in,' and settled down to watch the procession of riders filtering up from behind me and gliding by.

The long descent from the Moss is spectacular, and what's best about going *down* it, apart from the majestic view opening up, a broad perspective of the High Peak district, is reflecting on what a real bastard it must be to ride *up*.

The Chunal climb out of Glossop is evil. Phil had been off the bike for five weeks before the 2004 ride, he and Paul Sherwen following the Great Bike Race, cooped up in a car, a commentary box and hotels, and we rode up the soulless drag together. With three weeks of Pyrenees in my legs, I was cruising. 'What's this one called?' he gasped.

'Don't remember,' I said. 'Long Sod.'

There's a place above Glossop called Featherbed, the appellation of which ranks with the subtler examples of Yorkshire wit, if that's not an oxymoron.

On Chinley Head, the grousers were out, popping away on the hillside. Out of Chapel-en-le-Frith – asbestos town, home of the original Ferodo works, now home of Bradley Wiggins – we turned left towards Rushup Edge. That's a misnomer. Another protracted spell on the rack. At the top of the Edge, a side road swings left onto another winding strip of tarmac malevolence. Such cruelty. But stay, weary cyclist, harbour no complaint, for the way to old Mam Tor is short and not oversteep, the worst of the 100k is behind you, and the way herefrom is fast. You will go down the giddying steep descent up which Tommy Simpson flew to win the Mam Tor hill-climb before he turned professional.

A landslip in 1977 rendered the road unsafe. Now all traffic (except lorries) goes over Winnat's, and the Castleton defile has become virtually a hidden valley. That descent into Barber Booth, Edale and the lunch stop at Green Acres was hairy. I watched in wonder as Robinson, Liggett and Reid disappeared from view faster than did ever plummet stones. I followed timidly, then, flat out on the flat, reasserted my own governance and caught them in the valley.

I don't know what Green Acres put in their rice pudding, but Phil was a man reborn when we set off again down the lovely Hope Valley – winding road, leafy dells, the river running by. One year, there was no rice pudding, and he was too fagged to queue for lunch. As we lolled on chairs in the sunshine, in company with Brian, Louise and Isla, I offered Ligg an energy bar. His face took on the expression of a man who has been asked to adjudge which of *Finnegans Wake* or the Bible in Latin is the more readily accessible to the general reader. I said: 'Well, do you want it or not?' He hesitated further, then took the gift with the gesture of a man who is still very pissed off about missing the cooked breakfast that morning.

After lunch, feeling somewhat exuberant, I set off at a pace judged to test the recuperative effects of the energy bar I had so selflessly dispensed. The rest, apparently unaware that I had been handing out supplies of muscle-enhancing rations, tagged on behind as best they could without complaint, for a kilometre or two, until I detected the genteel silvery tones of Brian Robinson asking: 'Where's the fire?' I felt myself slowing down, inexorably. He has a remarkable way with words, Brian.

Coming up to the top of Ventoux, in the 1955 Tour, he came upon Ferdi Kubler close to collapse. '*Pushez* Ferdi,' gasped the Switzer, in all kinds of misery. '*Pushez* Ferdi.' Brian gave him what can only be described as a blunt rejoinder in his native tyke and pressed on. Kubler never recovered from the tongue-lashing and abandoned later that day.

The Audax route turns right at Hope, and, heading for Winnat's and Monsal Head, the stalwarts boldly leave Hope behind. Carlton did it first year, when he was preparing for one of his annual pain-fests, 24 hours non-stop, or some such folly, and he assured me that the longer ride is an absolute cracker. Right, Carlton, your word for it.

Under the waters of the Ladybower Reservoir lie the ruins of Derwent village, submerged in the late '40s, and Brian can remember, as a boy, seeing the drowned church spire. Speeding away from the water the first year, on something close to a flat surface, I said to Phil: 'This is more like it.'

'It's not round the corner,' he said. 'You'd better go to the front.' Obediently (gullibly) I went to the front and stayed at the front even as the flat road reared up into gradient like a bolshie kid in short trousers bristling to show he was a tough guy. Puce in the face and close to expiry at the top of the drag (past Cutthroat Bridge), I barely managed to splutter any kind of response when Keith Lambert smoothed up at my elbow looking as fresh as new lettuce and said: 'Just thought I'd check what you're on,' eyeing the sleek alu of my frame. Cynical old pro trick that: to nudge up and drain the last bit of oxygen you've got with an invitation to idle persiflage. A bit further on, Lambert and I, still chattering about this and that, insouciantly hung a left. Brian and three others in attendance followed, and Liggett, dangling off the back – he swore he was waiting for his wife Pat – watched as we took *the wrong turn*. He said he considered shouting out, then thought: 'Ah, bugger it.' We landed ourselves with seven miles extra, but hey, worth every supplementary push of the leaden pedals up the added slabs of poxy gradient.

In 2004, the four of us – Liggett, Robinson, Reid and I – came in together, which was oddly satisfying. Phil gave me a lift down to Sheffield station and thanked me for looking after him. The following year, he repaid my altruistic gift of a slipstreaming wheel in the only way a self-respecting ex-racing cyclist ever would: he dropped me on the Cutthroat Bridge climb and went hell for leather home, in company with Brian's son-in-law Martyn, a man who has ridden PBP but remains, otherwise, extremely approachable. When David and I eventually topped the final bloody steep hill after the *correct* turn-off, my legs felt like celery, my chest like a collapsed bellows spread across an Aga hotplate and the bike like a large section of scaffolding, but Liggett was disappearing over the horizon and I wasn't having that. Three miles to go. I told David it was straight in and set off in pursuit. Nearly caught them. They clipped me into the village hall car park by five yards. Liggett hobbled off the bike, masking his extreme fatigue with a to-camera smile and drawled in fading breath: 'I didn't know you were chasing, else I'd have made an effort.'

Nineteen

Music, War-Mongering and the Big Ride

In 2003, I had made a programme for Radio 4 about music inspired, even played, by the bicycle – Godfried-Willem Ries composed his futurist *2nd Symphony for Singing Bicycles* in 1980, the year his compatriot Joop Zoetemelk became only the second Dutchman ever to win the Tour de France. In the course of gathering material, I interviewed Alan Bennett at his home. We've exchanged greetings over a number of years – I remember watching him pedal away towards Camden Town after a brief confab at a West End stage door – but he has no attachment to the bike other than as a convenient mode of transport. 'I no more think of my bicycle than I think about a pair of shoes,' he said. The interview was, by that token, quite hard work. He did muse rather abstractedly on his auntie's renditions of 'Daisy Bell' but, otherwise, wouldn't be drawn. I prompted: 'Do you not have that experience of riding a bike, away from the work table, cutting loose and things just bubbling up in your mind? It happened to me the other day.'

He looked wistfully at me and in that dry Yorkshire brogue said, deadpan: 'No, nothing ever just bubbles up. It's more or less a constant grind,' making that *grind* sound like the stony rasp of revolving mill wheels.

I also interviewed Phil Liggett and two of our finest ever women racers: Mandy Jones and Yvonne McGregor. Mandy, who finished alone on the Goodwood circuit to become World Road Race champion in 1982, still rides and goes for family holidays on tandem and trailer for the kids. She spoke of the quietness of early morning rides, birdsong, the soft whirr of transmission . . .

Before the last day of editing and shaping the programme, I was down in Oxfordshire at Simon's, and we went for a ride. Cresting the brow of a hill, he warned me: 'This is really steep,' and was off. Like a black ski run: plumb straight, hellish pitch. I followed. He was sitting bang in the middle of a fairly narrow road. I was going faster and would inevitably have to pass, with very little room, when the front wheel started to wobble. This was trouble. The bike was shaking. I dared not brake. I thought I was going to turn a cartwheel smack onto the tarmac and in a paroxysm of fear but somehow calm managed to steer the bucking wheel towards the right-hand verge. The bike and I crashed over and we slid along the grass. I blacked out and came to, lying over the machine, bruised but breathing. I lay some while before getting up. The bike seemed to be OK. I had abrasions on my leg, arm and face; the bidon had gone. Simon reappeared up the hill, I got back on the bike and we rode on, another 40km. His computer was reading 80kph when I came off. Next day, I went into the BBC for the final session with the producer looking a fright and mused on the plangent irony of it: rhapsodising about the joys of cycling after what might have been wipeout. (The headset had worked loose.)

It's always a puzzle why we are preserved. That encounter with the Lotus . . . the unexpected, unasked-for lift I had to Stansted on the morning of 7 July 2005 that saved me from being in Liverpool Street station exactly when the bomb went off . . . near scrapes with death under the wheels . . . What was I thinking of that day in Norfolk, at the crossroads near Wells-next-the-Sea, when I launched across the main road from a side lane? I looked both ways, I know I did, and the way was empty, quite empty, until, nearly across, I looked left to see a car heading straight for me, full on, straight for me. I braked, straddled the machine, and the driver, with no time to slow down, swerved round the front wheel, by inches. Had I not stopped when I did . . . another quarter of a wheel and I'd have been obliterated.

Being in the condemned cell concentrates the mind most wonderfully, it is said, but shouldn't our mind be concentrated anyway? In a sense, we are all thrust into the condemned cell the moment we are born. Life may be seen as a mystic process of remembering what we knew then. As I wrote for Lucy, when she was but two days old:

> Lucy knows why
> There's blue in the sky
> And green in the sea
> But she isn't saying.
> Between you and me
> It's not that she's shy
> Of how? When? Or why?
> She's simply not saying.

In the First World War, the soldiers at the front had a grim saying, that they were all the same age because they were all the same distance from death. My generation is the first in recorded history not to have been required, or made available, to go to war. We, uniquely, have been spared that appalling onus. We have not had to grapple with what Wilfred Owen (who died a few days before the 1918 armistice) called 'the old lie'. Horace's *dulce et decorum est pro patria mori* . . . it is a fine and proper thing to die for one's country. Despite Dr Johnson's caveat that 'every man thinks meanly of himself for not having been a soldier or not having been at sea', I harbour no such qualms. My youthful flirtation with the military sufficed, and I have never felt the need to dice with death on the battlefield to confirm my manhood. As to going to sea, well, that I do want to do and soon. When my friendly neighbour Adrian gets his offshore fishing boat, that I *shall* do.

Quite early on in my sentient years, I did think that it was to be our generation's job, our duty, to learn to live the peace, real peace, not truce or armistice but lasting struggle in a forum without weapons to enforce might, law or ownership. A socialist once defined a bayonet as 'a weapon with a worker at either end', and, whether toff or cloth cap, it is our immense bounty that we have not had to learn its use. Accompanying that gratitude for release from one of the more disgusting burdens of manhood, the inhumanity of the battlefield, comes a horror that the war to end all wars seems only to have implanted a lasting nostalgia for conflict. The fact is, the ugly fact is, that men go to war because, by some irrational impulse, they choose to, want to, yearn to. It fits their vanity, their lack of imagination, their belief in the lopsided logic of their own compelling insistence that they are *right*. Think how many emotional cripples, intellectual dwarves and ideological maniacs never entertain *doubt*. They argue that everyone else is wrong because they have to be right. Doubt is the true arbiter of moral sense. Doubt, for the self-consciously upright, uptight and ever right, is like having a woman tell them what to do. When Lucy was quite small, I took her up to her cot after lunch, to rest before taking her to Bridget, our childminder. She cried, as often she cried, and I did not go up until the time to go came. She was kneeling, slumped in the corner of the cot, asleep, covered with shit, as was the cot. Even as I cradled her and took her to the bathroom to clean off that foul-smelling, slimy, feculent paste of her excrement, I thought: 'If more men had cleaned up more shit, there would be fewer wars.'

It would be interesting to find out.

Though the equalising influence of the bike has indubitably less resonance than the *obiter dicta* of our heroes of human rights and freedom, I do not shy away from its humanising quality. Top men in the Tour de France, club racers elite and lower rank, club time-trial casuals, advocates of the beautiful machine of all stripes, down to the frankly embarrassing antediluvians of the lunatic fringe of slow-wheel CTC, we all ride the same fragile machine, and its rhythm and simplicity are closer to the beat of our heart than can be any more powerful, engine-driven conveyance. For the beautiful machine is driven by another beautiful machine, the human body, an engine controlled by the most complex computer ever created: the mortal brain and the immortal spirit.

There are some people of whom we might say: 'If ever there is a crisis, I hope you're not anywhere in the vicinity.' I don't know many cyclists of whom I would say that. Most of them bear out the plain truth of the poet James Russell Lowell's dictum: 'It is by presence of mind in untried emergencies that the native metal of a man is tested.' For there is another aspect of those who *ride the bike*. The unthinking generosity. On the return leg of the Old Ports' Eastbourne run, February 2005, the wind was bitter cold and blustery. The chill was on my lungs. I stopped to adjust the new blade mudguards, remounted and set off after the receding bunch. One of them, Chris Whitelock, stopped to wait for me. Riding up to him, I went too hard too quickly, blew quite abruptly and completely and, by the time I reached him, could hardly breathe. I tried to hold his wheel but couldn't; my whole chest seemed to have caved in. I barely stayed upright. Chris waited; he coaxed me back, not minding how slowly I was going, waited still and, at last, brought me back to the shelter of the others. I had never met the guy before. It was spontaneous uncalculating kindness in him. Yet, we cyclists almost take such kindness for granted, because we do the same, whenever appropriate or necessary without stint in giving nor proud complaint in receiving. How cheerily Chris guffawed at me, nearing Cerbère on the Old Ports Raid, as we hurtled along the twisting corrugated coast road, its profile like the graph line of a thumping pulse, when I had shot past him downhill, only to succumb on the rise: 'Miss you on the down, get you back on the up,' he cried, full of the glee.

In the Pyrenees on a wet and dowly day, riding with a bunch of Liverpudlians, I and one of the number elected to continue after lunch and take in a big extra arc via the climb to Guzet Neige. On the lower slopes, we found an Italian struggling to inflate a new tube. He had a cylinder pump, and it had run out. We administered some elbow grease with our handier pump, gave him some more water and I offered him a bar, which he declined. Having sorted him out, we rode off, and, as we swung round the nearby hairpin, I said to my companion: 'Did you get his wallet?' The Merseysiders later thought this wonderfully funny and so very *them*.

In early 1999, my phone rang. It was Luke, then editor of *Cycle Sport* magazine. 'How do you fancy riding the longest ever stage of the Tour de France and writing it up for the mag?' he said.

Les Sables d'Olonne to Bayonne, 482km, in 1919, when the Tour covered the entire west coast of France in two hops. When Luke's partner June asked: 'Why the 1919 Tour now?', Luke answered: 'Because it's got a 9 in it.'

There are many considerations which weigh constantly upon the mind of a freelance writer, but the greatest, the most pressing, of these is money. I said 'Yes'. I weighed neither the pros nor the cons, the desirability of such an undertaking nor the consequences. Now, while 'Yes' is what I almost always say to an offer of work, it also accords with my more general approach to everything: first decide what you are going to do, then work out how to do it. Practicalities will always serve up problems, more or less thorny, but these are as nothing to the larger, radical, ingrained, negative, overriding psychological problem, that of the all-too-common readiness to make practicalities an excuse for *not* doing something. The positive 'will do' attitude is not necessarily bound up with confidence; it comes out of a basic mindset. Often bred in the bone, it can be developed and made instinctive.

I'd met Luke after he bought my translation of a series of reports on the 1924 Tour de France made by one of the pioneers of investigative journalism, Albert Londres. The despatches he filed for the French daily *Le Petit Parisien* are eccentric, quirky, droll, perceptive. I've read all his books, on a diverse range of subjects – the abuses of French colonial rule, trafficking in prostitution between Marseille and Rio de Janeiro, the miseries of the pearl fishers of the Horn of Africa, the horrors of the French penal settlements in Cayenne and the punishment battalion of North Africa and much besides – but his *Tour de France, Tour de Souffrance* (*Tour de France, Tour of Suffering*) was the first. A friend had loaned me her apartment in Paris while I was researching a book and left me a copy of the text as a gift. I translated it onto the page as I read, and, although Londres later called the Tour assignment 'an idiocy', my version introduced me to Luke, and when we did meet, at the magazine's office in town, we sat down for a coffee and he spoke the phrase which is like a springtime dawn chorus to ears numbed by the winter of no lolly: 'Welcome aboard.'

Clearly, such a ride called for a companion, and I rang my good friend John Partington, with whom I made my first forays into the Alps, Dolomites and Pyrenees. He's a steady man, John, quiet, unassuming and strong. I put the idea to him, he agreed and, as a way of paying for the trip, contacted Richard Hallett, then technical editor of the magazine, to see if he could road test a bike. Richard provided him with a Litespeed.

John is one of those people who takes a keen interest in frame angles, depth of dish in the rear wheel, spoke weave. It's all much of an enigma to me, and I cheerfully acknowledge my debt to the technical enthusiasts, even if the simplest task, like changing a tube, in the presence of one can be a trifle unsettling. I once did that with Hallett in attendance. He's been in the army, so he knows all about intimidation techniques – and unarmed combat, incidentally, usefully deployed against a road-rage motorist on one occasion, but that's another story. Richard is a sardonic individual, and he doesn't do sympathy well. As I struggled to remove then relocate the tyre at the side of the road in rural Kent, he somehow magicked my fingers into a set of unopposed thumbs and induced a sheen of sweat on my chilled brow. 'Is that how you do it?' he asked, as if I were trying to get the bloody thing off, not on. He later told me how to change a tube, and here, for the clots like me, is the method: remove the tyre starting at the valve; replace it starting opposite the valve. Having put one side of the tyre back inside the rim, seat its edge in the very bottom of the well so that the loose edge has the least distance to travel in lifting over the rim.

On the subject of car-owner v. bike-rider, intervention and retaliation: there are belligerent cyclists who have been known to lean into what they deem to be an offending car, remove the keys and hurl them into the nearest field, building site, cabbage patch. Such action is not always to be recommended. As witness Dave and a small party of the Old Ports out for a club run, heading back on the climb away from West Wickham up Beddlestead Lane towards the ridge round Tatsfield. It's a tight, wood-enclosed road, fairly steep, and they are in jovial mood when, behind them, they hear the whine of an over-revved engine. The car, probably nicked, screams past at about 70mph, a crophead troll with HATE on his knuckles at the wheel, three other troglodytes in the vehicle. The Old Ports, applying themselves to the high verge, manage to escape collision, but one, in the spirit of chirpy defiance which is the incautious mark of the feisty cyclist, makes an extravagant 'wanker' gesture with one hand.

'That,' says Dave, 'was a mistake,' even as the car went into a 40-yard skid, juddered to a halt and immediately began to reverse straight towards them, shaking, shimmying and juddering as if it were being electrocuted.

It slammed to a halt again, and driver and passengers disgorged, prehensile arms swinging and their eyes buckled into a curiously malevolent squint.

Dave thought that they were almost certainly in for a right kicking, but there followed, he records, merely 'an exchange of words', whereupon the driver and passengers embarked once more. Maybe the sight close to of those weirdos in the clowns' outfits, ungainly as ducks on land, helmets and shades rendering head and visage somewhat unhumanoid, deterred them. 'Wha've fuck? Martians?'

As the boarding party drove off, the 'wanker-gesture' culprit turned to the others and said: 'A thousand apologies, men,' and the Old Ports rode on.

There are happier stories of such roadside melees. A suit was cycling peaceably across London Bridge towards his office in the City when he was confronted by a carload of those ruffians in motors who object to the existence of bicycles on the grounds of . . . what? . . . their lack of petrol . . . CD player . . . furry dice swinging from the bars? Whatever. They initiated a campaign of physical intimidation. The suit told them, politely and in quiet tones, to back off. Pushing, shoving and shaking his bike, they tried to elicit more robust response.

He refused. Again they provoked, and finally, the suit, who, unbeknownst to them was a black belt in karate, moved in and sorted them out with exquisite force, skill and economy, and then rode on. Ah, but wouldn't we all like to have that packed under our jacket, if push comes to shove?

Sables d'Olonne to Bayonne, 482km, 30–31 July 1999
Our first problem was *how to get there.*

For the class of 1919, the journey to Les Sables d'Olonne was straightforward: they cycled, 412km from Brest. We needed to catch trains, which meant bike bags, which meant extra baggage, which meant we would be pushing the sort of dead weight of the machines that the men of the early Tours rode.

John borrowed a couple of lightweight bike bags which would roll up small enough to be strapped to the saddlebag, all other luggage reduced to bare minimum. I booked the tickets, he collected the Litespeed from the magazine office and we were set to leave on Thursday, 29 July.

Les Sables d'Olonne, bang in the western middle of what used to be the English half of France, and once a flourishing port, spread sideways out along the sands early in the twentieth century and is still a popular holiday resort – lots of postcards with bare-boobed lovelies pouting 'Kisses from Sables'. In 1919, it offered the weary Tour riders their first respite – sea, sunshine and a refreshing swim. A number of fine riders had not returned from the First World War, most eminent among them: François Faber, first Luxemburger to win the Tour (1909), shot through the head while trying to rescue a wounded comrade in the French Foreign Legion, Carency, Pas-de-Calais, 1915; Octave Lapize, Tour winner, 1910, a fighter pilot, shot down over Verdun, 14 July 1917; and Lucien 'Petit-Breton', winner 1907–8, died on a military mission when his car crashed.

Around 1.3 million Frenchmen had perished – the highest proportion of any of the combatant nations. Of her 38,000 communes, only one did not lose someone to the war. There were, in addition, three million men disabled or crippled, over a third of them permanent invalids, and 200,000 civilians died from shellfire, bombs, the stray violence of combat. In the office of his newspaper *L'Auto*, 10 Rue du Faubourg Montmartre, Henri Desgrange pondered a 13th edition of his great bike race. Severe rationing was in force: Desgrange would need to secure exemptions for petrol, food and other commodities. The roads of north and eastern France were in ruins, bridges destroyed, signposts disappeared, the roads in the interior were dilapidated after five years of neglect. Moreover, European cycling had been bled dry. The loss of so many good men was bitter, emblematic of the terrible waste the war inflicted, but Desgrange could not, *would* not, give way to sentiment. If anything could speak of France's redemption, inspiring her to heave herself like a phoenix out of the ashes of war, then it was his Tour. Unprepared the riders might be, but they would have to shoulder this crucial burden of *renewal.*

Desgrange billed the race as the Tour of Regeneration.

By Sables, of the 68 who'd left Paris, 47 had already quit, 26 of them on the first stage to Le Havre (388km), including the Belgian ace Philippe Thys, the first triple winner (1913–14–20). His teammate Rossius took the stage but was penalised 30 minutes, for handing Thys a water bottle.

The weather was unremittingly foul, riders were puncturing, taking heavy falls, giving up in states of collapse, extreme fatigue and horror of what lay ahead. A journalist in the official Tour paper, Henri Desgrange's *L'Auto*, wrote that it was 'the first time the opening stage of the Tour de France is accused of murdering our riders'.

On the next two stages, they rode into a headwind 'strong

enough to take off a bull's horns' and incessant rain. Leaving Brest at 2 a.m., the fog was so thick that the official car headlamps – the only illumination they had – hardly penetrated more than 10m. When the fog did lift, it revealed not a road but a string of lakes of mud. They were soon coated head to foot, machines and all. They rode into Sables and straight off to the beach.

On the approaches to Sables, Henri Pélissier had found his brother Charles, a colossus of a man, sprawled, glassy-eyed, sobbing with fatigue at the side of the road, incapable of taking a tow. 'The Tour is an abomination,' he said. 'I'll never ride it again.' (He rode four more.) Henri rode on, and when he eventually climbed off, amazingly a mere 34m 52s adrift of the 'worthy old routier, Christophe', he said: 'The Tour de France is for penal convicts. That's it for me.'

'We thought he had more stuffing in him,' said the others, but they weren't sorry to see him go.

That feeling is familiar, isn't it? Those times when the beautiful machine has transmogrified into a sort of punishment rack on wheels and you think: 'I am never, ever, going to get on a bike again.'

Both Pélissiers turned up at the Sables *départ* control in the Café du Commerce, off the central town square, in suits. The crowds had been gathering there since 7 a.m. to see the 'giants of the road' arrive to sign on, but the brothers headed straight off for the same station into which the local chuffer, John and I aboard, chugged at 5.40 p.m. in clammy heat. The original Café is now the *Bar* du Commerce, local HQ for the PMU betting syndicate for trotting races and sponsors of the green points jersey.

We nearly didn't make it. Waiting for ages at the Gare du Nord metro as the already clogged platform filled with ever more people, I paid no conscious heed to a couple of announcements. Then I did listen and turned to John: 'We're in trouble. There are no trains. We need to get a cab.' We scrambled back past the turnstiles, through the luggage chute, into a taxi and on to Gare Montparnasse by a whisker. As we boarded the TGV, a woman asked me if we were carrying musical instruments. 'Harmony of the road,' I said.

Monday, 7 July 1919, 9.45 p.m.
Eighteen riders roll the 500m from the Café to the Porte de Talmont, a gateway in the *octroi*, tariff wall (long-since demolished). At 10 p.m., the start is given and they set out for Bayonne, through a thick fog rolling in off the Atlantic, on what was, and remains, the longest ever stage of the Tour de France (included from 1919 to 1924), though only by 14km. (Stage 14, Metz–Dunkerque, weighed in at 468km.) Best time: 18h 47m 26s in 1921; slowest: 20h 16m 26s in 1923. The only benefit derived from the first seven hours' riding till daybreak would be cooler air and no sagging view ahead of the hills as they come.

We got up at 6 a.m. and sat moodily in the hotel room trying to salivate over fruit juice, bananas, yoghourt, cheese sandwiches. Duty breakfast done, we rolled out through the marina, chockful of motorised dinghies and floating gin palaces, via the Commerce Café onto the Talmont road.

I'd been off the bike for a week, having been to Paris for the *arrivée* of that year's Tour followed by a rapid write-up of the whole race as a new chapter for the book. I had accumulated enough miles in my legs hitherto, no doubt, but my system was sluggish, and I foolishly made it even more sluggish: instead of going out on the bike in the few days I had, I rested. Effectively, my body shut down, went to sleep and took not a little of my brain to bed with it. Much joy they may have had of their slumber – for sure they were, neither one, eager for the recall to physical action. Apart from the sense that my head and legs were complete strangers, my back brake was sticking, my musette, stuffed with food, was cricking my back something rotten and I felt altogether as fluent as a blocked drain. Plus, for all the waffle about a *dead flat road*, it wasn't. The original profile published in *L'Auto* proves it: an interminable succession of those sick-making undulations which, if you're not on song, squeeze your lungs like a cider press and replace the blood in your legs with a sort of vascular treacle. I was most decidedly not on song, more of a tuneless drone, and I really thought John was going to give up on me: he kept offering me slipstream and I kept slipping off. The very road seemed to be jeering at me, like a tarmac reincarnation of Pélissier.

We hit Luçon in about the same time as the Tour men (1h 40m) and sat outside a café in warm morning sun. The caffeine put a little more spark in my ignition, and a madeleine tweaked the corners of my mouth into something more closely resembling a smile than I had so far managed that day. We pushed on into the marshlands of the Marais Poitevin, the July heat intensifying, past one farm called Wet-the-Feet and the latticework of small creeks where were moored flat-bottomed boats called *acons*, said to have been introduced by a shipwrecked Irish sailor in 1235 for mussel-fishing. The 1919 route, along the one decent highway then in existence, took in La Rochelle, Rochefort and Saintes, where 'despite the early hour – approximately 04h20 – the crowds lining the road were dense', but it's all motorway and *routes nationales* now. We rode parallel insofar as we could: precise historical accuracy didn't matter, and there were none of Desgrange's loss-adjustor *commissaires* lurking about to dock us time or money for inauthenticity. Heaviest sconce, 500 francs, was imposed for hitching a ride in any car, official or spectator's, even if the rider were delirious with fatigue or his machine irreparably broken. A stage win was worth 350 francs.

Our route, through small towns and villages, on dustblown roads, traversing the verdant bocage of the Vendée, the plump vineyards producing wine (red, white and rosé), *eau de vie* and *pineau*, a blend of both, was certainly closer in actual feel to what *they* had passed than clocking off antique kilometre stones along screaming highways. Much easier to imagine them riding through the succulent cow-munched pastures of Cognac and the Charente Maritime, waved at by knots of bewildered villagers and hamlet-dwellers.

In that long trajectory of morning into early afternoon, it took me about 160km to warm up. John, ever polite and unabrasive, said he thought this a shade too far. I thought it was outrageous. Lunch and lemonade seemed to jolt me into life, at last. Perhaps I had simply been riding off the resentment at having had to commit eating so early in the morning. My stomach is recalcitrant and pliant by turns. Anyway, having got through the artificial suffering, when riding ought to have hurt but didn't, except in the disgruntlement of my spirit, I could start turning the pace on and get some response from, and tax on, my legs.

The 1919 bunch, bent on honouring the memory and reputation of the great men of the *peloton* killed in the war, had been warned by the Tour organisation 'not to hurl themselves like madmen at the feeding stations', but there was a general truce this ultra-long day. Doubtless reflecting on the impending ordeal of the mountains – Pyrenees, end to end in two stages – they passed through the controls more or less together. At Luçon, the 18 survivors were reduced to 17: the Belgian Urbain Anseeuw vomited his way off the bike and out of the race.

On one particularly vicious bit of uphill on the picturesque roller coaster between the RN137 south of Saintes towards Blaye, I went through one of those dreadful three-minute patches which last a virtual hour, when your brain leaks in a rush, like a blowout, when you might be trying to do step-ups in quick-drying cement and the gradient (not *really* much) looks like a sheer rock face. John, mannerly as ever, stayed with me as I strove to jump-start the mental circuits whilst maintaining upright position and forward motion, my inner voice raging and cursing at my lack of punch.

At the top of one hill, in blistering heat, we pass a sign which reads: 'Smile . . . Breathe deeply: you are in Aquitaine'. I didn't much care where we were, nor did I take kindly to self-help instructions affiliating soppy grins with topography.

John came alongside me and held out an energy bar. I told him I wasn't hungry. He continued to hold out the energy bar.

'Do you think I should eat?' I said.

'Yes,' he said. I ate it. It tasted sickly sweet and disgusting.

We got to Blaye, on the Gironde, with 1¼ hours in hand before the ferry across the Gironde. They buried the paladin Roland, hammer of the Saracens, in Blaye after his death at the pass of Roncesvaux in 778, and we sank two of the coolest tangiest beers ever as we waited by the dock.

Across the water, we turned left on the minor D2. The fingerpost read 19km to Bordeaux. (The original route followed the right bank of the Gironde: we avoided the three-lane lorry drag strip and opted for the quieter left-bank route.) In some ways, I found those 19km the worst of the whole ride: knowing we had bags of time, I was savagely impatient to get them done and had to fight like hell against a deep instinct to relax and take the distance easy. I simply couldn't do that, but nor could I allow myself the credit for the pretty decent speed we were carving up, either: 34kph, despite luggage and 260km in the legs, nonetheless felt slow, ponderous. 'That the best you can do?' my sniffy racing ego was saying to my humbler tourist-routier self, clogging away like a good 'un.

Skirting several illustrious châteaux of the Médoc peninsula – Margaux, Lafite, Pauillac, Mouton-Rothschild – we grimaced through Bordeaux's evening traffic and one-way systems onto

311

the Esplanade des Quinconces, one of that year's Tour finishes. Average for the day by John's bar computer: 28kph.

The 1919 Tour came into the city through a control at the Café Mazarin – start-point of the Bordeaux–Paris race – across the stone bridge and along the quais (now a *périphérique*). We picked them up – and I punctured – on the route de Toulouse, down part of this year's Tour itinerary from Mourenx. We followed the 1919ers more or less exactly from here on, and, quite against expectation, it turned out to be a great ride.

The flat coastal Landes are thickly afforested with pines, to inhibit the loss of the sandy topsoil to the offshore winds. The landscape is largely deserted, the dense thickets of towering pines slightly oppressive, the sense of general absence of identifiable destination quite insistent, yet the supposedly monotonous Landes roads were a joy. With 280km done and 200km still to do, long stretches of uninhabited roads through empty pine forests might very well have been the soul of tedium, but, unlike the Tour men, we had had a night's sleep to refresh us, plus a lavish dab of corticoid cream on badly chafed, acid-sweat-scored buttocks and groin. Performance enhancing? Certainly. It meant being able to tolerate the pressure of the saddle, *just*, as opposed to *no frigging way*. That and the decongestant fragrances of conifer resin and sun-baked pine cones: we were flying.

There was cloud cover thin enough to keep the day still bright, but the temperature was a mite cooler and we were riding bit and bit with occasional side by side for a chat. I felt marginally polka-dot sick crossing a painted tarmac message: 'Thank you Richard. Allez Virenque' just south of Hostens, and we avoided the ominously named town of Sore to launch into some 15km of sandy track leading to a rough road of compacted aggregate, not dissimilar to the surfaces of 80 years ago. Feeling that we had really cracked the challenge, we made a leisurely lunch stop at Labouheyre, second of their feeding stations, 385km, in Gascony, home of the fourth musketeer, d'Artagnan.

To show solidarity with the 1919ers, we put ourselves through a 12km calvary round the lake by Soustons, on a remote twisty road so uneven and corrugated we had to do virtually the whole way out of the – by now *excruciating* – saddle. Then, a bizarre moment: we stopped to check the map by a large gate in the middle of nowhere, attended by a soldier standing by a sentry box.

'Is this a military installation?' I asked.

'No, a private house. Belonged to the former President of France.' He meant Mitterand: his widow still lives there.

What a job: sentry-go on a forest byway.

Out of the forest, we rode into Capbreton, once an important harbour till the river silted up, now a popular resort. The vineyards along this bit of the shoreline produce a good *vin de sable*, and we began to dwell on the celebration to come that evening. Journey's end only 13km distant. (*Vin de sable* comes from grapes of a vine which grows in sand. In winter, the vineyards are flooded with water to kill off parasites and disease.)

The RN10 gave us smooth tarmac and a blast of 38+kph for the run-in to Bayonne. We had blazing sunshine, they had pelting rain which let up just before the finish atop the last kilometre of hairpins onto the Côte de St Etienne. Here the local *vélo* club had erected two stands: one for officials, one for the press. That road is a broad sweeping climb now, but the descent into the city is just as sweet, down across the bridges onto the Place de la Liberté and the *arrivée* control in the Brasserie Schmitt.

In 1919, Alavoine took the stage, and 350 francs, in 18h 54m 7s, and breezed over, fresh as fizz and debonair as ever, to shake hands with the veteran journalist Mercier: 'I didn't want to keep you in suspense,' he said. 'I'll gladly come and do the obligatory interview every day if you can guarantee me victory every day. I went great guns, no bad spells – should go well in the Pyrenees. After the early fog broke, I was glad not to be riding in a box of cotton wool. OK, poppa Mercier, off to entrust my little old legs to Pano [the masseur Panonetti].'

Chassot took second, and 200 francs, by a length, and Christophe, at 13 seconds, rode himself into the overall lead. The luckless Nempon – punctures and a fall – trailed in three hours down. He plugged away, though, the lone category B rider (i.e. without sponsorship) to survive, and carried the *lanterne rouge* into Paris, last of only 11 to complete the course, won by the Belgian Lambot.

All over France next morning, news vendors were mobbed as they had been from the start of the Tour by punters snatching copies of *L'Auto* for the latest episode of the saga and to stare in amazement at the profile of the next stage, to begin after 24 hours' rest: 327km to Luchon across the cols d'Osquich, Aubisque, Soulor, Aspin, Tourmalet, Peyresourde. Still to come: 323km to Perpignan, seven big cols.

From Bayonne, Henri Desgrange telegraphed his despatch: 'The race makes its unpitying selection and soon we will have to admit only those who have the strength *and* the heart to ride it.'

Elated as we felt, and, after some 18 hours all told in the saddle, remarkably fit, it was in the awesome appreciation not of what we had achieved but what we hadn't had to do before it and would not have to do after it.

That night at supper, we toasted my mother on the second anniversary of her death.

Twenty

Cinder Hill

The title I originally proposed for this book, in reference to a remark Claudine Merckx made about her husband's obsession with the bike, was *The Hypodermic Spoke*. 'The problem with Eddy,' she said, 'is that he was vaccinated with a bicycle spoke.' The idea had a certain slickness, but the inevitable association with doping was maladroit. Though I am required, professionally, to deal with the subject of drugs in sport and once interviewed the then French drugs tsar in Paris at considerable length, animadversions on the pharmacy, from anabolic steroids to zero tolerance, are out of place here. 'Cinder Hill' needs some explaining, however.

The area of Kent in which I live has a goodly catalogue of hill names: the climbs up to the North Downs ridge, Sundridge, Brasted, Hogtrough, Shoreham, Titsey and White Lane Hill (old Titsey), are extreme and awful; Star Hill is fractionally less unpleasant to traverse; only Botley, side-stepping slantwise along and around the contours, gives anything like an unstressed ride to the escarpment and big panorama over the Darenth Valley. I saw a rider interval-training on Sundridge Hill once and thought, briefly, of the intervals we did on the River Wear at Durham – 12 x 500m flat out and paddling back to the start in tightening spirals of physical decomposition and mental fragmentation, our coach cycling along the towpath as the twilight closed in, bellowing through a megaphone: 'Drive. Drive. Your legs will never give up,' and me thinking *how can he possibly know whether my, our, legs will never give up?* They never did. Wonderful conditioning, but the days for such craziness are long, long gone. I did not envy that lone devotee turning at the bottom of the descent and churning up again, but I knew what was in his head. And there is always the curving of the 1 in 5 to the shallower brow and the realisation that, once more, against all odds of declining powers, you've made it. On the high pitch of Hogtrough, just as your mind begins to cave in to the belief that your legs have taken all the lactic acid they can hold, the road suddenly eases a fraction through a spinney of ancient beech trees. A fine sunlit view back down over the valley, the low murmur of the M25 traffic almost inaudible now.

Another climb to the ridge, Polhill – a link I have to use for journeys to Orpington station – though once famous in club road-racing lore and still used for time-trials, is now blighted with traffic, most of it 'late-for-work' or 'bloody-cyclists' aggressive.

Elsewhere, Bayleys, with its languorous curves, and Yorks Hill, in a straight upwards run – an abject fury of gradient – rise out of the Bough Beech trough in the valley of the River Eden. The Catford use Yorks, by Hanging Bank, for their autumn hill climbs.

Suffixing the word 'Club', by the way, is redundant, infra dig, intensely uncool. Personally, I don't give a toss, but I am a sucker for linguistic oddity expressive of an emotional reflex, and saying simply 'The Catford' and so on is a linguistic oddity which comes out of a distinctly male vanity: that of belonging, the group instinct, the clubby 'us' discrete from the unwashed 'them', the joiners.

A pal of mine at the Highgate Men's Pond, Ken, is a lovely bloke and he's a joiner, he likes the cosy feel of belonging, of having an identity which comes out of an attachment to shared interest rather than the riskier process of allowing identity to float, as it were, on a public exchange where it may not have any purchasing power at all. One raw Saturday morning in February, high wind-chill factor, snow on the ground, the surface of the pond showed a skin of thin, thin ice – it makes an eerie bewitching low hiss and sizzle as the plate bends and lifts over the ripples when you swim through water which, at that low temperature, has the oily consistency of chilled vodka. Four of us repaired to the local café for breakfast after the arctic dip. A warm fug of heaters, cooking vapours and steam off the cups of coffee as we sat at the table waiting for our food: full English twice, liver and bacon once, sausage, egg and beans, fried slice once. Ken rubbed his hands and grinned at us, each one in varying stages of hypothermia, according to our tolerance of the cold. 'I tell you what,' he said, a boyish light of playing hookie in his eyes, that mischief which comes from being in a secret gang at school. 'I tell you what, we'll call ourselves The Polar Bears, and I'll get some T-shirts made up.'

I looked at him. 'No, Ken. We do it, that's all.'

He seemed not to mind. He's Jewish. He smiled, shrugged, there'd be other follies, other times, and the food came. Ken likes to belong. Except that this morning had been no more than an unofficial extraordinary chance meeting (no quorum taken) of the committee-less sodality of all-year-round pond swimmers over breakfast in the Parliament Hill greasy spoon run by Greeks.

The southern approach to Toy's Hill, to return to my miniature galaxy of potential eponyms, is a brute, a real poser, belying the charm and innocence of its moniker, and the narrow rustic western lane that joins it halfway up, through the back door up from French Street by Bardogs Farm past Puddledock, isn't much kinder. Magpie Bottom is a twisting, steep, lost-valley climb, so overhung with trees that the surface never gets completely dry and the rear wheel slips on the harder sections. Off Gover Hill, leading on past Rats Castle to Roughway, the road plunges apprehensively down down down into the leafy dell of Swanton Valley – hillbilly country, this: blind-windowed, remote, neglected homesteads draped with weather-torn faded Union flags . . . not a place in which to puncture, one feels. Sheet Hill and Yopps Green cradle the old Golding Hop pub, a throwback to slower-moving times when beaded bubbles of the cool ale winked at the rim of straight glasses ranged on a tray passed through the hostelry's hatchway.

On the village green at Ide Hill, I sat, once, waiting for my pal Geoff, when a man bearing a tray loaded with plants in pots walked up and told me he'd been a cyclist in his youth. His son was a keen rider, too, and he was thinking he might give it a go again. He had a mind to buy a bike, could I give him some advice? I said sure, I'd be glad to help, and scribbled my number on a piece of paper. Three months later, the phone rang: 'Hello, this is Bob Cash. You perhaps don't remember me, but on Ide Hill in May . . .' I loaned him a bike that I was intending to sell. It was vastly over-geared for him, but he kept it some time and its seduction worked. He bought a hybrid as well as copies of my Tour book. We became friends. He told me that Brian Robinson had inspired him as a kid, so I got Brian to send a card. Out of that chance meeting, our common ground the beautiful machine, Bob and his wife Linda became a cherished part of the confraternity of Low House, where I now live. That Geoff and Gill should live so close to where I came to settle was another happy coincidence, and the friendship with Dave and his wife Carol another instance of the great good fortune which has followed me to this Garden of England. Even the hills.

Hubbards Hill is an unlovely straight steep disgorge of

reinforced concrete up from the Kentish Weald to Sevenoaks Common. A bit to the east, River Hill, the main A225 to Sevenoaks from the south, is horrible, graceless, a real bully, to be avoided if possible.

I first picked One Tree Hill, further east, not much liked even by the best down here, as the juxtaposing place name in the book's subtitle, until I was told that it's the title of a popular American television show. Having no box, nor inclination to own one, how was I to know? Lucy didn't tell me, though she might have done, so that particular three-stress lead-in to the full stop (OK, for the purists: the rare triple-note in prosody called a molossus) had to go. To my annoyance. The name was perfect, and Old Riverhill, another name for the same long, tough, narrow, winding haul up from the village of Underriver with the false flat just over halfway, isn't on the map, and I didn't feel I could use a fiction. As to Plaxtol Hill, it didn't have quite the punch, quite the ring, albeit, for those of us who live between the escarpment of the North Downs and the hilltop Greensand Way overlooking the Weald and the flatter lands out past Tonbridge, Plaxtol Hill is a fact of life.

Tonbridge is where my friend Luke, former editor (*Cycle Sport, Land Rover World*) and now freelance, lives with June. They were my first new friends in Kent and have become a very dear fixture in my life here. For our occasional breakfast visits to the famous Knox Bridge Café, venue for the Sydenham's Christmas club run – turkey lunch and cross-toasting – which I always try to join, Luke and I ride past the hop fields around Hadlow, Laddingford and Collier Street. We do not cross either Winchet Hill or Worms Hill, and the circuit is, by and large, level and speedy, the roads quiet enough to allow side-by-side riding and animated prattle. For other rides, our habitual meeting place is by the butcher's shop in Plaxtol itself, halfway down the hill. Sometimes, needing more miles, Luke will ride back up the rest of the hill with me.

One grey March day, when I was in the thick of researching and writing the book about the French revolutionary Terror, we did an extensive ride, four hours or so, the Luke Evans tour of the potholes of east Kent, I recall. By the end of it, I was finished, not so much physically as mentally – drained and feeble. On Plaxtol Hill, nearing home and beginning to wilt at the thought of more strain, I struggled, and, in the gesture of friendship we all know by giving and receiving, but is never less than pure generosity, Luke rode up alongside me, put his hand in the small of my back and cruised me up the last torsions of the slope. Incidentally, that book on the Terror, researched and written in around 15 months, 15 months during which I spent all my waking hours and not a few of the sleeping hours, too, in the virtual company of some pretty dodgy characters, nearly did me in. It destroyed one relationship, although that was probably doomed – she was a smoker, her sweat after sex was stale with nicotine and I had lost nearly all levity. In fact, the labour of that book alienated me to the extent that I couldn't bear the company of anyone I didn't know quite well. Sundays were worst. As I growled mirthlessly back to the workroom after lunch, I thought of the Sabbath slackers, just sipping their first glass of chilled preprandial Chablis before a hearty roast lunch and, further lubricated with blackcurranty Rhône, maybe, repairing to bed with beloved for a lubricious siesta. From the crabbed solitude of the writer's cell, I notionally brandished my fists and hollered: 'Bastards.' No jokes about cycles of violence or parallel revolutions seemed to lighten the mood, either.

Luke was born in the western half of the county, a Kentish Man, therefore – east of the Medway live the Men of Kent – and one day as we slogged up the rise from Apps Hollow, off Gracious Lane, a cruel hill I knew well from the time when I worked at a pub on Coldharbour Lane, I moaned rather. 'I hate this bastard hill,' I said.

Luke rejoined: '*You* can choose the routes, you know.'

'Ah,' I said, 'I know my place.' He has been riding these lanes since he was a kid. I am but a late arriviste. That hill and the stinker which follows it form the closing section of a vile Kent clubs hilly time-trial, and good luck to them.

We were out in snow one wintry Saturday with Kevin, a high-octane club racer, in search of the hairier arse-kickers of the Gemini, who foray out from Chislehurst. We'd done a couple of hours, slithered up Plaxtol and on via some assorted bits of nastiness around Kingsdown, Knockmill and Knatt's Valley, by way of Tinkerpot Lane, down Crackenhall Lane towards Shoreham, and reached the T-junction at Eynsford. (*En passant*: there are some real brutes of climbs around Shoreham.) Hanging a left, we saw the Gemini hurtling along towards us, a tight-packed swarm of villainy, knitted together with competitive venom and no-quarter speed. Kevin immediately jumped the white line, turned about and was on their back as they swung into the right turn. Luke and I got caught in the oncoming traffic and, by the time we had slipped over to the far carriageway and regained the junction, the Gemini, like pounds, shillings and pence, were gone.

'Do you feel like chasing?' said Luke.

At such moments, admitting the simple truth that actually you *don't* feel like chasing has no place in the dictates of the code of honour which enjoins that you *must* chase, in whatever state your legs, lungs or head happen to be. We chased.

After about five minutes on the rivet, knowing, as well I know myself, that my part in the pursuit was futile, I came up alongside Luke and said: 'Too old, too fat, too cold, too shot.'

'And that's just me,' he replied. Such is the man's kindly and forgiving temper. We rode on for another couple of hours, in broadening sunshine, frost sparkling on the hedgerows, the roads wet with melting snow and ice. I made acquaintance for the first time with a real crusher along Penn Lane, up the back of Ide Hill past Brook Place, and so, gratefully, home, suffused with a tiredness which is close to deep contentment and fullness of being. I have heard people say that certain aspects of cycling, in particular achieving mountain summits, are as good as, even better than, sex. The two sensations are not remotely comparable, unless your idea of good sex is emerging from a protracted bout of bodily and psychological distress during much of which you'd been thinking you'd rather be anywhere else doing anything else. Besides: 'Comparisons,' says Dogberry, 'are odorous,' meaning odious, and my feeling is that if anyone thinks getting to the top of a mountain, even a big brute steeped in a century of cycling history, deserves inclusion within the same catchment of the sensations, physical and mental, triggered by lovemaking, they are not paying close enough attention to either sex or mountains. The two forms of bonking are poles apart, and *vive*, as they say, *la différence*.

Just to prove how illogical some comparisons can be: after running the 2006 New York marathon, Lance Armstrong called it: 'the hardest thing I have ever done, worse than the Tour de France', which seems to me to be not only nonsensical but a silly slight on the bike race.

The road from Leigh takes Luke and me up the steady drag of Cinder Hill to where a view, left, opens up of Penshurst Place, the ancestral home of the Sidney family, built in 1552. It's no great crunch of a ride. Nevertheless it has the piquant distinction of familiarity. Hardly a Poggio, that final obstacle before the run-in to the Via Roma at the end of the springtime classic Milan–San Remo, La Primavera, but Cinder Hill nicely concludes our habitual run to the famous Quaintways tea rooms. From the top of the hill, the descent is quick and always charged with the unspoken challenge of racing to the village sign, that old club routine. Never having been in a club, it took me a while to catch on. Now I have the same

Pavlovian instinct, if not the same cunning. From a mixture of ignorance and brash zeal, I almost always lead out, from some distance. And Luke, almost always, clips me on the line by as little as a tyre-width – all it takes. He has been a racer all his life and can judge when to jump in a way that a novice never can. It gives me such pleasure to observe that play of racing nous, to hear him chortle: 'Hey, beating Cipo [Mario Cipollini, the sprinting ace], not bad,' as he wins another of our two-up sprints. I have beaten him on a couple of occasions but neither time with any great skill or subtlety. Raw speed and impatience are my sole gambit, and, I suppose, sheltering in his slipstream so that I could read what he does would make me feel a bit like a wheel-sucker, the rider who never gets a tan because he is always in the shade cast by the man in front. Such an attitude is, of course, puerile, and, were I bothered, I could acquire the knack and hone the guile. But, winning the Quaintways sprint on the down of Cinder Hill simply means less to me than the exuberant joy of being with one of my best friends, on a bike, in Kent, at a midway point of another gleeful ride, at speed, merry as grigs, talking as we go, and the shiver of delight at Luke's kick for the line, overlapping me by inches. Although we do ride hard, there is no rivalry between us, more than the keeping up to the mark which comes naturally to any of us out on the road, in company. The Sydenham Christmas club run . . . the Old Ports weekend in Eastbourne . . . the Phil and Friends . . . mutual kickings are (generally) taboo, friendly competitive hot pace and the last push to the destination at accelerating tempo are not. However . . .

In July 2004, I was, as I said earlier, in the Pyrenees, showing American visitors around the climbs of the Ariège, taking in three mountain stages of the Tour de France and, this particular late afternoon, pitching up in a bar in Saint-Girons to watch the last half-hour or so of that day's stage in company with a bunch of riders from the Hounslow. They were installed in the bar before we arrived, rather untidily, taking up far too much room, as I remember. They were lodging at an auberge down the road from us, the anonymous summer casuals, in Biert, 32km away up the valley towards the Col de Port.

Some of our party went off to find a cyber café, and the remaining three of us settled in to watch the close of the racing. Whether from lack of interest, itchy twitch muscles or a spasm of Francophobia, the Hounslow decided to move on before the end of the transmission. They trooped out in a body, cleats clacking on the tiled floor. I was relieved. Let them get safely up ahead of us, out of the way, out of sight, no possibility of any stand-offs, the feral competitive urge kicking in to mash a nice quiet evening ride into the unholy dog's breakfast of an eyeballs-out scrap for precedence over the tarmac. Pooh to that.

We, meanwhile, Larry and Peter from Pennsylvania and I, took in the professional eyeballs-out scrap of the stage finish and then ambled out of the bar, remounted and set off. We pedalled lazily out of town, dawdling south onto the D618, which follows the route of the old coach road across the Pyrenees, along the course of the Salat River. Salat seems to be an old Languedoc word, akin to the Catalan, for pleasant, genial, and the valley deserves its name. Broad green meadows at the lower end gradually taper into the narrower gorge, and the curvy road itself, swaying its hips on a steady uphill, actually feels more like a downhill much of the way, planting the illusion that you can hit the pace harder than is sensible. Further on, the ups begin to multiply and take their natural toll.

The overspill of Saint-Girons, a quiet town which comes to bustling life on market days, peters out eastwards into a small clutch of industrial buildings dominated by the paper-making factories which stand either side of the road in Eycheil – a distinctive, dry, fibrous, cereal, faintly sour odour of the tissue sold as paper for rolling cigarettes. Apparently, it's the biggest supplier in France for Job and Zigzag and whatever other brands there are.

Out of Eycheil, the road shakes off the vestiges of the town and, like a dog out for a walk in the country, starts to roam and pry into the corners of the fields and the hedgerows. This was most agreeable: a comfortable ride up the valley home, sun shining, us contentedly weary after a long day in the saddle, and, hey, no hassle from the Hounslow or anyone else, for that matter. (I did once gaily ride past another lone guy on the way into Saint-Girons, about 20km out. I said good morning, so he had nothing to complain about on the social niceties side, but for some reason he took umbrage and stuck mutely to my wheel for about 15km till I managed to shake him off and ride on into town on a rising surge of resentment . . . wheel-sucker.)

As we rounded one corner with a longer view ahead, chatting happily, I saw something which sent a tremor of apprehension down my shorts: the Hounslow, in a bunch, taking it easy, apparently, except that we were taking it easy, too, and we were gaining on them fast. This wasn't in the quiet-ride-home plan. It's a curious moment, this sudden rumble of excitement and dread, tension spliced with merriment, when idiot folly pounces on common sense and gives it a scragging. What were we going to do? Take them on? Tag on at the back? Mingle? Please . . . you know exactly what you're going to do, fuck it.

We moved up nicely, the chains rolling off the cogs onto the overtaking gear like stocking tops peeling away from suspenders. The Hounslow hadn't heard us. We breezed up in sweet silence. Campag can do that for you. When we were about 10m from the back marker's rear-tyre tread, I turned briefly to the compadre at my elbow, Larry, an enthusiast to his twinkle toes, and said: 'Right, let's take them.'

Was there another option?

In such circumstances, there is never another option.

We took them. A cursory 'Hi, guys' and raced on. An innocuous enough remark, and spry enough in tone, but there is nothing you can say at such a juncture which doesn't carry the message: 'Is that the best you can do?' Anyway, we swooped past and the jockey wheels whirred. Good break. Working well together, bit and bit, Larry and Pete, his buddy, chipping in.

It took the Hounslow about two minutes to claw us back, but claw us back they did, and in the sudden flush of adrenalin when they did surge up and round us like a gang of queue bargers, the thrill of the chase simmered through me. And then it simmered back out of me. This was serious. We'd asked for it and we'd got it. I was on the front and the tempo was high, the pressure from behind my back quite as urgent as the intoxicating lure of the twisting road ahead.

Someone came through and I was on his wheel. This was better. Hey, we didn't ask the Hounslow if they wanted to come out to play, but here they were mixing in. The guy on the front swung off and dropped back. I was on the front again and the bunch got ever more vocal and restless, raring to go. This was the hammer. Then I heard a voice behind me saying: 'Let's get a chain gang going.' Good idea, I thought, very sound. Another of them came through and the pace stayed high, and, as he swung off, another came through and I was relishing the nice momentum of the chain-gang groove and full of the racing toxins as the front man swung off. Ain't this the business? Everybody sharing the pace. We'd be home in no time. Sharing the pace. Another guy sneaked up, got a feel of the open road, but I could see his heart wasn't in it. He lingered long enough for the breeze to dry his brow, and then, like the Cheshire Cat, he faded into invisibility. The clamour behind me continued. The action forward did not. Shouldn't someone be coming through? No one came through. I saw: I was re-elected. Perhaps, I reflected, they were uncertain whose turn it was next. Perhaps the Hounslow had strange protocols unknown to the generality of cycle-kind. Chris Boardman said that the day he was allowed to ride at the front of the bunch – not a privilege accorded to newcomers – was the day he knew he was a professional. But not vice versa, presumably.

Still no one came through.

Then it dawned on me: this was the Hounslow version of the chain gang, as applied to interlopers who tried to show off, a man-powered industrial-strength titanium and carbon lemon squeezer, and I was the lemon. The Hounslow weren't sharing the work, they were policing the break, and most of them were at least 20 years younger than me with aerodynamic haircuts, polished knees, kangaroo-leather shoes, top-of-the-range ultra-light machinery and components and impenetrable attitude. I was on a 30-year-old, steel, hand-built Shorter, its headset fused into the stem with age, brakes as stiff as a tax inspector's sense of humour, lugs and balloon tyres – wonderful handling downhill but, in the context of this encounter, me versus the Hounslow, strictly a museum piece with all the potential for turning me into the same. Not so much a chain gang as ganging up.

I lasted about a quarter of an hour, praying for a puncture, before age, punished lungs and the monstrous roar of the bunch flying away up a sudden cruel snap of gradient got the better of me. I watched them go, Larry and Pete with them, and knew I would not get back on. Too fast, too strong, too past, too young. When the speed goes up a click above what is just on the brink between manageable and unfeasible, you're done, cooked. We were still about 10km from home, and I found myself in company with two of the senior men of the Hounslow. We commiserated with each other on the discrepancy between what we could live with against what the youth up the road could and made our own way, more of a daisy chain than any sort of gang.

As it is, we mopped up several stragglers who had been

shelled out in their turn, and there was a kind of satisfaction in that. We came in no more than a minute adrift, unashamed and unembarrassed. Honour served.

To an outsider, it may all seem a bit silly, childish, unnecessary. Well, so what? We thrive on pushing ourselves to the limit and as far beyond as the limit is elastic and will give. When the elastic will give no more and snaps, we stop, that's all, we have to stop, there is no choice, and the day we stop pushing ourselves we have crossed forever a frontier which only physical failing can keep at a distance, not mental. The great running trainer (of Herb Elliott et al.) Percy Cerutti had his men running up and down loose sand dunes, for stamina. He joined them, even in his 70s, and was wont to say: 'You may go faster than me but you won't go harder.'

That, in my view, is what we're here for: to go harder, ever harder. There is, too, the uncomplicated sense of gratitude that we can still go at all. For, nothing much gets done in the comfort zone. Risk, chance, exploration of what others timidly call impossible, are the gearing ratios of our momentum.

In the Quaintways garden – cyclists welcome but not bikes – or inside, if there is no sun or warmth in the day, Luke and I sit and talk, about cycling, about psychology, about current causes for concern, about cadence and the life and times of various riders, laced with verdicts on races and riders, stratagems and stories in the ether. 'I've decided to try to like Armstrong this year,' says Luke.

'Hmm, I don't think I can,' I say. 'Perhaps I should try. Maybe I take my dislikes too personally.'

We talk of earpieces and how they have crucially changed racing. The spontaneous attack in the saddle is almost gone now, except among the small fry, released from *domestique* duties on a flat stage. The grand solo gesture of past leaders independent of the *directeur* in the car must now heed the incessant voice in the ear. Merckx in the 1969 Tour des Flandres, for instance. With more than 70km of the race to go, a cold, wet, blustery day, he went on his own. 'Driessens [his *directeur sportif*] came alongside me,' he recalled, 'and asked me if I'd gone completely mad . . . I screamed back: "Go screw yourself," carried on and won. Then, after the finish, I heard that Driessens was rabbiting on how "We've pulled it off yet again; we saw our chance once more and took it," and it infuriated me.' I cherish the moment when, on the final climb to Luz-Ardiden in 2001, Ullrich took out his earpiece and let it dangle.

Luke rode the Étape du Tour in 1999 and says it was that ride which taught him why he never wanted to be a pro. To be a pro, 'You have to be old at 17,' he says, 'and know that's all you ever want to do.' It goes beyond commitment, dedication: it's a state of mind, like taking religious vows. Talent isn't enough. Sean and Chris Yates are friends of ours – Chris refurbished the workroom where I write this – and although probably equal in talent, they are unequal in desire for the life of a professional bike-rider. They ride two-up time-trials, and Chris is a star of the south-eastern leagues. It's probably in the Yates genes that neither brother feels pain in the way *we* feel pain, but Chris simply had not the desire for racing at the professional level. I might liken that compelling need to what drives me to this job I do for a living, but I can't be absolutely sure of it – only that once I decided I would be a writer, there was never any question I would be a writer, come what may, no pact with the Devil required. If there is something we alone can do, whatever that something is, then it behoves us to do it or let it go to waste, and that is morally criminal.

A pot of coffee arrives together with that staple of the cycling provender, the toasted teacake. Componentry slinks into the conversation occasionally, and I make the routine disclaimer that, possessed as I am of one or two reasonable bikes and a fair bit of decent kit (it wasn't always the case), I will be found out one day. Custom-built Tifosi? Made-to-measure, pale peppermint-green Pista from Condor? Goblin-silver titanium without decals? Lipstick-red Vitus? Each one far too poncey for the likes of me. Of *course* I will be found out one day. Luke says 'you can never have too many bikes', though at one stage I did have seven, here, which was excessive: the aforementioned stable plus the Shorter, brought back from its long-term home in France, the Condor I bought from Phil Liggett and the town machine which I use for everyday travelling and shopping, an old Claude Butler. On two occasions while I was refurbishing and renovating Low House, it conveyed sizeable loads of furniture, rugs, candles and assorted items from the Croydon IKEA in panniers and rack.

Although the cycling-magazine offices are located in Croydon and trips there were sometimes necessary, I do try to avoid Croydon: it's one of those places that isn't really anywhere, and in the view of many ought *not* to be anywhere. The route I used to take – no more – included transit of New Addington. Here stands a large 'Welcome to Croydon' sign (believe me, *anyone* is welcome to Croydon *and* New Addington, suspecting or unsuspecting) on which is appended: 'The natural choice, twinned with Arnhem'. That says it all. On the second of those IKEA runs, the bike was so heavily weighed down that I was almost crying with effort going up the last hill.

Luke and I also delve into the masonries of cadence and *souplesse*, and it was he who urged me to get a fixed wheel. I held off for some while, largely because I didn't have the money. I'd converted the Coventry Eagle to fixed in my teens, so had had a taste, and took note of a recent surge in enthusiasm for the fixed, particularly among urban cyclists. Then came my friend Matt Seaton's masterly analysis of riding the fixed wheel in the second issue of *Rouleur* magazine: his loving description of the symbiotic relationship with the fixed was so enticing that I decided, finally, a fixed it had to be. A promised job had just fallen through, leaving me skint, but, at such times, economising is like giving in or up. I phoned Grant Young at Condor's. Grant and his dad, Monty, are good pals of mine. We meet periodically at the Pickwick luncheons, the Pedal Club, here and there in the manor of our two-wheeled circulation. I love their shop, and they are part of the wider world of bike-riding to which the writing of these books introduced me some while ago.

It took me a few outings to get used to the technique again – the instinct to stop pedalling, especially over a rut, a drain grating, a manhole cover, is wilful. The remorseless *perpetuum mobile* of the fixed punishes that lapse instantly and, to begin with, perilously. However, Luke told me the best thing to do was to stop deliberately a few times so that I was acquainted with the shock and would not panic. Soon, I was pedalling quickly and smoothly and am now a proselytiser for the cause. Winter conditioning. Fluent rhythm. Low maintenance. Hey, purist stuff.

Matt came south on his fixed with Tim Krabbé and a few of his buddies from the Dulwich one murky midweek morning. We met in Cudham Lane, the usual conduit for the London boys into the green lanes of Kent. (This was my second ride with Tim. He came first to Low House in the autumn of 2003. We did a wide loop out past Chiddingstone and back for supper.) We got pretty wet, did a circuit over some roads I didn't know, above and around Westerham, introduced Tim to the staple teacake at a café stop and said our goodbyes at the foot of Westerham Hill by the Pilgrims Way. I watched them go up that bastard of a climb – Matt pushing the fixed as if it were triple-ringed – without a flutter of remorse in my black heart, then headed off along the plain-sailing magic flying carpet of the old route leading eventually to the shrine of Thomas à Becket, the martyr, at Canterbury.

Luke also says, very wisely, that one shouldn't be sentimental about bikes – attachment is not to the object but to its history. Being a relative latecomer to laptop and mobile phone, this was in some conflict with my more sluggish sedate instincts, but I am a wholesome convert now. My town bike freights a deal of history. I bought it from my friend John, companion of Continental tours. It carried him, alongside me, over Alps, Dolomites and Pyrenees. Some pedigree. But, it does me service no more: its history is separate. The Shorter, about which I might have been expected to feel pangs, having decided that its day had come, has, like a faithful working horse, been put out to grass, so to speak. I could not think of selling it – who would have bought such an antiquated machine anyway? – and gave it to my dear friend Richard Divers, who is not really a cyclist but loves riding a bike. He keeps it at his house outside Presteigne, in Wales. Nice to think that my first real racing bike which had given me so much pleasure was still giving pleasure. I could not bear to think of it being trashed. As a gift to a friend, it kept its integrity, its specialness, its role.

'This may sound odd to you,' Richard said after he had been out on it a few times, 'but it goes straight.'

Having seen the lolloping machine he had been used to, I wasn't surprised. 'The technical term is "responsive",' I said. When I visited him down there, I took Shorter out for a ride and wondered how on earth I had managed still to be climbing Pyrenean mountains on it so late in the day. Sheer obduracy, no doubt. Did it really take advancing age to teach me the obvious lesson about keeping stride with advances in technology? After all, my credo in other spheres is that we all need all the help we can get. Why not, therefore, from better gearing, lighter frames? Good God, I didn't even have overshoes till Luke gave me an old pair a few years ago.

And saying that Richard is not a cyclist is no disparagement, simply that in his enjoyment of the bike there is no trace of obsession, and it is obsession, of whatever intensity, which defines us. Our life embraces the bike – the idea of it, the fact of it, the significance of it, the freedom it imparts, the joy, the pain, the inexhaustible delight – and without the bike the life would be, in an essential element, incomplete. That is *cyclist*.

It is, therefore, to celebrate what Tom Robbins calls crazy wisdom, fun and high spirits, pursuing the true impulse, that I apply myself to riding and writing, both. Who rides with flat tyres? The truth is what we are, and that truth is ultimately inexpressible, changeable, centred and diverse, non-transferable, unique and therefore without general significance. Recognising this is the beginning of wisdom and the wholehearted embrace of contradictions. For, like the bike, we must keep moving, ever moving, in order to function.

At the time I went down to the Pyrenees to live, in 1998, I was working for a Dutch production company on a big project. However (to simplify a more complicated story), the film script I wrote for them was shelved, I had to fight to get paid and, suddenly, felt altogether rather unstuck. But, the setback, though very hard at the time, delivered pure luck. The revision of the Tour de France book and its subsequent publication changed everything.

Since then, I have written much about what has been a passion since I can remember. The coalescence of an intellectual, physical, even emotional embroilment not only with the beautiful machine itself and with those who ride it for a living but also with those for whom it is as central to life and being as it is for me has brought pleasure and privilege in unexpected bounty. For example: in January 2007, my girlfriend Susanne and I went out to the Bremen Six Day race, she to help with interviewing German spectators and officials. Ron Webb had put me in touch with his old friend Patrick Sercu, the Bremen Six director, and on the Monday morning I sat at the trackside with Sercu, 'The Flemish Arrow', as he used to be known, to talk. Since the Bremen trip was an assignment for *Rouleur* magazine, I had recording equipment and notebooks with me, but some instinct prompted me not to regard this as an interview, rather simply to enjoy the conversation, and not to formalise the encounter.

And so I found myself caught up in another part of the great fraternity of cycling into which we all fit, one way and another. Sercu is highly intelligent, his *palmarès*, on track and road, are illustrious, he is modest, gentlemanly and utterly charming, and we talked and talked and talked for about 40 minutes. (I went off afterwards to lunch with Camille, the photographer, and scribbled down everything I could spring from my brimming memory.) If I was conscious of the rare privilege of spending so much time with one of the sport's finest exponents, it was unalloyed friendly pleasure, too. Why did we meet at all? Not because I was a journalist (I'm not) looking for copy. Nor was I a dayglo fan, brushing up self-consciously against greatness. Love of the bike is what drew us together, and we met: the rest followed.

The first letter I had from Chris Boardman, in response to a 'Get Well' card I sent after his horrific Prologue crash in the 1995 Tour: he thanked me and said how much he appreciated my message, especially because it came 'from a fellow cyclist'. Imagine.

Of course there are big egos on two wheels, but the fragile bike is a fine leveller. There are probably sons-of-bitches and hard-case Neanderthals on two wheels, too, but I can't recall meeting any. We all ride the bike and . . . that's about it, really. For all that it has brought me, this beautiful machine, I rejoice and sing praise and look forward to the next time, as to every time, that it takes me out on the road.